PRAISE FOR *LEADING FOR JUSTICE*

"Rita Sever combines personal insights and relatable experiences with practical and implementable recommendations in *Leading for Justice*, to create an immensely readable book on how to create an equitable, mission-driven, and high performing organization. Every manager who wants to sleep better at night and wake up excited to face the challenges of a world in dire need of change, should buy this book."
—DONNA NORTON, Executive Vice President, MomsRising

"In this clear-eyed, practical guide, Sever, an HR professional, urges managers and HR teams to take the "time, energy, focus, and leadership" to ensure that organizations committed to working for justice in the world develop a culture and practices that also foster justice within the organization itself. . . . *Leading for Justice* offers insights and advice that would benefit any supervisor or HR professional committed to an inclusive workplace. . . . This vital guide, peppered with provocative questions and insights, will aid any supervisor or organization eager to work to live up to their mission."
—BOOKLIFE REVIEWS

"*Leading for Justice* is a timely business guide for leaders looking to develop awareness around equity issues, both in themselves and in their organizations."
—FOREWORD REVIEWS

"Rita Sever's *Leading for Justice* provides us with a roadmap to know when to step up and when to stand back when supporting, mentoring and uplifting our BIPOC team members while striving to dismantle a system created to sustain white supremacy. *Leading for Justice* is a treasure trove of resources to be incorporated into our leadership repertoire that can be referenced time and time again."
—HEIDI STRUNK, Presider

Leading for Justice

Leading
for
Justice

SUPERVISION, HR,
and CULTURE

RITA SEVER

SHE WRITES PRESS

Published 2021
Printed in the United States of America
Print ISBN: 978-1-64742-140-3
E-ISBN: 978-1-64742-141-0
Library of Congress Control Number: 2021906579

For information, address:
She Writes Press
1569 Solano Ave #546
Berkeley, CA 94707

Interior design by Tabitha Lahr

She Writes Press is a division of SparkPoint Studio, LLC.

Names, situations, and organizations are pseudonyms or composites when I write about my work with clients to protect their privacy.

To Mark, who created space for me to write—literally and figuratively.

And to Barbara Love and Roberta Hunter, past coworkers in the field of social justice and personal mentors in the power of speaking truth and love in the face of structural injustice in the world and in organizations. Barbara, a Black woman, and Roberta, a white woman, first introduced me to white privilege and invited/instructed/encouraged/exhorted me to use my power and privilege for justice.

Author's Note: I am not an attorney, and therefore nothing in this book should be construed as legal advice.

I have chosen to use the acronym BIPOC (Black, Indigenous, People of Color) throughout the book. I recognize that language, context, and understanding changes. At the time of writing this book, BIPOC is the most frequently used term within the groups with which I work most closely. It is reflective of this time and this context. That context and that language may change.

CONTENTS

Foreword, *by Mala Nagarajan* xv
Introduction xix

Chapter 1: How Do You Show Up as a Manager? 1

Sordid Words. 2
Working in Partnership 4
Different Roles, Different Responsibilities 5
The Sauce of Supervision 9
Who Asked You? Unwelcome Advice 11
Gotcha! 13

Chapter 2: Bottom-Lining It—Mission, Vision,
and Values 16

Why Are You Going? 17
Where Are You Going? 19
How Are You Going? 22
Actively Highlighting the Mission, Vision,
and Values 24
Touchstone 27
Mission Touches Everyone and Everything 28

Chapter 3: Day-to-Day Practices 31

Prepare Your Staff to Be Successful. 32
Regular Meetings 34
Respect Boundaries. 37
The Relevant Question 41
Supervising Staff Who Aren't There 43
The Danger of Hidden Rules 47

Chapter 4: Supervision Is a Team Sport 51

Ten Questions for Supervisors on the
  Path to Justice 52
How People Are Treated 57
Consistency as a Tool of Equity 59
Positive and Negative Impacts 61
Burnout. 64
Liability. 67
The One-Vent Rule. 70
Squeezed in the Middle 71

Chapter 5: Look in the Mirror 74

The Journey of Reflection, Awareness,
  and Management 75
Practices of Self-Reflection 78
Ground Truths. 81
Managing Your Buttons 83
Owning Your Power.   87
What We Don't See: Hidden Dangers 89
Owning Your Shit (Primarily for White Folks) 91
When a Man Talks 94

Chapter 6: HR as a Justice Partner. 98

The Wide Umbrella View of HR. 99
Transforming HR for Justice 103
HR Stands Alone 110
Connecting the Dots 112
Infrastructure to Hold Up the Work 116
Try Saying Yes. 118

Chapter 7: Hiring for Justice 123

Watch Out for the Mini-Me's 124

Do You Know Who You Are Looking For? 128

Affirmative Hiring 132

Team Input on Hiring 134

Compensate More Justly 136

"There's Your Desk" Is Not Enough:
Onboarding New Staff 141

Chapter 8: Holding Accountability 146

It's About Clarity 147

Success as Motivation 149

Accountability Tools 151

*Some Good Coaching Questions to
Support Accountability* 157

Every Which Way 158

You Can Decide, but You Might Decide Wrong! 160

Delegation Questions for the Supverisor 162

Evaluation Trauma 163

What Makes an Evaluation Fair and Equitable? 166

"We Never Fire Anyone" 168

The Challenges with Flat 170

Chapter 9: Culture—Walking the Talk 173

Culture Happens 174

Culture Invigorates Values—or Not 177

A Culture of Respect: The Seeing Triangle 180

Pen or Pencil Culture? 186

Is Pretending Undermining Your Culture? 190

Support Through Hard Times 196

Zero-Tolerance Culture re: Harassment 199

A Culture of Inclusion 202

Culture Snapshot 207

Chapter 10: Issues of Power and Privilege 212

Let's Talk About White Do-Gooders
(Primarily for White Folks) 213
What Are You Willing to Give Up?
(For White Leaders) 216
I Could Not Be Complicit (For White Leaders). 218
Insubordination and Other Dated Concepts. 221
Strong Teams Require Pushback. 224
Sticks and Stones 226
Being "the Man" 230
Deer in the Headlights. 233
Disrupting Sexism. 236

Chapter 11: Misses and Messes 239

One Supervisor per Person, Please! 240
Your Staff Has Personal Troubles—Now What? 243
Valuing People *and* the Work. 247
The Impact of Ignoring Rules. 249
Breakdown!. 251
Avoiding Conflict 256
How Did No One Notice?. 258
Don't Look the Other Way for Too Long 261
Avoid the Triangle 262
Getting Stuck in Guilt. 266

Chapter 12: It's a Marathon, not a Sprint. 269

Respect the Drops; Recognize the Bucket. 270
Recognition Sticks 271
Sustaining Passion 273
Making Play at Work Work. 276
Another Name for Morale Is Belonging. 279
Grief. 283
Keeping the Conversation Going 285

How Can You Dance When the World Is Burning? . . . 292
PS: Thank You! 293

Acknowledgments 295
About the Author 299

FOREWORD

by Mala Nagarajan

Rita and I met in 2017 as members of the RoadMap consulting network, an incredible treasure trove of movement activists, organizers, academics, and strategists turned organizational consultants. In fact, ever since my wife and I joined the network and connected with other network consultants, Rita's name came up repeatedly. Her reputation preceded her. Seasoned consultants like Brigette Rouson, our transformational JEDI warrior and cross-network pollinator, or Margi Clarke, who published RoadMap's People-Centered Supervision Practices and Salary Policy Discussion Guide, would all refer me back to Rita as the HR expert in the network. So I was part of Team Rita well before we formally met.

Rita's previous book, *Supervision Matters*, was the go-to supervision resource that RoadMap consultants would send to their clients. I soon got to witness her wisdom and counsel firsthand, when our colleague Nijmie Dzurinko encouraged a group of HR consultants who were deeply interested in racial justice to organize. I was nervous and excited at the same time to get the chance to work with Rita.

The thing about Rita is that she is incredibly down-to-earth. As I read through this latest book, I was reminded of the bite-size kernels of wisdom she would share in our working group. She practices the partnership role she speaks of here in *Leading for Justice*, and she helps us walk with her as she weaves together poignant stories, her breadth of experience, her lessons learned, and her curiosities.

Rita tackles the historical shackles of supervision and invites us to reconceptualize super-vision in perhaps its lesser-known root form where *super* means "beyond, besides, in addition to" (vs. "above, over, on the top of"). How would we experience supervision if its meaning were not to *oversee*, but to *see beyond*? That leads to her inviting supervisors and managers to see themselves as *partners* to staff, with different roles and different responsibilities.

Rita sets forth the larger context for leading for justice, highlighting how to make mission, vision, and values the connective tissue that feeds and unifies the work. Rita the trainer appears throughout the book, wherever she shares how she infuses group exercises with fun and creativity. And she demands we not abandon the need to balance the seeming polarity of *serving our people* and *observing the law*, both of which are critical to any of our efforts to move us toward justice.

Rita reminds us to not just teach the job or position, but to set staff up for success by investing time with each direct report, respecting boundaries, and focusing on what is impacting the work—whether in person or remotely. She emphasizes supervision as a team sport, and the need for a unified organizational approach to supervision.

Rita begins to break down the importance of developing self-awareness and self-reflection about how your identity shows up, especially in places where you have privilege (as a white person, as a man, as an able-bodied person, etc.), and about our implicit biases and tribalism (that we tend to recruit and hire people who remind us of ourselves).

The book is chock-full of practical advice, such as how to set up candidates well from the get-go, letting them know to expect explicit discussions about racism and explaining that if the candidate is not comfortable with that, they may not be comfortable working at the organization. Or, as another example, letting candidates know the extent to which statements regarding your organization's values and practices are aspirational, in progress, or integrated.

Rita notes up front that she is not an expert in justice. She leaves that expertise to you. Truthfully, none of us are experts in justice. We are only experts in our own experience, and at best, we can use our own experiences as portals to empathize with, *not* compare our experiences to, the experiences of others. And like a true ally, a lifelong learner, and an HR partner in solidarity, Rita starts from where you the reader might be, and she works on building trust and inspiring courage. She brings in examples of personal experiences that elicit strong moral and emotional responses that many readers will relate with—having rules applied unequally on a plane ride, for example—and then skillfully pulls the reader into how staff feel when rules are applied differentially. And while Rita does not always explicitly address racial justice in every story, the broad principles of justice are still useful for leaders who are seeking to supervise and lead others with, through, and for justice.

Along with *Supervision Matters*, I'm excited to learn from and share this new book with my clients and colleagues. Rita's partnership and mentorship have meant the world to me. She is my go-to person when I'm looking for practical, in-the-trenches, and hands-on HR advice, and I trust as you read this, she will become yours, too.

....

Mala Nagarajan is a principal and partner at Vega Mala Consulting. As a senior HR professional, she works with small-to-midsize nonprofits that center social justice. She approaches HR from a holistic, people-centered, movement-oriented, and values-driven lens and works with organizations to radically shift the structures and assumptions that embed and deepen inequities in the soil of their workplace.

Mala works at the edges of innovation. She has developed a highly customized management tool to support organizations in creating a mission-centric compensation system that lifts up unseen and undervalued labor, reveals patterns of inequities, and supports the reengineering of structural compensation practices that have contributed to the further widening of the wealth gap. She is also part of a team creating an app to support cross-class collaboratives, collectives, and communities with interpersonal reparations through voluntary income redistribution.

Mala is a member of the RoadMap consulting network.

INTRODUCTION

This book is for all the leaders who care about justice. This book is about what happens inside organizations. There is a direct connection between what happens inside organizations and the work that is done by the organization in the world. The more staff feel seen, respected, empowered, and safe to be who they are, the more likely they will be to do their best work—which will in turn directly impact the mission of the organization. When organizations and their leaders actively work to reimagine and recreate structures and processes in order to disrupt oppressive practices, transformation will occur. And this transformation does not stop at the door. For example, when a staff person builds their skills of applying an explicit racial justice lens to their internal work and learns to address conflict constructively within the organization, that also translates into forming more effective campaign strategies, having constructive relationships with external partners, and replicating fewer oppressive habits with community and partners. This book is written primarily for nonprofits and specifically for social justice organizations, but anyone who cares about justice is invited to join us.

My focus in this book is on the internal work of organizations, in particular through the three functions named in the subtitle: Supervision, HR, and Culture. I am not an expert in antiracism or other structures of oppression. I am an expert in supervision, human resources, and organization development and that includes responding to how oppression impacts the staff and the work.

I refer often in this book to the dominant or mainstream culture. What I mean by that is the embedded structure of hetero-patriarchal white supremacist capitalism.

Here's how I got here. In 1997, I interviewed for a job as a human resources director at an organization staffed primarily by people of color. In the midst of a fairly routine interview, I was asked what I understood about systemic racism. I am a white woman. I knew about systemic racism as a concept and answered, in part, using the fish-in-water metaphor. Fish live in water and therefore it is normal and absolute; they know no other way of living. This is how systemic racism works; it is so much a part of our society that those of us with privilege often do not even see it. Through that job, I learned so much more about the realities of racism and the impact of systemic practices in general and in HR in particular. I saw how the concepts affected my colleagues. As an organization, we dedicated significant resources to the work of equity and inclusion, including training, compensation adjustments, accountability to this value, updating our hiring process, and much more. My colleagues were generous and patient as I learned and applied this new understanding to my work. The entire workforce was on a journey together to become an organization that centered on equity. When I left that job nine years later, I not only knew I was white but had a much better understanding of what that meant in the world and in my work and how I could contribute to racial justice. I have never stopped learning. I know I can never know the experience of people who identify differently than I do.

This book is dedicated to my husband who has always supported and celebrated my work, and to my mentors in this vital component of working for justice. I appreciate all who have continued to teach me and think with me about how to lead for and with justice, especially my colleagues at RoadMap Consulting. (A national network of experienced consultants committed to strengthening organizations and advancing social justice.)

I wrote this book to support the leaders and the organizations working to build a more just world. To help you be more effective in reaching the goals you strive for, to help you work well together to move your mission forward. I want to encourage leaders to lead intentionally and to build just organizations while they work to build a just world. In order to do that, leaders must look carefully at themselves first and then at their teams and organizations. Where is white supremacy culture leaking into your leadership and organization practices? When does the lens through which you see the world get in the way of the work? How can you show up and do your best work to lead with and toward justice?

This book offers stories, thoughts, ideas, and techniques to support your leadership. It does not offer prescriptions nor an explicit game plan. I trust you to make these ideas your own—to build on them by applying them to your leadership and your team.

It is vital to remember that you can control only what you can do. You cannot make others change, although you can invite and persuade. You may have a small window of influence, or you may have a wide platform. Be the leader you can be from where you are. See what you can see, change what you can change, and show up as the best possible leader you can be for your team and the entire organization. Be a strong, fair, and collaborative supervisor who keeps the work moving forward and supports your staff. Notice and address racial, gender, and other injustice when you see it. Change HR, if necessary, and if you can't, then raise questions and change how you interact with HR or how you frame challenges. You won't be able to change the entire culture on your own, but you can have an impact on your team and you can raise concerns and start conversations. You can invite your organization to work collectively to shift how things are done—and to celebrate what you are already doing well.

The sections in this book overlap and interrelate. I may suggest something in one chapter and then remind you of it in another chapter. Some of my ideas will probably be familiar to you, and others might invite a shift in your approach. You can read the book sequentially or dive into a topic that interests you. If something resonates with you, try it out or talk about it. Just as we can't change the world overnight, don't try to change your organization all at once. It takes time and it takes patience and it takes collaboration. And in the journey, you are building the foundation for any other work that needs to be done.

Each section ends with a list of questions. I call this "Make It Your Own," because it's how this work becomes real. Pause at these questions. Consider them. Use them as coaching prompts for yourself or your team. You might want to pick one that appeals to you and write about it for five to ten minutes or ponder it while you go for a walk. Keep a running list of ideas you want to implement.

If you lead an organization, consider taking action that can impact the whole system. Do an assessment or hire consultants that can help you see and address oppressive systems that are at play in your organization.

Make this book your own. Make it work for you and for your organization. Make it work for our many social justice movements.

I have learned so much from my clients and my colleagues. When I tell stories about them, the names and the situations are adapted or compiled from situations I've seen. I have been honored to do this work. I am grateful to all the skilled and dedicated leaders I have known.

I also want to acknowledge that my learning and my work in the field of justice is not only professional. My work and my life are aligned in this work. On a personal level, my daughter is queer and has a trans partner. While I have always been fully accepting of her and him in my mind and heart, I have to admit that I have also caused harm. I have acted from learned norms and unrecognized heteronormativity. I appreciate that my daughter has confronted me (and my husband) about these actions and behaviors and invited us to grow into better parents and better people. I am also heartbroken that I/we have caused her this pain. I cannot undo the pain, but I can do and be better. And that too is a part of this book.

Let us all continue to rise up, make room, and surge forward together—for justice.

CHAPTER 1:

HOW DO YOU SHOW UP
AS A MANAGER?

One of the most difficult tasks I face as a coach is when a leader does not recognize how they show up. The way you show up includes the words you use, your tone, your attitude, and your understandings and assumptions, as well as your personality and privileges. I am often there as a coach because they have received feedback that their staff feel undermined, disrespected, and frustrated and the leaders do not understand what they are doing wrong or how to manage in a different way.

It is not enough to simply intend to be a good leader. You must act with intention and awareness of how you approach your role. You cannot just do what has always been done. You cannot just act like a stereotypical boss. You need a plan and a practice to lead with integrity, purpose, and justice. You need to recognize that your words and your actions matter, that the way you show up matters.

For some people, this means they have to unlearn bad habits and re-create how they show up. For others, it means adjusting their approach and acting with more intention and understanding.

Sordid Words

"Supervisor" and "boss" have a bad reputation. And it's no wonder—these words have a dirty history, and some of that history clings to them. For too many people, these words (and the positions they represent) have been used to mean authoritarian, arbitrary, harassing, dictatorial, racist, sexist, oppressive, and controlling. These words have historically been linked with societal hierarchies of what leadership "looks like," including with male privilege and white supremacy. They also have a taste of rigidity, bureaucracy, abuse of power, and authority.

Especially for people who do not have institutional or societal privilege, these words can make them nervous and cause them to move into defensive mode, and rightfully so.

Supervisors have been abusive and power hungry. Some still are.

Bosses have been micromanagers or authoritarian. Some still are.

Hierarchies have been bureaucratic. Some certainly still are.

And power has absolutely been oppressive and blind and debilitating. Definitely a serious threat that continues.

Authority has been usurped and misused. And still is.

I want to reclaim these words, not to deny their sordid history or tainted reputation but to remind all of us that words, just like people, are not just their past. People can change, and so can some of the concepts that infuse our workplaces.

All of these concepts can be reinterpreted in service and in support of good work and strong partnerships. These words, and a reimagined, equitable framing of these concepts, can be used to serve justice. Other words may work better, but for most people, these words will continue to lurk in the background, creating distrust and disease if we do not actively reclaim them in service of better organizations and a better world.

My vision of supervision is 180 degrees from the traditional, top-down, power-hungry crew boss that the word might bring to mind. My vision of supervision is of a partner working with their staff for a cause that is bigger than both of them. This partner is a supervisor not because they are better than their staff but because they have a different role and different decision-making responsibilities and a different vision. Not a *super*vision that implies "better than," but supervision, meaning wider or further along the path. This kind of person offers a different perspective. These supervisors are guides and are focused on supporting their staff to be successful in their work. They are in relationship with their staff. They respect and support and appreciate their staff. They work in partnership with them, not in mastery of them.

Likewise, the other terms often correlated with supervision can be effective and respectful concepts if they are used in an organization that embodies respect and partnership and a united focus on an important mission. Power can be a term of responsibility and presence, not a sword to cut people down. Hierarchy can be a simple recognition that not everyone can be involved in every decision and every action when an organization gets to a certain size or level of complexity. Authority can be a direct connection to the ultimate responsibility of decisions and actions.

Held and used by thoughtful people, these terms can help an organization move forward. But to do so, we must reclaim and redefine them so that the taint of their burdensome history does not infect the organization. This takes training and direct conversations. Otherwise, such words can stink up the place with their sordid reputation.

Make It Your Own

- How can you actively reclaim tainted words like supervisor and boss? Tylenol reclaimed its brand after someone poisoned bottles and killed seven people in 1982. The company rebounded by recalling all of the Tylenol bottles on the market and then telling the truth about what had happened, what the company did, and what it was doing to ensure that the same catastrophe wouldn't happen again. This approach ultimately built brand loyalty, rather than destroying it. How can we apply this lesson to reclaiming tainted words?

- Is there a way in which reclaiming the words can contribute to an understanding of their previous harm and therefore be part of a greater good?
- How might an organization symbolically reclaim these words to recognize a new approach to work?

Working in Partnership

Working in partnership is not just a vague idea. It can be an active reframing of roles and responsibilities that infuses the work and the organization. It has to be authentic, though, or it will be worse than being authoritarian. If you pretend to be working in partnership but then erupt into micromanagement or authoritarian commands or paternalistic condescension, you will break trust and be seen as hypocritical, which is one of the worst things you can be in a social justice organization.

Your organization was formed to make the world a better place. In some form or fashion, the intention is that this organization is to contribute to leveling the playing field, to fighting oppression, to supporting justice. And justice has no place for hypocrisy.

This work demands that the workers are respected. This work demands that equality is not just a phrase or a concept. Every staff member expects to be recognized as a partner in service to the work. These principles have not just a theoretical value but a working, day-in-day-out value.

This does not mean, however, that the work is the same for every person or that there cannot be some level of hierarchy—if that hierarchy serves the mission and not the ego at the top.

Working in partnership recognizes that we have different roles. My role may be director, and yours may be receptionist. But

4

we are, first of all, equal as persons and, second of all, both there to serve the mission. We do that work in different ways, however.

Our job descriptions outline our roles. We have different levels of decision making and responsibility, but we both recognize that we are working for the same mission, vision, and goals. And we bring our best selves to our work.

As part of a partnership, we recognize and respect that we will bring different ideas, thoughts, solutions, and skills to our work. And we will listen to each other. Everyone has a voice in a social justice organization, but every voice may not be a vote when it comes time to make some decisions. We are not a democracy or a collective—unless we are!

Make It Your Own

- What are the positives and negatives of working in partnership?
- What are examples of strong partnerships that you've witnessed, and what is one thing they did that exemplified their partnership?
- How do partners act when they face problems or challenges?

Different Roles, Different Responsibilities

Part of working in partnership is recognizing that each person has their own role and that each role has a level of authority and responsibility. This does not make any person or any position better than any other person or position. All the roles are important and necessary to meet the needs of the organization. Each person is entitled to respect for who they are and the work they do.

When I worked at an organization offering support for people with AIDS at the height of the epidemic, we did not have a big staff. For a period of time, we relied on volunteers to staff the front desk. But, of course, the volunteers needed breaks. We would have two volunteers every day—a morning shift and an afternoon shift. That left an hour in the middle of the day wherein we needed to either close the office or figure out another way to staff the front desk. At that point, we decided that we would rotate that lunch coverage throughout the paid staff. Each staff member would work one lunch shift at the front desk every three to four weeks. It gave us all a greater sense of appreciation for the important work the crew of volunteers did for the organization. The amazing thing was that this rotation applied to every staff member, from the administrative assistant to the executive director. We all worked a lunch hour and covered the phones and greeted clients. On one level, this didn't make sense. Could we really afford to pay the ED's salary while she answered the phones? She could have been doing more important work in her office or out in the community. But, whether intentionally or not, we recognized the message that this one hour sent, internally and externally, was worth every penny. Staff knew the ED was one of us, working in conjunction with us and on the front lines with us. And the community and clients knew it too. When she stopped covering lunch breaks, we all did. That was a powerful message of working in partnership.

Different roles come with different responsibilities, authority, and decision-making opportunities. That is the most common interpretation of the work, embodied in organization charts. But it does not have to be value-laden. It can be a simple recognition that in order for the work to be done, we each work within our strengths and our roles to get the work done. Reframing the work as responsibilities helps to clarify the distinction. It is not a perk to get to decide how to balance a budget; it is a responsibility. If the budget does not balance, that responsibility is someone's to own and accept, just as it is a receptionist's responsibility to own and accept how they treat people when they walk into or call the office. Every person has their sphere of influence. Every person has their role, their authority, and their responsibility. Every person has their job description.

Job descriptions are sometimes seen as archaic and cumbersome—and they can be. But they can also be a road map that offers clarity and understanding. When a job description is thoughtful and comprehensive, without being restrictive, then each person understands the parameters of their role, the depth of their responsibility, and how their work interrelates with all the other work of the organization. They can use this well-hewn document to clarify their priorities and boundaries.

A job description is not written in stone. In fact, the staff member and supervisor should review it periodically to make sure that it still captures the actual work that is being done. This review can also ensure that the work being done is still what needs to be done. Is this person in the right job? Jobs tend to morph and drift—sometimes because of the skill of the person in the job and sometimes because of the lack thereof. I have seen a case manager who was also responsible for IT, public speaking, and accounting. That may make sense at some initial, grassroots stage of organization development, but you don't want to codify that kind of job description simply because an early staff member has all of those needed skills. On the other end of the spectrum, I have seen case managers who actually no longer met with clients. That made no sense either. So the systematic review of job descriptions is an important part of building a strong infrastructure of support for the work. I recommend tying this job review to a recurring event, like a budget review, a performance evaluation process, or the new year.

Infrastructure is another concept that is incredibly important but not sexy. It does not immediately bring ideas of justice and equity to mind. Yet it is critical. It refers to administrative and operation-focused work as opposed to direct client-focused work. I think of infrastructure as the skeleton of an organization. People don't always see it as valuable, but without that behind-the-scenes work, any other work is not going to move smoothly or effectively. I once worked with an office manager who felt unappreciated and invisible to the rest of the staff. They were out in the field, organizing and holding press conferences and staging protests. Staff members tended to see her as a bureaucrat and subtly looked down on her as a less important member of the team.

While coaching her, I offered her the image of the skeleton and suggested she share that idea with her team. She did talk about her role at the next staff meeting and brought up important facts about skeletons: how strong they are, what they make possible, and so on. But then she went one better. She went out and bought a big roll of skeleton stickers and started putting them on documents to remind people that her role mattered: on time sheets, on expense reports, on grant reports, on light fixtures . . . She said this approach made a big difference and that she finally felt respected as part of the team. In fact, she sent me a thank-you note that read in part, "Your encouragement and skeleton analogy have made a big difference in the entire staff's attitude (including mine) toward the admin work of the organization."

Making an organization succeed requires different roles and different responsibilities, including behind-the-scenes administrative and fiscal work. Justice would take a lot longer to achieve if those roles were not part of the team.

Make It Your Own

- Do you, or does your organization, currently value some responsibilities as more important than others?
- If different levels of responsibility are not interpreted as "more important," how does that shift the internal landscape or culture of an organization?
- Is there any internal snobbery regarding positions or importance in your organization that needs to be uncovered and discussed?

- Do you have current and complete job descriptions? If not, what assumptions have led to their lack of importance? What would be the positives and the negatives of taking time to update them?
- Where do you see patterns of who fills the different positions and how they are treated based on race, gender, class, ability, or other identity?

The Sauce of Supervision

A good sauce can make or break a meal. When it's good, the flavors linger and keep you engaged. When it doesn't work, the whole meal can fail. And when you first taste unfamiliar sauces, the reaction can often be negative, until you learn to appreciate the different flavors.

The same can be said about the tone that a supervisor uses, especially in times of feedback or trouble. A supervisor's tone can convey enthusiasm, patience, and respect. It can also convey disdain, impatience, frustration, and so much more. Too often, I have heard employees tell me, "It's not what they said; it's how they said it." That's tone.

Watch your tone. When you're not careful, your tone can send staff running out the door. This kind of tone sounds condescending or punitive. I have coached men who did not recognize that when they became agitated, their voices became a little stronger and deeper, which their female staff interpreted as "yelling," even though the men had not technically raised their voices.

When your tone is respectful and appreciative, it can keep staff engaged. This kind of tone often holds pauses and lifts a bit at the end of a sentence, like a question, which invites people to respond.

When your tone is neutral during difficult conversations, you let staff know that this is information only, not a judgment. Neutral does not mean robotic; it means free of emphasis or pushiness.

The other way your tone can betray you is when your tone does not match your words, such as when your words say, "I'm fine" but your tone says you're angry. Or when your words say, "I have no news to report" but your tone is excited. This kind of mismatch between tone and spoken language can be very unsettling and lead to mistrust.

At the same time, it is important, and sometimes tricky, to not automatically interpret other people's tone. The point is to monitor your own—not to judge others. People who have different backgrounds from you may very well bring a different tone or inflection to their work. In too many workplaces, Black, Indigenous, and people of color (BIPOC), immigrants, and poor people have been shamed for their tone. If you hear tone, check it out. Ask questions—starting with an I-statement. "I am hearing a challenge in your tone. Am I right?" Believe what people tell you and listen for how they use tone.

Learn to expand your appreciation for different tones that you may not be used to. Pay attention to your own alignment, use your tone as the sauce of your approach, and let it flavor your interactions in a positive manner.

Make It Your Own

- When have you experienced the feeling "It's not what they said; it's how they said it"? How did you react to that situation?
- How does a mismatch between tone and spoken words lead to mistrust?
- How do biases—race, gender, class, culture, and others—influence how people experience tone? What are things you and your staff can do to learn about different biases and constructively interrupt them?

Remember:

Remember that tone can be influenced by cultural differences. Where and how we grow up can give us different interpretations of what tone is sincere and what is sarcastic, what tone is inquisitive and what is condescending, what is patient/neutral and what is disinterested. So if you find yourself giving or receiving repeated feedback about tone, be curious about that possibility.

Who Asked You? Unwelcome Advice

It was a stunning day to hike by the ocean in Northern California. It was warm and sunny and sparkling. I was minding my own business, hiking and thinking, and suddenly someone walking the other way stopped and told me, in a very firm and authoritative way, "Keep hiking up."

Huh? It wasn't a suggestion or an invitation. It bordered on an order. It was unwelcome and extremely irritating. I didn't let it ruin my hike, but I lost a couple minutes yelling at this person in my head.

That is often the way unwelcome advice is received. Supervisors assume that they know better, that their staff wants your input, or that it is simply their job to tell their staff what to do and how to do it. And sometimes all of that is true.

If your staff member is brand new, then you probably do know more and better and you are in training mode. This is the time to offer advice, help people learn their job, and familiarize them with the organization. While doing this, don't forget that they bring their own skills, experience, and knowledge. That's why you hired them! If your staff is struggling and not reaching their goals or keeping their agreement, it is absolutely appropriate to give them feedback and let them know what's working and not working. When you are establishing priorities and clarifying expectations, it is your job to state clearly and directly what is needed and how it needs to be done. (None of this needs to be done in a "bossy" manner, however.)

But when your staff *do* know what their jobs are and how to do them and are moving forward to accomplish goals and get the work done, back off. Let them do their work. Keep meeting with them and checking in, but be careful with giving unwelcome advice. Don't be one of those micromanagers whom people dread.

Here's what to watch for:

1. The biggest signal that people want advice? They will ask for it. Remind them often that you expect them to let you know when they want your input. And make it safe for them to ask you for help.

2. If you see someone struggling or moving in the wrong direction, offer input. But even then, present it thoughtfully. The struggling person may have a plan and a method that gets them to their goal in a manner that is very different from your method or plan. Instead of saying, "That's not going to work!" try saying something like, "I don't see how these actions are going to get you where you're going. Tell me how you see it."

3. If you're not sure what they need, ask them, "Do you need any help?"

In my aforementioned hike on the coast, I would have welcomed a friendly invitation, such as "The path up is gorgeous." Although probably well-intentioned, the bossy advice to "keep hiking up" was not welcome or appreciated.

Make It Your Own

- Think of a time when you received unwelcome advice. How did you react?
- What patterns do you see in your organization related to advice and race, gender, class, and other identities? What could you do to constructively interrupt them?
- What are the dangers of waiting for someone to ask for advice? How could your organization mitigate those dangers?

Gotcha!

Some people love strategy games like chess or RISK®. They love the logic and the planning and the eventual "Gotcha!" when the winner claims victory. Those moments when both players have agreed to the rules and respect each other's skill can be joyful, whether you win or lose.

In the workplace, however, there is little room for "gotcha" moments. Some supervisors do love those moments, and others inadvertently spring them upon their staff, but rarely do such moments help your staff to learn or grow. At its worst, "gotchas" can reinforce dominant race and gender dynamics.

"Gotcha" moments happen when you set up a staff member to be caught in a mistake. It may not be an intentional setup, but it is nonetheless harmful. Let's look at the way Warren confronts his staff member Kayla when she turns in her expense account.

"When are expense reports due?" Warren asks.

"On the fifteenth of the month," Kayla answers.

"And when did you turn yours in?"

"The fifteenth."

"Then why is it date-stamped the eighteenth?"

Warren displays implied glee in showing Kayla that she was wrong. Instead, he could have just asked, "What happened with your expense report? It looks like it was late this month."

The inadvertent "gotcha" happens when a supervisor doesn't understand an action that a staff member took and tries to find out what they were thinking. Questions can be a valuable tool, but you must bring genuine curiosity to the questioning; otherwise, it can come across as interrogation.

Interrogation

"Why did you speak to that client in that manner?"

"Don't you know the procedure for updating the website?"

"Haven't we discussed this several times previously?"

"Did you think you had a better way to do this process than the rest of the staff?"

Curiosity

"Tell me what was going through your mind when you spoke to that client."

"We have a procedure for updating the website. Has anyone ever reviewed that with you?"

"Tell me what you remember about our previous discussions, and I'll fill in any gaps."

"What led you to do this process in a different way?"

When you are in interrogation mode, you assume that you know everything there is to know about the situation. You don't really care what the staff member has to say. You just want to make a point. When you are curious, you genuinely want to hear what the staff member has to say. You recognize that you might learn something. And your intention is to help the staff member be successful.

Not only are the curious questions less aggressive in the initial exchange, but they set up the staff member to have an honest exchange with you, to keep talking to you, and to trust you. The interrogation tells the staff member that there is only one right answer and you know it. So they won't bother to tell you what they were thinking or why they tried something new; they will just try to get the "right" answer and move on. Over time, the interrogation questions erode trust, impact the work in dramatic fashion, and replicate the oppressive systems we are seeking to dismantle.

Don't practice Gotcha with your staff, unless you're playing chess.

Make It Your Own

- How do people react when they have been challenged or interrogated?
- What are the signs of an organization that tends toward blame? And what are the signs of an organization that leans toward curiosity and learning? Where does your organization fall on that spectrum?
- How is playing Gotcha different than holding someone accountable?

CHAPTER 2:

BOTTOM-LINING IT— MISSION, VISION, AND VALUES

M ission and purpose seem to have a bad connotation in some leadership circles these days. I don't get it. Maybe because I work with nonprofit organizations, mission has always been sacrosanct. The bottom line is not money or power; it is a better and more just world. How can that be a bad thing?

It is important that organizations know why they exist, it is important that all stakeholders know where their organization is going, and it is important that they have principles about how everyone will operate on their journey together. These are the bottom-line priorities for organizations concerned with justice.

Support for organizations forms a three-legged stool: mission, vision, and values. When people don't pay attention to all three components of this stool, things get out of balance. When an organization lacks a clear focus on its mission and vision, its destination can become vague or transitory. When an organization does not pay active attention to values, the organization can lose their integrity and sense of identity—or even become hypocritical. All three legs are necessary to support the work.

Why Are You Going?

When I worked internally at a community action agency, its mission was "to partner with low-income families and individuals to help them achieve economic and social stability, to build community, and to advocate for social and economic justice." I knew it by heart, I referred to it often, and I saw it every day when I walked into our office, because it was written on the wall in the lobby. It was the reason I worked there.

The mission took on a whole different level of meaning to me, however, when I hired a man who didn't just know the mission but *loved* it. He loved the mission so much that when our executive director asked him about it during his interview, he cried. And when he passed his introductory period, he got a tattoo of our logo on his shin. I loved that guy!

No doubt your own mission is on your website and other relevant places. Maybe you even allude to it in ads for open positions. And hopefully, someone discusses the mission when an official orientation occurs.

But when do *you*, as a manager, mention the mission? Do you discuss it when you bring someone new onto your team? Do you refer to it regularly during staff meetings? Do you invite staff to talk about it? How does the mission speak to you and show up for you?

In justice work, the mission needs to be the be-all and end-all of everything you do as a leader. The mission is the bottom line of nonprofits in general and social justice organizations in particular. If not for the mission, there is no "there" there. There is no work. There are no grants. There is no guiding light to inform the work.

I believe that every employee should be able to draw a line directly from what they are doing at any given moment to the mission. Writing a grant: I hope that connection is obvious. Working with a client: The mission should be front and center. But what about when staff are filing, writing reports, doing trainings, learning about harassment, sweeping the floors?

How do those tasks support the mission? People should know and be able to explain it in twenty seconds.

And this won't happen if you do not make the mission real. If you, as a supervisor, never mention it explicitly, that sends a very clear message. It may be theoretically important, but if it were *really* important, you would talk about it. You would talk about it at least as often as you talk about the budget or grant numbers.

If you don't talk about it, the mission remains hypothetical and vague. But when you talk about it, early and often, it becomes part of the lifeblood of your work. When you spend time during orientation talking about what the mission means to you and why it matters, that sticks. When you mention it during staff meetings, it becomes a valid criterion for success. When you ask staff to think about how their work is furthering the mission, you underline its importance.

In these ways, the mission becomes real. You don't have to have it tattooed on your body, but it should hold a place in your heart.

Make It Your Own

- Take a relevant news story to a staff meeting and ask your staff to discuss how this story could support or challenge your mission.
- How, if at all, would it impact your work if you knew you might be asked to draw a line from what you are doing at any given moment to your mission? Is there anything that comes to mind that threatens that line?
- If you have not routinely mentioned the mission, why not? What assumptions, fears, or concerns underlie your omission?

Where Are You Going?

Do you know the story about the fisherman and the banker?

An investment banker was taking a much-needed vacation in a small coastal village when a small boat with just one fisherman docked. The boat had several large, fresh fish in it.

The investment banker was impressed by the quality of the fish and asked the fisherman how long it had taken to catch them. He replied, "Only a little while."

The banker then asked the fisherman why he hadn't stayed out longer and caught more fish.

The fisherman replied that he had enough to support his family's immediate needs. The banker then asked, "But what do you do with the rest of your time?"

The fisherman replied, "I sleep late, fish a little, play with my children, take siesta with my wife, and stroll each evening into the village, where I sip wine and play guitar with my friends. I have a full and busy life."

The banker scoffed, "I am an Ivy League MBA, and I could help you. You could spend more time fishing and with the proceeds buy a bigger boat, and with the proceeds from the bigger boat you could buy several boats, until eventually you would have a whole fleet of fishing boats. Instead of selling your catch to a middleman, you could sell directly to the processor and eventually open your own cannery. You could control the product, processing, and distribution."

Then he added, "Of course, you would need to leave this small coastal fishing village and move to a big city, where you would run your growing enterprise."

The fisherman asked, "But, mister, how long will this all take?"

The banker replied, "Fifteen to twenty years."

"And what then?" the fisherman asked.

The banker laughed and said, "That's the best part. When the time is right, you would announce an IPO and sell your company stock to the public and become very rich. You could make millions."

"Millions! Then what?"

The banker replied, "Then you would retire. You could move to a small coastal fishing village, where you would sleep late, fish a little, play with your kids, take siesta with your wife, and in the evenings stroll to the village, where you could sip wine and play guitar with your friends."

This story illustrates how important it is to know where you're going. If you don't have a clear picture of that, things can go awry.

1. First of all, you might not recognize when you get there. The fisherman in the story did know where he was going and what he wanted, and, importantly, recognized that he was already there.

2. Second, if you don't know where you're going, you won't realize when you start to drift off course. You could get distracted by shiny objects (or big grants) and end up veering away from your destination.

3. Third, you can get bored or frustrated. You may start to feel like you're in a rut, doing the same thing over and over and not making headway—because you don't know what headway looks like. And when people feel as if their work doesn't matter, they may find themselves apathetic or despairing.

4. Fourth, the work becomes a goal unto itself. The fisherman could become so focused on fishing that he forgets to spend time with his family and friends. The work in front of you becomes the only thing that matters.

Many of these issues happen in organizations.

1. Okay, it isn't common that organizations succeed in fulfilling their missions and don't recognize it. But it is possible. Maybe a dance company wants to put on shows to support local programming. The company succeeds at that and immediately moves on to a statewide and then a national goal. That's great, but it needs to stop and acknowledge that it fulfilled its initial vision and has now expanded that vision.

2. The shiny thing in nonprofits is most often funding. "Ooh, here's a grant for a food pantry. We could do that." "Could" means "should." That's how the mission and vision can keep the organization on track.

3. Organizations can get bored as much as people can. I've seen entire organizations where the work is routine, the funding is flat, the work is done in a formulaic manner, and turnover is both high and low. What often happens is that a cadre of long-term employees who have been there for years and are happy to have steady jobs don't care to rock the boat. And then there are new staff, who are drawn to the mission and want to ask questions and wake things up, and when that leads nowhere, they quit, so there ends up being new staff and long-term staff and no mid-tenure staff.

4. Some organizations get focused on their day-to-day work and survival to the exclusion of forward movement. These organizations have a standard way of doing things and not much incentive to do things differently. This does not mean that people aren't working hard. In fact, they are often overwhelmed, and that too becomes part of their day-to-day reality. No one has the time, energy, or inclination to look up and see where they're going.

All of this is to remind you to build a clear vision of success. What will it look like when your mission becomes a reality? Why does the mission matter? The vision is the picture of where you're doing what you're doing. Often the vision has a broad scope that is part of a wider movement that includes other partner organizations. You may have a similar vision but a different approach to or segment of the vision. This too is important to recognize, so you don't end up sabotaging your shared vision by becoming competitive with a valuable partner.

So paint a picture, with and for your staff and your constituents. Share a vision that you all yearn for and want to work toward. Hold that vision at the center and help them see that there is movement forward.

Make It Your Own

- What will the world be like when your mission is fulfilled?
- In what way, if any, are you falling prey to any of the four pitfalls described in this section?
- Who are your valuable partners that have the same or a similar vision, and how can you support each other's work?

How Are You Going?

A former coworker of mine who is a Bangladeshi woman once told me that when she came to my organization for an interview, she felt confident while sitting in the waiting room that we would have a place for her. When she saw that we had a diversity display in the lobby, she felt herself relax. This was in the late 1990s, when "diversity" was the nomenclature for the work to build equity. The work and the nomenclature continue to evolve in order to expand the focus beyond demographics to practices of inclusion.

Although the example is dated, the commitment to values is not. Values speak to *how* an organization does its work. What matters? What guides? What checks the work?

Let's say a new organization hires a campaign organizer. She knows how to organize and is committed to the mission, but her supervisor still needs to talk about the "how" of the work. Maybe she is used to working solo and going for short-term maximum numbers. Your organization's values would have her working on teams and building relationships for long-term impact. As a supervisor, you cannot assume that the "how" is going to be the same, because the values of the organization determine the "how" of any job. And while many values of progressive organizations are the same, they are not identical—either in prioritization or in practical action. So *how* does this employee need to do her job, relative to the values?

My organization implemented the late-'90s value of diversity through hiring, promotions, evaluation, signage, displays, trainings, difficult conversations, books, orientation, and state-of-the-agency talks. It was very intentional and multifaceted. No one could get away from it! And that is how it should be. A value needs to be real and lived and tangible, not just theoretical.

So, what are the values of your organization, and how do they show up? The answers to this question may or may not replicate what the written values of your organization are. Many organizations claim inclusivity or equity as a value, but when you look at their practices, you may discern that their lived values actually replicate mainstream oppression. If you can't answer how an organization's values are implemented, you need to look at what *is* implemented and see what the actual values are.

As a supervisor, you need to model, teach, and monitor the values of your organization. How *you* do things is how the organization will do things. If the values are not showing up in the work, that is a problem that must be addressed. How staff do their work, how staff are treated, and how the organization interacts with the community all attest to how the organization displays its values.

Will someone recognize at least a hint of your organization's values when they walk into your space? Does your staff know the organization's values by how they are treated? Is the organization known in the community for walking its talk?

That's what values come down to: how you do things, and whether that is aligned with who you say you are. Only then can people feel confident that they are in the right place, doing the right work.

Make It Your Own

- Does your organization have stated values? Do you all know what they are?
- Do our values specifically speak to racial justice, gender justice, and other forms of justice? If so, do we have a shared understanding of what we mean by those terms?
- What are ways that our supervisors and managers are embodying our values? What are ways that they are not?
- Are the values reflected in job descriptions, evaluations, and expectations so that staff are held accountable to them?

Actively Highlighting the Mission, Vision, and Values

There were more than two hundred employees in a huge conference room in Santa Rosa, California. We came together from five different divisions and twenty locations. Once each year, we brought the entire staff together for one day. This was my big annual event as HR director. I had mandatory topics to cover, I wanted people to feel engaged and have fun, I wanted to bridge some of the silos that inevitably develop between programs, *and* I wanted to ground us all in our shared mission. Staff tended to have primary allegiance to their program, but our common mission united us, even when we didn't think about it. It was a lot to cover and a very stressful period of time. I loved it!

I loved the challenge of fitting all of those goals into one day. I loved inventing new ways to address safety and harassment and time sheets year after year. And I loved the creative challenge of connecting a diverse crowd with our shared mission, vision, and values.

One year, we filmed a video celebrating the work we had done, as an entire organization, to enliven our value of diversity. The video was dedicated to our coworker who had died the previous year. She had been our diversity leader and was well loved. Her death was shocking and heartbreaking. Barbara had the skills, at a time when diversity was not yet a mainstream topic, to challenge all of us (leadership and line staff) to walk our talk in a real and vulnerable way. The video was made in-house and managed to celebrate all the concrete steps we had taken and challenge us to do more, while also honoring Barbara, who had led us down this critical path. When the video ended, there was not a dry eye in the house, and the conversations that followed about our next steps were rich, deep, and challenging.

Another year, I started the meeting by passing out a copy of our mission statement printed on card stock. I asked each person to put it on the ground and stand on it. "This is not in any way meant to disrespect our mission; it is to remind every one of us that these words are the ground that we stand on. This is what unifies our work. This is what feeds our work. This is the beginning and end of our work." Then I had them talk to each other in small groups about how the mission fed their work. After that, we rolled out a banner with our mission statement on it and asked everyone to sign it at some point during the day to indicate their commitment to our shared work. We kept that banner posted at our central office for several years, as a powerful statement of our common ground.

One visioning we did was to work in teams to create a newsletter headline for a period in the future when our mission was declared complete. The headlines were alternately inspiring, funny, and poignant.

One of my favorite activities was when I printed up various icons and placed them under each attendee's chair. When our executive director finished her welcome/annual report/

appreciation speech, I had the staff find their icons and gather into groups based on their playful depictions. We had a team of unicorns, a team of kittens, a team of fire trucks. . . .

I asked each team to do four things together in fifteen minutes:

1. Introduce themselves.

2. Explain their program and their jobs.

3. Find a common value that all of their jobs demonstrated.

4. Come up with a unified way to demonstrate that value to the other groups.

After the fifteen minutes, I asked for groups to volunteer to show each other their unified value. One group showed a human-powered machine working smoothly together; one group made a heart; one group read a statement together. It was inspiring, fun, and connective. One of the best parts was seeing people talking to (and playing with) other staff members whom they had not known when they walked in that morning.

Our mission, vision, and values came alive every day within the work. On the day of our all-staff meeting, they became visible to each of us. As soon as we completed our annual meeting, I started thinking about how we would highlight our mission, vision, and values the next year.

Make It Your Own

- How does your organization highlight your mission, vision, and values?
- When did you last explicitly mention your mission, vision, or values, and how was that received?
- What difference does it make if people feel inspired by the mission, vision, and values? Is it really necessary if they are doing good work?

Touchstone

My business was not always called Supervision Matters. When I first went out on my own and imagined my business, trying to define my niche and be creative and inspiring, I launched it as Touchstone. I loved the sound of it and the idea I had of the concept: as something to help people be more authentic. But then I looked it up in the dictionary and changed my mind about it as a business name.

Merriam-Webster's online dictionary defines "touchstone" as:

1. a fundamental or quintessential part or feature;
2. a test or criterion for determining the quality or genuineness of a thing.

My reaction was to the "test" part at the heart of the second definition. I did not want my work to be a test; that did not fit the image I had of myself or my business. But the word does work very well as an image of how an organization can use its mission, vision, and values. These can, and should, be tests.

The mission can be a test to make sure an organization is on track, that it is being true to its key purpose and the reason for its existence. This can be a critical asset when staff are weighing new programs, funding sources, and strategic plans.

The vision can be a test in the form of looking at progress and focus. Are we inching closer to the ideal we hope to achieve? How do we know? Are we moving forward in a meta fashion or by and through individual movement? Is that what we want to be doing? Are we doing what we are trying to do?

And values can be a test of whether we are walking our talk. Are our values obvious in the way we operate? In the way we treat staff? In our reputation in the community and how we partner with others? What does it mean if we say we value teamwork and then actively reward and promote individual achievers? What does it mean if we say we value inclusion, and all of our leaders are straight, white, and able-bodied?

Actively using your mission, vision, and values as a touchstone will help you determine your quality and genuineness as an organization. When you do this in a purposeful and regular manner, you will be a stronger organization, and your reputation will support your work in recruitment, funding, and partnering.

I had to let go of Touchstone as my business name, but I never let go of my love of the metaphor and the value of the tool.

Make It Your Own

- Certified B corporations are businesses that meet the highest standards of verified social and environmental performance, public transparency, and legal accountability to balance profit and purpose. What would their touchstones be?
- How do you currently use your mission, vision, and values as touchstones, and is there anything you'd like to do differently or more deliberately in their use as such?
- What is one personal touchstone you use in your life, and how does that show up at work, if at all?

Mission Touches Everyone and Everything

When President John F. Kennedy announced his goal of landing a man on the moon in 1961, America had spent barely fifteen minutes in space. Just over a year later, the story goes, Kennedy visited NASA. He saw a janitor with a broom, politely introduced himself, and asked the janitor what he was doing. The janitor promptly replied, "Mr. President, I am helping to put a man on the moon." And, of course, NASA achieved that incredible goal in less than ten years!

This story is often told to illustrate the power of a BHAG, a Big Hairy Audacious Goal, as defined by Jim Collins and Jerry Porras. It does that, but it is also a great anecdote about the through line of a strong mission.

As I mentioned earlier, every employee at any given point in time should be able to stop what they are doing and draw a figurative line from what they are doing to their mission. How is what they are doing impacting the mission? As the janitor knew, every element matters, from the engineers' mathematical calculations to the people putting together the space capsule screw by screw to the janitor keeping the NASA offices clean.

Every single thing they do. At any point in time. If they cannot draw that connecting line, why are they doing it?

This does not mean that every moment must be spent in serious, direct actions, with clients or members, but it does mean that every moment matters. If you are playing a game with your team, how does that help you work better together? If you are filling out a report, how does that information make a difference? If you are in a meeting, are the right people there to impact the mission?

Is this a critical and real challenge? Can you and your staff connect the dots between your work and your mission? Do you talk to your staff about how vital their jobs are to fulfilling the mission? If you randomly asked your staff or your peers, "How does this action impact the mission?" could they answer quickly, authentically, and meaningfully? And if not, what does that tell you?

The story about the janitor may be apocryphal, but I hope not, because I love the pride, audacity, and full teamwork that it illustrates. Does your mission deserve any less?

Make It Your Own

- What do you think of this idea of the through line from any action to the mission? How do you react to it intellectually? How do you react to it emotionally?
- Write down the last five things you did before you left work yesterday. Can you connect them to your mission?

- If you can name things you do, as an individual or as a team or organization, that do not support this through line, how can you change that? Can other people see and name the through line, even if you can't?

CHAPTER 3:

DAY-TO-DAY PRACTICES

Beware of the once per year supervisor. This is the in-name-only supervisor who shows up only to conduct your annual evaluation. The rest of the year, they function with the attitude "No news is good news" and "I'll let you know if we have a problem. Otherwise, carry on." Staff turnover rises when little to no supervision exists. The work can get off track, and even when it's great, staff feel disengaged and devalued. I hope this is a dying breed of leadership.

The actions of a supervisor and a leader contribute directly to the success or the decline of any organization. This is not because staff can't work independently or need monitoring but because collaboration, clarity, and connection need to exist throughout the organization. The best supervisors show up for their staff on a daily basis. They may not do so via direct communication or action, but their staff know nonetheless that their supervisor is behind them, as well as how that person is going to show up and support them.

It is through consistent practices that supervisors build effective partnerships that support collaboration. By establishing regular meetings and recognizing boundaries, good supervisors build connection. By understanding how their staff can be successful and knowing when (and when not) to intervene, they build clarity. And by uncovering hidden rules, they build trust that supports the entire organization.

Prepare Your Staff to Be Successful

Imagine that you are starting a new job as an outreach worker in a youth-violence-prevention program. Your supervisor reviews the "why," "how," and "what" of your job. Then he says, "So, I think you understand the obvious danger points of this job. We've talked through how to respond to those kinds of situations, and I know from your experience that you can handle them. There is one more kind of danger that we haven't talked about, but I want you to be ready if this happens. At some point, a parent or a youth is probably going to flirt with you. They may even blatantly come on to you. Here's how you should handle that. . . ."

Darryl, the supervisor in this scenario, told me about this conversation, which he has with all new staff during a training. We were talking about clear expectations and the idea of setting up staff for success. One of the prompts that I offered was to think about what might get a staff member in trouble, or what might happen that they are not prepared for. Darryl shared that he used to feel embarrassed to talk about this before it happened, but it kept happening and new staff did not know how to respond. They were afraid that they would drive someone away if they responded too strongly, and they also knew they couldn't go along with it. So he started adding this conversation to his orientation. And staff weren't embarrassed—they were appreciative. They felt protected that he was preparing them for the realities of the job. They knew they could talk real shit with him.

I love this example of setting up your staff for success. The more you can prepare them for both the day-to-day demands of the job and the wrinkles, surprises, and traps, the safer they will feel, the more ready to step fully into the job, and the less fearful of doing something wrong.

Of course, no one can download all of this information in one sitting. You need to pace the conversations so that you don't overload staff. Lecturing new people until their eyes glaze over is not helpful. Instead, make a list and set them up for success.

The job description will be the primary tool to help you unpack the success factors of the job. Break down each bullet point and explain what it means, what it looks like, and what the timing is. Explain the "why" and "how" of each activity. Maybe the staff member was an outreach worker in their last job, but that doesn't mean that the job is done the same here. How do you conduct home visits? How does teamwork matter here? The "how" and the "why" are not usually in the job description, but they are incredibly important if you want your staff to understand the big picture and be successful.

Beyond the job description, here are other things you can help make clear with your colleagues:

- What is the day-to-day pace of this work?
- How, when, and whom should staff ask for help?
- What is the hardest (trickiest, most confusing, most ambiguous) part of the job?
- What has gotten other people in trouble in this job?
- When do staff need to run things by you before acting?
- What are the top three priorities if they get overwhelmed?
- How and when can they bring suggestions to you if they find a better way to do the work?

I'm sure there are more, but these questions will help you think through how to set your staff up for success. You don't have to address all of them. Some won't apply, some can wait, and some might be better addressed after they've done the work for a few weeks.

What does success look like for this staff member in this job? Frame that as a big part of your role as a supervisor.

Make It Your Own

- What is not in the job description that every employee needs to know to be successful in this organization?
- How, if at all, does your role shift when you think of setting up your staff for success, instead of simply teaching them how to do the job?
- When you consider Darryl's example, what comes to mind that you might want to warn your staff about?

Regular Meetings

The best way to embody this style of supervision is by establishing regularly scheduled one-on-one meetings with each staff member. "Regularly" means "in a consistent, predictable manner"—e.g., once per week, once every other week, or once per month. "Scheduled" means these meetings are planned and written on both of your calendars and made a priority. They don't get moved lightly or replaced very often by something more important. Of course, you may have to reschedule occasionally, but when that happens, apologize and change the date immediately.

By establishing these meetings, you do several things at once:

- You show each staff member that they are worthy of your time and attention.
- You build the relationship by having regular and ongoing conversations.
- You have a set time to check in on how things are going.
- You can celebrate successes close to when they happen.
- You can catch problems or confusion sooner, rather than later.

- You continually fine-tune and expand expectations.
- You normalize feedback because it happens routinely.
- You find out how best to support each person.
- You build awareness of each staff member's strengths, style, and challenges.
- You build a stronger team.

Pretty impressive investment of about an hour per week or month, right?

The timing of this meeting will be based on a number of variables, including:

- Tenure in the position (you'll meet more often with new staff)
- Skill in the position (you'll meet more often with staff who are developing skills or having trouble)
- Complexity and/or time concerns regarding the staff member's job and/or current projects
- Impact of any potential mistakes on the organization
- Confidence of each staff member
- Autonomy of position
- Questions each staff member has

No matter how senior, confident, independent, and trusted a staff member is, these meetings should happen at least monthly—remember, scheduled regularly. If all is going well, the meetings can be updates and time to connect. If you or your staff have questions or concerns, you'll voice them.

It is essential that you construct these meetings as conversations, meaning that they involve two voices. You must listen at least as much as you talk. This is not a meeting where you bark out a list of tasks and your staff member takes notes. This is not a corrections or counseling meeting, although that may happen sometimes. This is a meeting between partners. Each partner has a voice.

The content of the meeting will vary according to each of your particular needs, but a good basic format is:

- What's working?
- What's not working?
- What's next? (This makes sure you are in agreement about the priorities between now and when you meet again.)

These questions are open-ended, so the answers might range far and wide. That's okay. What's working might be about the immediate work. It might be about skills that are being developed. It might be about your working relationship. It might be about members, the organization, or the team.

The same goes for what's not working. You may get some feedback in these meetings, and you need to hear it and consider it. What's not working might include skills that the staff member wants to be able to use in her job, or it might be performance that is not meeting the necessary criteria. Remember, you're still the supervisor, even though you're working in partnership with staff.

Some people need more guidance than others, so you may find that some staff members work well with an hour every other week and that other staff find that an hour per week is not enough. These meetings do not have to be open-ended. You do want to give each staff member enough time that they can move the work forward, and it may be appropriate to have different times with different people. But it is also okay for you to say, "We've got an hour. What is most important for us to talk about?" At the end of the hour, wrap it up and schedule another time if you still have pressing business to address. If you just let the meeting go on, the meeting will always go on.

Let me underline this important point: These meetings are scheduled. You may talk to your staff members every day. Questions and emails may flow back and forth all the time.

That's okay, *and* that is different than these meetings. And these meetings are different than staff meetings. Those are important, but those are not this!

Here are a few things I've heard from supervisors who have tried this regular meeting format:

"It made all the difference. I could relax between meetings and know what was happening. And my staff member no longer felt like I was breathing down their neck."

"Feedback simply became part of the conversation, instead of a big deal."

"It truly was an investment that saved time."

"Instead of asking me questions all the time, my staff member now manages her time and saves her questions for our weekly meeting—and she became more clear about when it was appropriate to get guidance in between the meetings."

"Our staff meetings became more efficient because our individual meetings dealt with more questions and more work."

This works!

Make It Your Own

- What has worked in your one-on-one meetings with colleagues you supervise, and what has not worked? (Ask these same questions after conducting one-on-one meetings for a specific period of time—e.g., six months.)
- What does support specifically look like to you?
- Some people tend to think of one-on-one meetings as micromanaging. How could you reframe them to emphasize their supportive, investment-focused, and mission-imperative nature?

Respect Boundaries

A supervisor named Kelly was very frustrated because her staff member was not understanding Kelly's workload, yet wanted her own work to be understood and supported. "It's a two-way street, right?" Kelly asked me during a coaching call. "No, it is not a two-way street," I replied. "Not in that way."

I'm all about working in partnership, but this is not a partnership between peers in the work. If you are the supervisor, your role is different than your staff member's role. It is part of your job to support and guide your staff's work. It is imperative that you show respect and appreciation for that work.

It is not, however, your staff's job to understand and support your work, unless their work is intricately connected to your work. If their job is to be your assistant, then, yes, their role is to support your work, but otherwise, no. This is *not* a two-way street. As a supervisor, you must carefully navigate the issue of boundaries. Their job is to do the work, not to take care of you.

This dynamic can be tricky, particularly in small organizations, where friendships may develop. I would like to say, "Don't be friends with the people you supervise," but I know that is not always realistic. If that is too firm a rule, it can cause distance and weirdness. But ideally, the role is friendly but not a friendship. If you are friends with one or more of your direct reports, then you need to acknowledge that there is a firm line between work and not work. You cannot share confidences or treat friends differently than non-friends—you're going to have a hard enough time maintaining consistency and objectivity without friendships muddying the water. You can be sure that if you are friends with one or more staff members, people will be watching how that impacts your interactions with them and others.

Beyond the danger of friendships, there is the danger of invading privacy. One staff member I worked with told me, "Everyone is friends where I work, and so my supervisor feels free to ask me about my dating life and my relationship with my mom. I don't like it, but I feel like I have to answer her." Yikes!

Be careful. Follow the lead of your staff person. If you are curious about their personal life, ask open-ended questions, like "Did you do anything fun this weekend?" If they respond promptly and in a friendly way, giving you more detail about what they did and with whom, then you can assume (at least for now) that they are open to sharing some of their personal life. If they respond, "Not really" or, "Yay, I had a good weekend" but offer no follow-up comments, follow their lead and do not pry. *Do not* ask, "What did you do?"

Be equally careful about sharing details of your personal life. It's fine to offer a few general nuggets: "My kids and I went to the Giants game. It was a good one." But do not add, "I had the kids this weekend. I'm divorced, and my ex-husband is being a real asshole about sharing custody." TMI!

It is also important to be attentive regarding what is welcome in these general comments. Too often this is an area where heteronormative/nuclear-family assumptions exclude people. Make sure that when someone shares something that reveals them as queer or as having a non-majority lifestyle, you receive that information with the same welcoming manner as you do with any other shared information. Don't let heteronormative or race-normative or class-normative ideas dictate what can and can't be shared. This is an area where inclusion or exclusion is felt in an immediate and real manner, and where norms and customs of what is appropriate to share, and what is too much (or too little) information, vary.

Some of the ways in which supervisors have been known to cross boundaries are:

- Asking prying questions or expecting staff to share details of their personal life
- Sharing details of their personal life when not invited to do so
- Giving or asking for personal advice
- Sharing/using confidential information
- Spreading gossip/talking about what is happening with other staff

- Asking a staff member for advice about how to work with a coworker (or a boss)
- Invading personal space; assuming it is okay to hug, pat, or touch a staff member
- Not respecting cultural/ethnic/race/class differences and/or expecting staff to explain things about their identity
- Talking about your team as a family and/or acting parental (e.g., giving advice on dating or other relationships)
- Making inappropriate jokes or innuendos
- Engaging in unwelcome teasing, especially anything related to a protected class—e.g., age, color, gender, religion, political affiliation, hair, or dress. (Even if these are not all "protected classes" in your state, they are still areas to be respectful of and to avoid joking or teasing about.)

The difficulty with boundaries is that they are often invisible. Tread carefully, and notice any signs of discomfort or hesitancy. Be especially careful if these are areas that your organizational culture accepts as fair game. There are many ways to connect and be friendly without venturing into such dangerous territory.

Make It Your Own

- On a spectrum from detached to enmeshed, where does our organizational culture fall on the question of boundaries?
- What can supervisors do to make the line between work and friendship clear, so as to avoid favoritism and the perception thereof?
- Are there any areas on the "teasing" list where we have let our guard down? Why/how is this such a dangerous and tricky area?

The Relevant Question

Megan and Sam were good friends. They often spent time together on weekends and always had lunch together. Their laughter frequently rang through the office when they shared jokes or teased each other. Their friendship was obvious but not exclusionary.

Then one Monday, Joanne, who supervised both Megan and Sam, noticed that the women were not laughing. At lunch, they headed in different directions. At the staff meeting, they did not sit near each other or talk about their weekend. They both seemed subdued and distant. Joanne checked in with each of them, "Is everything okay?" They each told her everything was fine.

This went on for more than a week. Joanne called me, frantic, and told me about the dramatic shift in their relationship. I asked her, "How is this impacting their work?"

She was taken aback and replied, "It isn't impacting their work. They seem to have had a fight or something."

"But they are talking to each other enough to get their work done?" I asked.

"Yes, I think so. I haven't noticed any problems with their work. What do I do? How can I help them?"

"You don't do anything," I told her. "You are their supervisor. If the work is proceeding, then it's none of your business."

"But it's so quiet. They're barely speaking to each other."

"If the work is proceeding, then *it is their business*," I repeated. "Have they asked you for help?"

She sheepishly admitted that they had not.

"Then leave it alone," I said.

This was hard for Joanne. She liked people to be happy. It made her uncomfortable that two of her staff were barely talking to each other. Besides, she was dying to know what had happened. She had to manage her own feelings. These were her colleagues' personal lives, and their issues were not work-related.

One of the most important questions for a supervisor to ask is, how does this affect the work? When something isn't working, when staff are not meeting your expectations, when people are not getting along, when results are not what you expect, this is the basic question that will help you figure out how to respond. Until you can clearly answer this question, any directives or suggestions or even expectations might be confused and irrelevant, or appear to be irrelevant. In most situations, this question will help you understand what needs to be done and how to address the situation.

Ask yourself this question often, especially when you don't know how to talk about something with your staff. If the answer is that their circumstances do not affect the work, then the situation might not need any intervention from you. But be open to a wide answer. It may not impact a direct work product, but if it impacts the team in a way that affects their work—for example, if people are working around a negative staff member because no one wants to talk to them—then that *is* impacting the work. The work can be impacted in any number of ways, including productivity, morale, teamwork, clarity, trust, time management, and priorities.

Start with this question: How does this impact the work? Once the answer is clear, you will have a better sense of how to intervene, if at all. Make a plan about what to do, when to do it, and how to talk about it, and then proceed with your plan. Focus on the clarity of how the work is impacted and what needs to be different.

Make It Your Own

- What if Sam or Megan had asked Joanne to help them work something out? When would that be appropriate, and when would it not? How does *the* question apply in that circumstance?

- When else might this question be appropriate to ask? At a staff meeting? Before you give feedback?
- What are the dangers of not asking this question? What happens when a supervisor wades into non-work-related areas?
- There are direct impacts on the work, in terms of productivity, performance, teamwork, etc., and then there are indirect impacts, such as bullying, gossiping, and high-maintenance employees. Which kind of impact do you find easier to address, and why?

Supervising Staff Who Aren't There

How do I know what remote staff are doing? How will they be connected to a team? How will I know if they are really working when they say they are? What if something comes up and I need to talk to them and they aren't available? What if they totally drop the ball?

These and many more are the fears that I hear from supervisors when staff are considering working remotely—and not so much from supervisors when staff *are* working remotely. Even before the world fell victim to a rogue virus, COVID-19, remote workers were becoming more common. Once we all got used to working from home, the world changed. Now, most of us have experienced working from home and supervising remote staff. All along, there were some workplaces that were entirely virtual; there was no *there* there. And they made it work. The work happened, and the organizations thrived.

The basic keys of supervision apply whether staff are in the next room or the next state. Build a relationship so that you know who these people are and how to help them be successful, and so that they know you and how you work. Communicate clear expectations about everything from their specific working hours and what you need to see and hear about their work to the mission, the outcomes, the benchmarks, the values, and the policies and practices. And provide clear and specific feedback about the work.

The need for regularly scheduled check-ins is even more critical and timely with remote staff. If you would meet with an on-site worker once every two weeks, meet with your remote staff weekly.

Here are some additional tips for supervisors who support remote staff:

1. **Stay connected.** One of remote work's most frequently reported downsides is a feeling of disconnection and/ or exclusion. This can show up in the form of staff not knowing new people, not getting updates that impact their work, being left out of meetings, and hearing from their supervisors rarely, or only for quick, urgent calls.

So schedule your one-on-one meetings and prioritize them. If you absolutely must cancel a meeting, reschedule it immediately. Allow time for some friendly chatting if the staff person is comfortable with that. Don't pry, but ask open-ended, inviting questions and step into the connection if they offer it. Talk about yourself in a general, friendly manner to model this dynamic: "My partner had two recitals this weekend, so I spent a lot of time hearing her play the piano. It was kind of boring and kind of wonderful." Schedule most of your meetings as video chats, so that you connect in some of the nonverbal ways humans employ when we are together.

Make sure that staff meetings (which should definitely be video conferences) include everyone, and that you invite your distant staff to join in, especially if most people are in the same room. Start with a check-in question or icebreaker to allow everyone to connect and belong. It's easy to forget that one person on the screen when seven others are in the room. Offer round-robin opportunities so that everyone has a chance to weigh in on questions or concerns. Include remote staff in training opportunities, ad hoc meetings, quick conversations, social events, and updates/changes that impact their work.

2. **Establish clear benchmarks and reporting.** Some remote staff value brief daily or weekly written reports, in which they answer specific, agreed upon questions. Find a system that works for you and each staff member and that is appropriate to the work. Some jobs may require daily check-ins, especially for new staff. Other jobs may require just a quick update before or during one-on-one meetings. Make sure outcomes are clear and that you agree on due dates and deliverables.

3. **Let go, but don't abandon.** If you are new to supervising remote staff, those nagging questions may haunt you, especially when your success is dependent on their success. Experiment (transparently and together) to discover what level of oversight/reporting/connection you need to feel mutually comfortable and confident that the work and the support are happening. Maybe you start out with a daily list of tasks and reporting, and when that works, move to twice per week, then once per week, and so on. You want to find a balance that gives the staff member autonomy and flexibility appropriate to their job and that doesn't leave you a nervous wreck or leave them confused and floundering.

4. **Build a budget to get together.** The most successful virtual teams host quarterly or semiannual in-person retreats when possible. It is essential that people connect as people, not just positions. The value of in-person meetings may be intangible, but that does not mean they are not important. Eating together and learning one another's body language and style, having a chance not to focus on work, and laughing together are all important.

5. Be transparent and trustworthy. Admit that this is difficult if it is. Do what you say you will do. Prioritize your meetings. Don't put off the hard conversations. Don't take your staff or their work for granted because they are not in front of you. Appreciate them and their work. If you are hosting a lunchtime staff meeting, send them takeout so everyone can eat together. If you are not sure they can accomplish their job remotely, name that concern, but also give them a fair trial. Make clear agreements. Apologize if you left them out of a meeting that they should have been in. Ask for their help if they need to manage some aspect of the off-site dance. And, of course, always listen at least as much as you talk.

Remote workers are an important part of the work world. Supervision still matters and can make or break the dynamic. Remote work can be a strong retention tool when it goes well. Don't be the reason it doesn't work.

Make It Your Own

- A danger of supervising remote workers is that many supervisors tend toward micromanagement or abandonment. The sweet spot is in the middle. What are the signs that a supervisor is finding the middle ground for any particular staff?
- What are the danger signs that remote work is not working? How are the deal breakers different when the worker and the work are off-site? (Deal breakers are behaviors that cannot be tolerated and will lead to termination if they continue.)
- Do you tend to respond more to intrinsic or extrinsic rewards? (Feeling good primarily about the outcome of the work would be an example of an intrinsic reward; feeling good primarily about earning a raise would be an

example of an extrinsic reward.) What do you notice about your staff's responses to rewards, and how do those impact their experience with remote work?

The Danger of Hidden Rules

Many years ago, I read a book called *A Framework for Understanding Poverty*, by Ruby K. Payne. The book describes the hidden rules of class and how they are used to identify insiders and uncover outsiders. Since then, I have observed many types of hidden rules. The classic example of a hidden rule is when someone is faced with three forks at a formal dinner and doesn't know when or how to use them, but knows that if they use those utensils incorrectly, they will be in trouble—or at least embarrassed.

When we start a job in a new organization—or even in a new department or with a new supervisor—we often confront hidden rules, sometimes even after we think we fit in. Most of the time, we can figure out these hidden rules through observation, by messing up and being told the "correct" way of doing things, or by asking about them directly. Typical questions include:

- How important are deadlines here?
- Do people show up for meetings on time?
- Is it okay to make jokes or tease each other?
- How are birthdays acknowledged here, if at all?

But sometimes the hidden rules are more insidious, and not catching on to them can lead to someone being ostracized or labeled a troublemaker. Examples include:

- Only the boss talks in staff meetings.
- Ask your coworkers any questions you have, not your supervisor.

- The leader does not want to hear criticism or concerns.
- No one talks about the elephant in the room.

If the leader is not able to hear feedback or concerns, then someone offering them could be seen as a troublemaker. The problem is that when the rules are hidden, we often don't even realize there are things we should know or traps that might get tripped.

So the question for you, as a supervisor, is how can you uncover the hidden rules for your staff to keep them out of trouble and set them up for success? In order to do so, you must analyze your department and look critically at what actually happens and what the unspoken rules are.

Sometimes uncovering hidden rules is easy. This happens when you hear people say things like, "Well, they should have known" or, "Who doesn't know . . ." or, "I shouldn't have to tell her that."

The most treacherous hidden rules are the ones that are actually the opposite of the stated rules. For instance, many organizations have a stated policy that leaders have "an open door" and want to hear from any employee at any time, when the reality is that no leader will consider an idea unless and until it works its way up the company's hierarchy. Other organizations may have a stated process of resolving conflict directly, but the reality is that no one talks directly and anyone who tries to do so is seen as a problem.

Of particular concern in this area are the hidden rules about values: "We say we value families here, but every time I take a sick day for my kids, I get the silent treatment." "We say we value racial equity here, but if I call someone out on something offensive, they just deny it and that's the end of the conversation."

Even more insidious are hidden societal rules that many people follow so blatantly that we often accept them (or might not even see them), but they cause all kinds of problems at work and in life. Knowingly or unknowingly, these hidden rules are often a gateway to the perpetuation of oppression and injustice. Examples of these rules might be:

- Talking about race is impolite, and calling some action racist is a personal insult and must never happen.
- Men dominate the meeting and the agenda, even when they are the clear minority in the room.
- Women traditionally don't negotiate their opening salaries; men do. (Guess who gets paid more?)
- Gender is binary, and the topic is off the table.

When you can uncover benign hidden rules that you can show your team, your staff will be better prepared to work for your organization and more likely to identify inequities and hidden rules when they see them in the future. They will also probably see you as a helpful supervisor who has your staff members' backs when you show them the ropes of navigating hidden rules. When you reveal hidden rules that undermine your company's values, you offer a chance for organizational alignment. Doing so might be uncomfortable, but most organizations will appreciate the opportunity to correct these kinds of unspoken practices. And when you call out insidious, oppressive hidden rules, you are offering your organization a chance to address deep and impactful problems. You might be seen as a rebel and a troublemaker for daring to uncover these issues. Be a troublemaker on the side of transparency, alignment, and justice.

Make It Your Own

- Have you experienced a situation like the three-forks example, when you realized you didn't know what you were supposed to do? What was the situation, and how did that feel?

49

- On the other hand, have you ever been the one to know the rules and see people who didn't know them struggle or embarrass themselves? What did you do and how did you feel in that situation?
- Uncovering the hidden rules in an organization can be daunting (and dangerous). What would need to be in place before you could freely uncover and discuss hidden rules in your organization? Whose voices might you need to listen to in order to learn what's hidden?
- What is at risk if you don't address the deeper hidden rules that replicate oppression?

CHAPTER 4:

SUPERVISION IS A TEAM SPORT

No one is a supervisor in isolation. Supervision is a team sport, whether it is played that way or not. When each supervisor in an organization works independently and does their own thing, trouble can brew. The door is open to different practices that can be unfair, or at least seem that way. Inconsistent practices can lead to inequity and mistreatment. Isolation can undermine intentions and invite danger.

On the other hand, when a unified approach to supervision is implemented throughout the organization, magic can happen. Consistency breeds safety. Shared experiences build improvements by addressing problems and amplifying successes. There is still room for individual styles and flexibility when the whole organization recognizes the importance of a supervisor's role. Supervisors and staff alike feel more valued and supported.

Make sure you have a plan for good supervision. Keep supervision as a topic of conversation, training, attention, and assessment. Never forget that it matters and that it is a team sport.

Ten Questions for Supervisors on the Path to Justice

I must never forget that I am white. I must never forget that my lens is the lens of the historically racial majority and the lens of the advantaged and non-oppressed. I grew up poor and I grew up female, and this led to some experiences of systemic marginalization. On a personal level, I experienced troubles that contributed to my having less advantages than others. However, I have always been white. I have always been straight and gender-conforming and able-bodied. With those identities come certain privileges that I have not always recognized as privileges; I just took them for granted. They were normal and routine and, as far as I knew, what everyone experienced.

And then, a long time ago, I started working with people who did not have those experiences of basic acceptance, routines, and norms. I started learning about differences and unearned advantages; I started learning about systemic oppression. I learned pieces from the other side of standardized American history. And I learned that I was, inadvertently, part of the problem. I also learned that I could be, intentionally, part of the solution. But I had to be ready to step up. I had to be uncomfortable and embarrassed and humble. I had to do some hard self-reflection. And I had to look through other people's lenses to get a glimpse of what it means to be "other" in our society.

Supervisors must bring self-awareness and self-reflection to their role—particularly regarding dynamics of race, gender, class, power, and privilege, and in terms of how they show up. How does your lens impact what you consider normal and appropriate, not to be ashamed or "politically correct" but to be empathetic and effective in your work? You must not expect others to know what you know, but meet people where they are and how they are.

Here are a few questions to consider:

1. When I am hiring, do I carefully consider which specific traits and skills a candidate needs to fulfill the role, or do I just trust my gut about who will be the best fit?

2. Do I automatically require a college or postgraduate degree for every job, without considering the possibility that people could attain the required skills through experience?

3. What do I identify as a "good work ethic" and "professional conduct," and how do I react to people who don't exhibit those qualities?

4. Do I expect people to complete assignments and projects the same way I do? Do I have a clear (or vague) understanding of how a particular job should be accomplished?

5. Should I pay people based on their last salary?

6. Do I believe that identity doesn't matter in the workplace? Do I consider how my own identity brings its larger history and its societal messages to the workplace, whether they are true for me or not?

7. Do I recognize the power that is inherent in having a supervisory position?

8. Do I speak up when I see systemic practices that can lead to silencing within the workplace?

9. Do I attentively invite and listen to the experiences of the people I supervise without putting them on the spot or expecting them to speak for their "group"?

10. Am I rigorously consistent in how I apply both positive and negative consequences with my staff?

Here are the dangers or values in each action listed above:

1. Without carefully considering the objective traits and skills needed to fulfill a specific job, we will be more likely to hire someone who is similar to us. We all unconsciously want to hire someone just like us; it makes work so much easier (but not necessarily more effective!). This practice also keeps workplaces homogenous and insular. (See more about this in chapter 7.)

2. When we automatically require a college or postgraduate degree for a job, without considering the possibility that people could attain the required skills through experience, we systematically exclude many people who grew up without the opportunities or resources for higher education. This exclusion disproportionately affects BIPOC and poor people because of historic and systemic economic and institutional decisions and actions. It also undervalues other forms of experience.

3. "Good work ethic" and "professional conduct" are often unrecognized shorthand for white middle-class characteristics and practices and therefore discount people who work hard and act professional in different ways.

4. If our understanding of how a job needs to be handled is based on explicit, nonnegotiable requirements (i.e., writing legal briefs), then it makes sense to teach people those rules. But sometimes the expectation to do things a certain way is simply how *we* would do it, or how we have seen it done previously. Consider whether there is another way to do something—one that looks different but is still effective and leaves more room for cultural and personal differences while building a more equitable work environment.

5. Basing the salaries of new staff on their past salary can perpetuate gender and racial discrepancies, which unfairly reinforce pay gaps. This practice is illegal in California, New York City, and other states and locales.

6. When we act as if we are all the same and as if our social identity has nothing to do with work, we deny history and the present conditions of systematic oppression. This is especially true for men and white people. Whether we like it or not, we have to own our identities as "white women" or "cis white men." White people have done great systematic harm to BIPOC in this country, and white people actively benefit from existing systems, policies, and practices. Our coworkers and staff may assume that we possess all the negative attributes of our identity. This may or may not be about each of us as an individual and may rather be about staff protecting themselves from their past experiences with people who look like us, either historically or in their lives or both.

7. The people we supervise will see us as people with positional power, and if we do not recognize, acknowledge, and accept that responsibility, they might consider us dangerous people who use our power with impunity and lack of awareness. That will impede trust and get in the way of the work, especially if we also display unacknowledged privilege of our identity.

8. When we remain silent when we see silencing or exclusionary practices, we are not just tolerating those practices but condoning them and aligning with systemic oppression. And the people we supervise will notice and remember our silence. This does not mean we always have the power, position, or personal ability to change the systems we see, but we can usually name them. It is also important to recognize

that this is another area where identity has an impact; for a woman in a male system, speaking up could be difficult. For a person of color in a white-dominated organization, doing so might be even more problematic.

9. If we do not proactively and routinely invite the people we supervise to share their experiences, and if we do not listen to what they have to say, then we will not hear what we need to hear and people will not speak their truth. It is critical that when we listen, we believe what we hear. We must trust that staff are speaking their truth, even if it does not match our intentions or our experiences.

10. Without rigorously and consistently second-guessing and reviewing both the positive and the negative consequences we give to our staff, we could be applying subconscious biases to promotions, raises, warnings, or even terminations. We must learn to add a filter of consideration to double-check the decisions we make, both as individual supervisors and as an organization: "Would I respond this way if this person were [white, straight, etc.]?"

We must all work to be a part of the solution. Speak up for justice. These questions will not, in and of themselves, end injustice in the workplace, but they will help you to be a better supervisor. It's not about being "politically correct" (see sidebar); it's about being thoughtful and fair and helping all staff members be themselves and be successful.

Make It Your Own

- Which of these ten suggestions resonates with you, and why?
- How does the lens of your racial, gender, and class identity and your life experiences impact how you show up at work?

- Are there aspects of your identity that you never have to think about? How could recognizing that privilege shift your internal understanding of yourself and others?
- How have you reacted when someone has talked about their identity and felt mistreated or discriminated against? Did your reaction change based on whether their identity was different from your own?

Note

"Politically correct" is a phrase that denies the power of language and behavior. Phrases and actions that are labeled as politically correct are hardly ever insignificant. It's not about just using the current trending language; it's really about recognizing that every person has a right to be seen and heard and respected for who they are—and that *they* get to say what that looks like. This is a facet of our constantly evolving language and culture. If I need to learn new language, like "cisgender," so be it. If that helps someone feel included, instead of excluded, why wouldn't I say/do that? Why would I intentionally choose not to care about people who are feeling alienated?

How People Are Treated

To most people, their supervisor embodies their organization, has the most influence on their day-to-day work, and makes it rewarding or stressful, productive or frustrating, worthwhile or inconsequential. People either feel respected by their supervisor or eventually leave their company.

While we can hope that nonprofits in general, and social justice organizations in particular, have higher engagement and satisfaction than many corporations, most issues of employee satisfaction still circle back to management issues. Organizations such as the Building Movement Project look at the racial and generational leadership gaps in the nonprofit sector and work to bridge those gaps.

To say that supervision matters is really to say, quite simply, that the way people are treated matters. People work in nonprofits and for social justice in order to make a difference in the world. They want to be instrumental in how people are treated; they want to create a more just and equitable society. When these same people feel disrespected, they are furious. And when they feel micromanaged or mistreated or left out, they feel betrayed. In the case of people who have faced systematic oppression—BIPOC people, women and gender-nonconforming people, LGBTQ+ people, people with disabilities, and others—this becomes another experience of oppression.

How people are treated matters. And people at work are most directly impacted by their managers' actions. Managers can make the values, the policies, and the practices of their organization real. They can hold people accountable for what they say and do. They can own their privilege and address aggressive and discriminatory actions. They set the priorities and the volume of work. They determine what actions are rewarded and who is supported. They model work-life balance. Or they don't do these things, thereby diluting or undermining the trust of staff in their supervisors—plural. If one supervisor is untrustworthy, it impacts all supervisors.

The way people are treated affects every part of organizational life. It is a matter of retention and integrity. And you can't do it alone.

Make It Your Own

- What is your reaction to the idea that to most people, their supervisor embodies their organization?
- Have you ever worked with a rogue supervisor who brought their team down and staff turnover up? How did that impact your work as a staff member?

- Do you conduct exit interviews? If so, what do they tell you about why people are leaving? If not, why not?

Consistency as a Tool of Equity

African Americans are incarcerated in state prisons at more than five times the rate of white people. The gap between white home-ownership and black homeownership is the highest it has been in fifty years, at more than 30 percent. The achievement of college degrees directly relates to earning power, so when 15 percent of Latinx and 23 percent of Black people have a bachelor's degree or more education, compared with 36 percent of white people, that has a long-lasting impact. This short list shows a glaring need for greater equity and consistency. And it points squarely to a systemic problem that is bigger than any jurisdiction.

When we are working in the shadow of that kind of systemic oppression, it is not surprising that some disparities show up in even the most well-intentioned workplaces. The unintended replication of external injustices can form an internal system through policies, practices, and individual actions that are condoned or ignored. And, as with so many other issues that drive internal dynamics, this dynamic often comes back to supervision.

While I trust that most people would not intentionally treat staff in an unfair or inconsistent manner, it often happens inadvertently. One supervisor looks the other way when minor rules are broken or when staff are late or need extra time off. She is loose and easygoing, maybe even an "easy grader" of evaluations. Another supervisor in another department plays by the rules and interprets guidelines strictly. When her staff are late, they make sure to mark their time sheets truthfully and get some pay docked. She follows the letter of every policy and thoughtfully weighs her staff against the organization's stated criteria at evaluation time. This inconsistency is made even worse when evaluations determine who gets raises. This is a situation crying out for consistency.

Or let's look at the way in which inconsistencies can show up in supervision related to our biases, which might play out along racial or gender lines. Perhaps white supervisors give the benefit of the doubt to their white staff and assume wrongdoing when BIPOC staff do the same things. Or they give male staff leeway when they raise their voices or get angry but speak to women who engage in those same behaviors.

It is important for organizations to train supervisors to all follow the same basic approach and game plan. They also need to apply the same level of oversight to lapses and interpret the rules in a similar manner. This isn't about making everyone conform to a cookie-cutter mold; it is to ensure fairness and consistency.

When I work with organizations, I often train their supervisors. The training is the start of building a uniform practice. It gives them all a standard language and a common approach to what is important and how to hold people accountable. After the training, I encourage the organizations to spend time developing standards of supervision. The standards are what the organizations expect all supervisors to do. They leave room for individuality and style but ensure that all staff are being treated the same in terms of opportunity and trouble. The standards address factors such as the role of a supervisor, the regularity of meetings, the availability of training and the process of professional development, the process and use of evaluations, how and when discipline and termination work, the importance of privacy and confidentiality, and what teamwork looks like.

When a supervisor's role and actions are carried out in a similar fashion throughout the organization, people feel safer. When people are treated unfairly, whether in reality or in perception, the seeds of distrust are sown. Staff need to be focused on the injustice in the world, not within their own organizations.

Make It Your Own

- It is said that "perception is reality." While that may not be fair, how is it true?
- What happens when people feel treated unfairly? How could those feelings undermine your work if they were to erupt inside your organization?
- What is your organization doing to set standards of supervision? What's working in this regard? What's missing?
- As an individual supervisor, how can you raise this concern if you see or experience inconsistencies between supervisors?

Positive and Negative Impacts

Supervision matters, both positively and negatively. A disengaged or micromanaging supervisor can drive people away from organizations. A supportive and clear supervisor can build strong teams and synergy.

When supervisors are allowed to phone it in (i.e., simply go through the motions of their job, with no ownership of or investment in the outcomes), bad things start happening. Staff become disengaged, often not immediately, but after feeling unrecognized or disrespected by their manager. In such cases, most employees tend to step back from their work, at least a little bit. Bad habits start to develop, like gossiping and unhealthy group dynamics that pit one faction against another. And still the supervisor does not intervene.

Supervisors who don't know how to hold people accountable in a respectful and constructive manner often get frustrated with people whom they consider "bad" employees. They revert to authoritarian tactics to try to get results. They start shaming staff, sometimes even debasing and humiliating them. They hope the "bad" people will just quit—and they often do.

All of these actions create a negative and toxic work environment. People stop trying quite so hard. They may still care about the work, but they don't care so much about the organization anymore. They might take shortcuts or bad-mouth the organization in the community. All of this becomes a disincentive for the staff who are working hard. It is difficult to do good work when others are undercutting your performance or not doing their part.

This toxic environment has a direct effect on the outcomes the organization produces and on the way staff show up in every aspect of their work—and ultimately on the mission of the organization and all of the movements for justice. If supervision is not effective, the organization has a hard time being effective.

On the other hand, when a supervisor is well trained and works in partnership with their staff, things go more smoothly. Fewer problems arise, because the supervisor has invested time in preventing problems and/or addressing them sooner, rather than later. Teams work well together because the supervisor has put time and attention into getting people on the same page. These supervisors know how to set clear expectations and give specific feedback. They connect the work, all the work, to the mission. The work moves forward. It doesn't mean that everything is easy, but it does mean that no duplications of effort occur, things don't routinely fall through the cracks, and staff are engaged and productive. And, very often, they also have a good time. These organizations are often full of laughter and joy.

A few of the specific signs that an organization values supervision are:

- **Time:** The organization recognizes that supervision takes time and that time is built into their supervisors' work and valued by other managers and executives.
- **Training:** The organization spends time and money to invest in supervision training and to keep the topic on the table as something to value and address.

- **Inclusion:** Supervisors and executives come from the same communities and life experiences as the staff and clients; there is not an obvious racial, gender, or other distinction between who leads and who is expected to follow.
- **Perspective:** Organizations acknowledge that there are different ways to look at things. They invite staff input before they make decisions that will impact their staff. When something is not working, they ask, "What's going on?" They listen, and no one, literally or figuratively, says, "It's my way or the highway."
- **Standards:** The organization is clear about what it expects of supervisors. It talks about, codifies, and holds supervisors accountable to these standards.
- **Modeling:** Good supervision is modeled from the top. An executive director does not just talk about good supervision but practices it. They set regular meetings with their staff, they define success, and they give and receive feedback.
- **Assessment:** Periodically, these organizations facilitate an objective assessment to determine how things are going. Are they accomplishing what they plan to accomplish? Are their values being implemented? Are there any gaps in compensation, hiring, promotions, etc., that indicate bias is undermining their workplace?
- **Accountability:** These organizations hold people accountable, including supervisors for how they supervise. They make sure people do what they need to do and follow up on agreements. Accountability is relevant to tasks, their work, their results, their values, and their agreements.

The impact of supervision on an organization can be like the slow erosion of a foundation, or it can be a solid structure of support to hold the organization together.

Make It Your Own

- What are the impacts on staff when a supervisor tolerates poor behavior?
- Is this an example of the author's thinking all things relate to supervision? What else could contribute to the impacts described in this section?
- What can get in the way of supervisors doing this kind of work even when an organization values supervision? Is there any way to mitigate those factors?

Burnout

I knew it was a bad sign when I found myself fantasizing that maybe I would have an accident and not be able to go to work for a while. I quickly amended my fantasy so that it became an accident that would not be too painful but would still require me to stay home and watch TV for a month or two. That, my friends, is a symptom of burnout.

When I worked at an AIDS agency at the height of the epidemic, I noticed that people had a hard time leaving. Every employee was there because they were passionate about the work. Whether they were a case manager or a fundraiser, being a case manager or a fundraiser for this particular organization was what mattered. And often, when people were ready to leave, it was not easy (or even possible, in some cases) to say, "It's time for me to go." Their values, their commitment, and their identity were too caught up in the work.

So, more than once, the employee found a reason to become angry at the agency. Sometimes the reason was valid and there was something that needed to be adjusted or addressed, like the staff member who said we were not paying him what his colleagues doing similar work at another agency made. Sometimes the reason was something that had happened countless times before but had never bothered an employee until now, like the staff member whose supervisor spoke to him about being late, as they did once or twice a year. Only this time, he became furious and used that anger and that reason to leave the organization. Sometimes they even burned bridges when they left. It took several incidents like this, as well as a conversation with a trusted organizational consultant, before I realized this was how these staff members were protecting themselves. They couldn't just give up on the cause. They couldn't be people who walked away from the work. But they were also burned out and suffering personally and needed to leave the organization. They found a way to do that.

Merriam-Webster defines burnout as "exhaustion of physical or emotional strength or motivation usually as a result of prolonged stress or frustration." "Racial battle fatigue" is a term that William A. Smith coined in 2003 for the additional burden that BIPOC experience from repeated exposure to oppression and mistreatment. Some of the symptoms of burnout include extreme fatigue, loss of passion, and intensifying cynicism and negativity. Some of the symptoms of racial battle fatigue include headaches, raised heart rate, depression, chronic anxiety, anger, frustration, shock, disturbed sleep, helplessness, and fear.

These are both factors that have a huge impact on social justice work. Burnout does not result from simply having too much to do, and racial battle fatigue does not result from an isolated incident. Everyone working in the nonprofit and social justice field has too much to do. When staff feel as if they cannot get anything done, face seemingly endless obstacles, and are not making a difference, that's when burnout happens. Racial battle fatigue happens in our organizations when BIPOC and others must be on constant guard against mistreatment based on their identity.

Supervisors have a role to play in keeping overwhelm from becoming burnout. They must make sure staff have the skills, the clear priorities, and the authority to get work done.

Supervisors are the ones who can offer support and clarify priorities when they become too many or when too much noise surrounds competing actions that are all important. When everything is important, you can feel as if it doesn't matter what you do or when you do it or even if you do it, because you are never going to catch up or make a difference. There are no clear priorities when everything on your list is important. Supervisors can offer the focus and support to keep overwhelm from slipping into burnout, or they can push it down the hill by ignoring, or even adding to, the overwhelm.

Supervisors can also work to disrupt the oppressive practices that impact BIPOC staff by monitoring their own language and practices, by learning more about the issues and concerns that their staff face, and by speaking up when they hear problematic language or see inappropriate action. As a group, supervisors can lobby for training and practices that eliminate (or at least reduce) the need for BIPOC, LGBTQ+, and other staff to protect themselves from mistreatment within the organization. Leaders can work with their staff (and/or racial justice consultants) to create a clear code of conduct that addresses the specific ways in which racism, sexism, and ableism invade our organizations and add an extra layer of fatigue for targeted staff.

There is another level of supervision required when someone is experiencing debilitating fatigue or burnout. It is the supervisor who must have the difficult conversations with the employee about the situation. The supervisor must not only encourage time off and self-care but model it, and occasionally even mandate it, without blaming the person who is exhausted.

Burnout is a dreadful malady. It can strike individuals and organizations. The antidote is often clarity, healthy boundaries, equitable practices, and a good dose of collaborative joy.

Make It Your Own

- How can you reconcile the amount of work that must be done with a commitment to self-care?
- What are structural changes within your organization that could make getting the work done and self-care both possible?
- How is a culture of overwhelm related to a culture of scarcity?
- What do leaders in your organization model that contributes to any unspoken rules that staff are expected to give until they have nothing left?

Liability

When organizations get in trouble, it can be devastating; it can decimate budgets and ruin reputations—of the organization and the leadership. Liability can come in the form of a lawsuit, a government investigation, a problematic monitoring visit from a funder, or an attack from a group that would rather you didn't exist.

When it comes to labor law, rarely does it matter whether the organization is a nonprofit or if it is focused on social justice. The law is the law, and every organization is expected to comply with it. Ignorance of the law doesn't matter much either. You are expected to know the laws that apply to your work.

Supervisors can get organizations in trouble, either by what they do or by what they don't do. They can do it actively or passively. A lot can go wrong: wrongful termination, wage and hour claims, discrimination, harassment, unfair hiring practices, and any of these factors and more could be the title of a claim against the organization. And when a claim is filed, the organization must defend itself. The liability and its repercussions are huge, but so is the collateral damage. The organization's reputation is often severely damaged, even if it ultimately wins the lawsuit. Its reputation, of course, impacts donations, hiring, morale, and services.

Make sure your supervisors are trained. Make sure they know the dangers they face. How they respond to a question from a staff member, an offhand comment, or acts of bias could get them in trouble. They need to know what they can and can't do, and they need to know what the danger areas are so they can get help. I don't expect every manager to be a human-resources expert or a labor-law maven. But I do expect them to know when and how to get help. The fact that many social justice organizations have no HR function underlines the need for staff to be trained in danger areas and in how an affirmative, equitable workplace can mitigate those dangers. They must know how to respond when someone asks for a leave of absence or an accommodation. They have to understand what constitutes harassment and discrimination. And someone has to make sure the organization knows and is following national, state, and local labor laws. Make sure no one tells people they can't discuss their jobs on social media. Anyone who has responsibilities to hire and fire has additional concerns to worry about. So, train your staff about HR dangers, and make sure they know whom to go to and how to get help when they have questions or concerns.

All of these precautionary measures will help protect you from liability. You know what else will help? Having good supervisors who treat people fairly and consistently. When staff feel respected and supported in their work, they are far less likely to sue their employer without making at least some attempt at correcting the problem. And if they are committed to your mission and have a relationship with leadership, that is even better. Connecting with people makes a tremendous difference in all kinds of ways, including in terms of liability.

Paying attention to policies, procedures, and practices can feel like a distraction, like it is taking you away from the *real* work of your organization. I challenge you to shift this mindset. Think of it as wearing a mask during the COVID-19 pandemic:

I need to protect myself and others. It's about managing your risks so that you can stay healthy and continue to do your good work. If you don't protect the organization as a whole and the staff as employees, the work will suffer.

Labor law is the floor of basic protection for your staff. Most laws were enacted because people were systemically mistreated. Therefore, staff who can't rely on the basic safeties of labor-law protections and fair and consistent treatment are not doing their best work. No doubt they are committed to the mission, but they are also employees. And when a lack of basic organizational infrastructure exists, staff will eventually start feeling used and resentful. I have seen good, solid social justice organizations undermined by distrust and perceptions of mistreatment. Once any level of distrust exists, the liability door is open. All it takes is a claim from one unhappy employee to attract the skeptical and prying eyes of government authorities who want to pore over your records and books. Or, even worse, a group that wants to take down your organization because of the work you do hears rumors about wrongdoing and starts a public campaign to dishonor you and disrupt your work.

Labor law gives you the guidelines to ensure basic protection for your staff and your organization. In most cases, however, you will want to do much more.

Make It Your Own

- Discuss the pros and cons of nonprofits and/or social justice organizations having the same rules as for-profit organizations.
- How do you respond to the following statements? Labor law is about protection and therefore is grounded in social justice. If exploitation hadn't existed at some point, there would be no laws in this area.
- When policies are seen as laws, enforcing them can make managers feel like police. How can that role be reframed?

The One-Vent Rule

Plumbing vents are pipes that extend from internal waste pipes to the outside of a building, often going through the roof. The vent pipes allow sewer gases to escape to the outside, rather than being released inside the house and leaving it susceptible to exploding if a random spark ignites.

Sometimes supervisors serve the same purpose. If supervisors are approachable and trusted, staff will sometimes use them to vent. This outlet allows staff members to express upset, anger, frustration, or disappointment without unleashing those feelings on the team. The supervisor can listen, talk the staff member down, and defuse the situation. This approach can be helpful in the short term.

What happens in the long term, however? If the supervisor is successful as a vent pipe, the staff member leaves the meeting feeling better and life goes on. The supervisor, meanwhile, is left with all the negative feelings and unresolved issues. Even more important, the issue is never addressed with the team.

I have been told that I am a good listener. I was an excellent vent pipe for numerous staff. They would vent, I would support, they would go back to the same dynamics. At some point, I realized that I was not helping much. So I started trying to coach staff to address their own problems. They often would agree, and we'd make a plan. Then they would return a week or a month later and vent again, frequently about a situation identical to the one that had happened the previous month. It still wasn't working. I realized I wasn't really functioning as a vent pipe; I was more like a vent hole in the wall. I helped in the moment, but that did not really address the problem.

That was when I instituted a "one-vent rule." I was still available and happy to listen and provide support and suggestions to any staff member about any problem—once. If they came back about the same problem, they had to do something about it. They could choose to let it go, or I would help them make a plan. I would even help them address the situation if they did not feel like they could do it themselves, but they no longer had the option simply to vent and do nothing and repeat over and over and over again.

Over time, this rule actually led to problem resolution and eventually reduced the number of venting sessions. I recommend this practice to all staff who find themselves serving as a vent hole in the wall. It's time to upgrade to a solution that actually addresses, rather than prolongs, the issue.

Make It Your Own

- When is venting enough in itself? When do people need to do more than vent?
- What happens when someone has no viable options for venting or for help in resolving problems within an organization? (For example, when anyone who approaches a supervisor about a frustrating problem is told, "That's yours to resolve; I don't want to hear about it.")
- What would eliminate the need for venting in an organization?

Squeezed in the Middle

Middle children are known to be peacekeepers, to possess traits like agreeableness, and to be good at relating to both older and younger people. At the same time, middle children often feel excluded, ignored, or even neglected.

I believe the same could be said about middle managers. They often feel squeezed from the top and the bottom. They try to be supportive of their staff and their own supervisors. Middle managers are expected to delegate to their line staff while also making sure they don't overload them. Executives often don't feel the same hesitancy to delegate to the middle managers because, they reason, they're managers, so they'll figure it out.

Middle managers are expected to relay information "down" from the executive level but often have trouble finding anyone to listen when they try to bring input from their staff "up" to the top leadership. It is an exhausting role. Middle managers have told me that they feel stuck, ignored, and in a lose-lose position.

Too often these feelings go unheard and unsolved because the director-level staff are usually externally facing and their priorities are outside the office. When the directors are struggling themselves, one of the first things to go is frequently their one-on-one meetings with their managers—even as they expect them to hold one-on-ones with their own staff members. I would guess that this middle management tier is where the largest area of turnover happens in an organization. It really is a difficult role.

All of these concerns are exacerbated because it is a rare organization that brings together middle managers as their own team. Besides enabling directors to have time to support their managers, creating a middle managers' group can be a way to support this critical role in an organization. Be ready, though, because these people will have a lot to talk about! The first few meetings might very well devolve into complaint sessions, but don't disband the group. Bring in a facilitator for them (internal or external or one of their own) and ask them to produce suggestions, requests, or questions after each meeting. After they have the release of being heard and understood, they will no doubt turn to problem solving. This group has a lot of information and a unique perspective in the organization. Let them put that to good use.

In my work, I have hosted many "supervisor circles" and found that they benefited the organizations. (I know because they told me so *and* they invited me back!) Some smaller organizations bring all supervisors together for these sessions and do breakout groups based on tiers. All levels of supervisors can do circles together, but don't expect the middle managers to speak their truth easily when their own supervisors are in the room. The directors must model learning by participating in their own circle. This is the only way the entire organization can move forward.

My supervisor circles would center on a topic of interest and relevance for the group. I would do a mini-presentation on the topic and then give the participants a prompt for individual reflection, followed by either dyads or small-group sharing. Then everyone would come back together to discuss questions, learnings, realizations, and next steps.

One group I worked with held quarterly supervisor circles for five years. Over time, the managers felt more supported, heard, and influential in solving problems in the organization, and thus felt less stuck and instead used their perspective to strengthen the entire organization. Then everyone was able to enjoy the agreeableness and peacekeeping skills of these middle managers.

Make It Your Own

- Discuss the assets and challenges of each tier within your organization. What works and what doesn't work? What unique perspective does each tier bring to the organization?
- Committing to a new meeting by creating a horizontal team of managers could be daunting in terms of both time and productivity. What conditions would make this investment worthwhile?
- When middle managers feel squeezed from above and below, something has to give. What does it usually turn out to be?
- If directors choose not to participate in any development process, how does that impact the middle managers and the entire organization?

CHAPTER 5:

LOOK IN THE MIRROR

Self-awareness is one of the most important skills of an effective leader, if not *the* most important skill. When self-awareness is lacking, actions may or may not match words, consistency will be neglected, and one's impact on others will be unrecognized and therefore irrelevant. A lack of self-awareness sows seeds of distrust.

On the other hand, when you are a leader who practices self-awareness and self-management, trust is strengthened. People will be more likely to give you the benefit of the doubt because you will have shown yourself to be a thoughtful work in progress. You are more likely to own your mistakes, act with purpose, and practice what you preach.

A leader who actively practices self-awareness is open to feedback, invites differences of opinion, and does not arbitrarily shut down innovation. Even more important, they act with awareness of their impact, their baggage, their identity, and their own strengths and challenges. They are not afraid to share power or recognize the strength and skills of others.

Some people are more prone to self-reflection; others must cultivate the practice. Developing this skill and making it an essential tool of your leadership is well worth the time, energy, and attention.

The Journey of Reflection, Awareness, and Management

We've all experienced moments when someone says the right words but we know they don't mean it. It might be when you ask someone, "Are we okay?" and they answer, "Sure, everything's fine," but their tone and their body language scream that things are not okay. This happens in supervision too. An authoritative manager who tries to work in a partnership mode might say, "I'd like to hear what you have to say." Good words. Good idea. But what the staff member hears, through tone, is, "I'd like to hear what you have to say, even though I know it won't make a damn bit of difference to my decision." Or the supervisor says, "How do you think it went?" when you know they can't wait to tell you how you messed it up. These are experiences when a person's tone and sometimes their body language betray an underlying message that belies the words that are said. The manager may know they are just going through the motions, but far more often they think they're doing the right thing. They are unaware of the conflicting message between their words and their affect.

Other times, a mismatch between words and subsequent actions is evident. Supervisors may be well intentioned and say what they think are the right things to say—things like, "It's okay to make a mistake" or, "Let me know if you have any questions" or even, "I'm here to support you." But then when something goes wrong, the supervisor comes down hard on the mistake maker or becomes annoyed with a person who asks too many questions. They make it clear, by their actions, that there is a limit to their support and that staff members will reach it pretty quickly. These people don't intend to break trust with their staff, but they do—and not just with immediately impacted staff but with every member of their team.

What these managers are lacking is self-awareness. They haven't been trained in self-reflection. They don't recognize the impact of their words and actions on staff, and their attempts to work in partnership have a far greater probability of failing. The dynamic is worse than if they had been direct to begin with. By "pretending" to work in partnership and not recognizing that they have not done so, these managers are seen as inauthentic and untrustworthy. That impact lasts a long time.

Self-reflection leads to self-awareness leads to self-management. All three are essential components of fair, consistent, and effective supervision in a partnership mode.

Self-reflection begins with taking time to consider how things are going and how people react to you. It is pausing to consider people's reactions to your words and actions. It can take many forms, but it must be active and consistent. It cannot be passive and random. If a manager just waits for something to pop up or for someone to point something out to them, then they are not being reflective and might do significant damage before they learn how to act more thoughtfully.

Active self-reflection requires designated time on a daily or weekly basis. This might be accomplished through meditation, journaling, working with a coach, contemplative walks, making reflective art, or simply setting aside time to consider how things are going. It involves replaying the day or the week in your mind and noticing how things unfurled. It's as if you are watching a movie but are not inside the protagonist (you); rather, you are watching the entire scene and watching to see what happens when you do x or say y. "Oh, when she popped into my office for the fifth time in half an hour, I sounded rushed and impatient when I asked, 'What do you want now?' I see how she shrank back a bit and chewed on her lip before she asked her quick question."

The next part of the reflection is considering what you could have done better, or whether there is anything you can do now to address something that happened. "I should talk to her about finding a better way to handle the questions. Maybe we can try having her bundle her questions for the day or the afternoon. I didn't tell her I didn't want to answer five questions in half an hour."

With a regular and consistent practice of self-reflection, most people will move into self-awareness, which is self-reflection in the moment. Self-awareness lets you see the impact of your actions in the moment, or upon reflection.

Finally, self-awareness is followed by self-management, wherein you recognize the impact of your actions before you do them and can choose to act differently. You can acknowledge that if you proceed down a certain path, doing so is not going to help the situation. You can recognize, "I'm feeling triggered. If I continue this discussion now, I will say something I regret. I'd better take time out and continue later."

These steps come more easily to some than to others, but everyone can develop their skills in self-reflection, self-awareness, and self-management. If you can't quite get the hang of it on your own, find a coach (or a mentor or even a peer) to help you. These skills will help you be a better supervisor, as well as a better partner, a better parent, and a better person.

Make It Your Own

- How do people tend to react when a leader's words don't match their tone or behavior?
- How can the practice of self-awareness strengthen an entire organization?
- When and how might self-awareness go awry and lead to problems?
- What self-reflection practices do you already have? Which form(s) of self-reflection appeal to you (e.g., journaling, discussions with a coach)?

Practices of Self-Reflection

I have a treasure chest full of journals—years and years of them. I doubt I will ever read them again—and I doubt anyone else would care to either. Sometimes I fill up three journals in a year; other times, one journal lasts me three years. I don't have many "shoulds" about them—no rule that I write every day or regarding what I write about or anything like that. Journaling is really just a way that I've found to figure things out. To think out loud with myself. For me, this is one of my practices of self-reflection.

Building a practice of self-reflection is a way to make sure you have some quiet, protected time and space to consider how you are showing up at work and in life. Without this practice, you might slip into some bad habits or not hear feedback you receive. You might not recognize an "oops" that needs correction or your discomfort about something that is giving you information but that you don't have words for yet. You also might miss a brilliant new idea about how to approach a problem that has been stymieing you for weeks. Your practice of self-reflection will let those thoughts, feelings, ideas, and considerations rise up and become actionable, or at least recognizable.

Ways to practice self-reflection include:

- **Writing/journaling:** You can dive right in and write whatever pops into your head. You can start by recounting what's happened since you last wrote and see what comes from there, or you can start with a prompt and follow that. A prompt might be a specific question you're wondering about (e.g., "Why did Maurice's comment upset me so much?") or a topic ("Write about sexism you've witnessed in the past week"). Wherever you start, follow your mind and see what comes up. Even if you start with a topic, just write and see where it goes—indefinitely or for a specific amount of time. Your mind will tell you what it wants to write about. If you've got ten minutes, set a timer and go!

- **Meditating:** Lots of resources teach meditation. I am not going to do that. For me, meditation is primarily about being quiet. Literally being still, for a specific, planned period of time. Countless studies demonstrate the positive effects of meditation. If it feels too hard and you think you could never sit for twenty minutes at a time, try a minute. Literally one minute. Prove to yourself that you can do it. And then, if you want, add another minute or two and slowly build up. Or make your practice one minute per day.

- **Painting/collage/drawing/coloring/playing with clay, etc.:** Do something that gets you out of your head and focused on something besides "thinking." Thoughts will arise in a free-form manner, and what you need to know will pop up, either during the activity or later. And don't let yourself get judgy about your product; this is a process activity. The product is extra, if anything.

- **Walking:** Walk instead of taking public transit or driving. Walk just to walk. In this form, it cannot include music or podcasts or talking with friends. If it is going to be reflective, it needs to be you and yourself having a conversation while you do it.

- **Dancing:** This may seem to contradict the idea of walking without music, but somehow it doesn't. If you are able to fully immerse yourself in dancing (or other physical activity), you will get out of your head and reflections will arise. Maybe. See what works for you.

- **Spiritual practice:** If you believe in a higher power and have a practice to support that, then this offers you another avenue for quiet and attentive listening. Whether it be through prayer, ritual, or a community of practice, you can capture awareness when it erupts.

- **Driving with no music/radio/podcasts:** Do this one only if you are an experienced driver who can stay focused on driving. Without music or talking, your mind will lift up what you might need to consider.

- **Counseling/coaching:** This is a more active approach to self-reflection, which can be particularly helpful when you realize you have some baggage to unpack or something that feels stuck. Find a counselor or coach with whom you feel comfortable, seen, and heard. Actively seek out a person who specializes in bringing a racially just, culturally affirmative, and liberating lens to the work.
- **Coaching circle/book club:** This can be a structured process wherein friends and/or colleagues come together to consider a topic or read a book together. It can be a combination of a discussion, a support group, and peer coaching.

Experiment and see what works for you, or take an activity you are already doing and designate at least some of that time as self-reflective time. Commit to doing it on a regular basis (at least weekly would be good). And take some notes either during or afterward so that you can remember and act on any relevant revelations.

At times, my journals have been a key component of my self-reflection. But you might notice that I said I journal whenever I want, and then I told you to commit to doing something on a regular basis. My consistent practice is meditation. After years of not being able to sit still, no matter what I tried, I finally tried a one-minute approach to meditation. Before that, I always felt like someone else was telling me I should do it, and I immediately would go into rebellion. When I decided to do one minute per day, I claimed it as my own choice. Eventually I worked up to five minutes, and from there, I could progress to any amount of time I decided to do. (Well, up to thirty minutes—I don't know about more than that!) Now, I have meditated every day for more than four years. While my nuggets of awareness are not always obvious, I know I am more aware and more calm because of the practice.

Make It Your Own

- Do you have a practice of self-reflection? If so, what do you get from it?
- What do you imagine the impact on an organization would be if every employee practiced self-reflection?
- How does resistance show up for you (e.g., my rebellion upon being "told" to meditate), and what do you do about it?

....

Ground Truths

I once worked with a group in conflict. Trust had been lost, and the organization was on the edge of collapse. As I worked with these people to help mediate the conflict, we turned a corner and started working toward solutions, instead of blame.

Sometimes that corner is clear, and other times it is reached slowly and gradually. For this group, I believe the shift happened when we acknowledged a few ground truths about interpersonal dynamics. I call them ground truths because they are fundamental to everything else. When we can recognize the ground we are acting from, we can shift our understanding, and from there, we can change the whole process. It doesn't always work that way, so this is not a systemic solution but rather an invitation to see things differently.

Here are the ground truths that contributed to a seismic shift for this group:

1. **We cannot change anyone but ourselves:** As much as we often wish we could change others, we can't. We can influence, we can persuade, we can ask, and we can hope that others will change, but we cannot make it happen. The only actions we can control are our own.

2. **No one else can "make" us feel or do anything:** We all can, and do, respond and react to what others do. We can be

triggered by actions; we can feel angry; we can feel hurt. It is important to remember, however, that those feelings and reactions are our own. We see others' actions through our own perspectives, interpretations, and assumptions about what happened.

3. **We are each responsible for our own actions, words, and thoughts:** We are each responsible for what we do, what we say, and, to some extent, what we think. There is volition in how we respond to triggers, hurts, and anger. We must each accept responsibility for what we do and what we say.

Realizing that we can influence our thoughts is tricky. They seem so random and organic that we often can't quite recognize that we decide what to focus on and how to think about things. I find it helpful to realize that thoughts do pop up but that I am responsible for what happens next. Do I nurture blame and judgment to keep negativity alive, or do I try to consider the situation from another perspective? Do I give people the benefit of the doubt or assume negative intentions?

4. **We cannot change the past:** As much as we might wish we could change what happened or change what we did or what someone else did, we can't do any of that. The past has happened; we cannot change what has already transpired. And focusing on the past can keep us stuck. The only thing we can change is our understanding of it. Acknowledging the past is important. We can learn from it and apply that learning to future actions.

5. **We can't always control what happens to us, but we can control how we respond to what happens to us:** This is a clear corollary to items two and three, above. We can't control what happens to us, but we can control how we

respond to it. We alone are responsible for how we act in response to what others do or to what life throws at us. People can experience the same events and respond very differently. We can practice choosing to respond more often in a way that aligns with our values.

When the group I was working with explored and embraced these ground truths, everything changed. The toxic blame that had filled the room dispersed. We did a short ritual to leave it behind, and then the group started working together to move forward. It was a powerful and healing process that helped the team save their organization.

Make It Your Own

- How do these ground truths land for you? Which one do you have the biggest reaction to?
- How do race, gender, class, and identity issues intersect with these ground truths?
- How does fighting these ground truths show up in the work of social justice?
- Is your organization stuck facing the past in some area? If so, how can you help your staff move forward together while still bringing the past with you in a constructive manner?

Managing Your Buttons

When you make your selection in a vending machine, you know what you're going to get. The twirling thing will start turning, and your Snickers bar (or kale chips) will move forward and drop down.

Similarly, when we talk about "pushing someone's buttons," we also know what we are going to get. Rarely is it as intentional as selecting a snack from the vending machine, but in hindsight we can usually say, "Yep, I should have known that was going to happen. Every single time I tell him he's not listening, that's the reaction I get."

The challenge is to learn not only how to work around other people's buttons but, even more important, to recognize, respond, and eventually defuse your own buttons. It takes practice. It is not a quick or easy process. Most of our buttons were installed years ago, and just like a vending machine, we react automatically, often before we know it. Further complicating our efforts to deactivate our buttons is the fact that they are often not directly related to what triggers them.

Following are three practices to address our buttons. These steps are not easy or quick or linear, but paying attention to what happens when we get triggered can eventually help us respond more consciously.

1. **Recognize:** In order to recognize your buttons, you must first become an observer. Notice when you feel bad about how you responded to someone or something that happened. Or maybe you realize that you reacted way out of proportion to an incident. Those are usually the first recognitions of your buttons. Over time, you will start to notice your own trends. "When people are late, I feel irrationally impatient." "When I am interrupted, I get furious." "When people cut me off in traffic, I scream at them." (Granted, I think we all share this last button!)

   After you've noticed a few examples, try to find what is being triggered for you. You might view lateness as a form of disrespect. Interrupting might feel to you like your intelligence is being questioned. Perhaps you interpret people's cutting you off in traffic as a message that they are more important than you are (but that's not what it means when you do it!).

2. **Respond more slowly:** The next step is to interrupt the automatic response. The primary method to slow your

reaction is to take a few deep breaths as soon as you notice your button, and/or to count to ten (or twenty or one hundred). Both practices buy your brain time before you react and allow you to realize that you are not in imminent danger, which is what our brains assume when our buttons are pushed. If possible, pause the conversation and return to it at another time. "I need to run to the bathroom; let's continue in five minutes." Or even "I'm feeling triggered right now; I need a short pause to gather my thoughts."

With the ability to interrupt the automatic actions, you are more likely to choose a more appropriate response.

3. **Figure yourself out:** This is the difficult step of figuring out what happened internally to cause these reactions and how you can address the underlying need they are trying to protect for you (respect, sense of being valued, safety, etc.). This process is often long and could involve a therapist, coach, or trusted and wise friend to help you figure it out. For your health and happiness, you might want to invest the time in yourself that this step requires.

In the workplace, you must stop yourself from overreacting and learn to control your reactions if those behaviors interfere with your work. Notice that I said "*over*reacting," not "reacting." I'm not saying you have to put up with inappropriate actions, but you want to be able to respond in a manner that will move the situation forward and not cause it to devolve into a situation in which your actions are the problem.

These kinds of button-pushing incidents are an area in which self-reflection, self-awareness, and self-management are required. Self-management is an important leadership action whenever your automatic emotions or reactions threaten to get in the way of a plan of action that you have decided to take, or a tone that you want to set for your team.

Examples of times when implementing self-management is important include:

- When you are extremely nervous about having a difficult conversation
- When you are too upset about a personal situation and fear you will cry in a meeting
- When you are frustrated and know you could lose your temper or respond sarcastically
- When you feel too impatient to listen to input or feedback—especially if you invited this conversation
- When you feel unappreciated and know you will have a hard time focusing on others

This is not to say that you cannot show feelings or empathy or sadness. This is about the times either when those emotions are beyond your control or when expressing them will make the situation inappropriately about you, when it should be about your staff.

Self-management might also be relevant in determining whether to push the button for a Snickers bar or kale chips, but that's a whole different story!

Make It Your Own

- What are the signs that someone is oversharing or overreacting, rather than simply responding or sharing feelings?
- What is the impact on staff if a manager or leader gets their buttons pushed and makes no attempt to address that reaction?
- How do power dynamics exacerbate the situation of button pushing and controlling?

Owning Your Power

Daniela was an organizer before she became lead organizer. She was a peer of her team, and now she's the boss. But she wants to maintain her friendly relationships with people, so she goes out of her way to tell them, "I won't lie—this promotion is great for my wallet, but I'm not going to let it go to my head. We're still the same people we were before I was promoted. Nothing is going to change. We'll still hang out, and I promise you I will never be bossy!" The team is relieved, and work proceeds.

This works great until a problem arises and Daniela must suddenly make some tough decisions. A grant the organization was expected to receive falls through, and Daniela has to lay off two organizers. She begs her boss to make the decision. But Daniela's supervisor tells her, "This is your decision. We can talk about it, but you have to decide." Daniela makes the tough choices and tells her team the news. Not only are they upset about the news itself, but they feel betrayed by Daniela. After all, you can't get much more bossy than deciding who gets laid off.

People who work in nonprofit organizations, and especially those who work in social justice organizations, are not always comfortable with their own organizational power and authority. They do this work to fight the oppression in the world, not to assume the mantle of power themselves.

It is imperative, however, that any manager understands their role and owns the attendant power and authority. I hope that by this point in the book, you know that I do not mean a manager must be authoritarian or punitive. I mean that they must understand that they have a different role in the organization as a manager. I mean that they need to accept that they will have to make decisions and convey messages that they may not like. I mean that they realize there are times when they need to be directive about what is okay and what is not. I mean that they own their power and authority and privilege.

Being "in charge" is not always easy or comfortable. People who are used to fighting the power and authority in the world don't want to replicate it. I understand that. This book is all about how to own your power and authority in a way that is collegial and furthers the organization's mission.

To be an effective leader, you must recognize the power of your position. Anyone who has power and does not own up to it can be a dangerous person. Being a manager gives you authority to do and decide things. This is a reality, and to ignore it is to work out of alignment. And being in a position of power and authority gives you privilege. You most likely make more money and perhaps earn more benefits. You are involved in decisions that others may or may not be involved in, or maybe you hear news before others. It is vital that you do the internal work of making peace with how you hold your power and authority and privilege. If you don't, you will damage trust with your staff. They know you have a different role now, and acting like you don't just complicates the issue (as does denying any other forms of privilege that you hold). This is especially true if you have both organizational power *and* societal or mainstream power because of your race, gender, class, ability, or other identity.

Owning your power, authority, and privilege in this way really comes down to accepting responsibility for them. Recognizing, accepting, and holding your responsibility with integrity and trust puts the mission first.

Daniela would have done better if she had been able to own her new role from the start. She should have told her team, "Things are different now that I've been promoted. There will be times when I won't be able to hang out or act the way I did before. I'm not sure what it will look like yet. I'm still me, and we're still a team, but I have a different responsibility than I did before." If she had done so, when the hard times came, her team would have been disappointed about the layoffs but would not have felt betrayed by Daniela.

Make It Your Own

- What are the particular challenges of being promoted over peers, and what can help address those challenges? What are the assets that offset the challenges?
- How might someone's discomfort with power, authority, or privilege show up in supervision?
- What are the signs that a manager is owning their authority and role, versus someone who is authoritarian?

What We Don't See: Hidden Dangers

My son recently bought a new car. It has a lot of bells and whistles, including seat warmers (which have nothing to do with this section, but which I think are a genius invention that should be standard in every car). More relevant to this topic are the bells and whistles that are safety related—specifically, the beeping sounds that tell you you're too close to other cars or objects.

We also have the low-tech version of these safety features—i.e., mirrors. Both warning systems are designed to alert us to dangers, especially the dangers that we cannot see while driving—what are commonly called our blind spots, and which present a considerable risk. The mirrors and the beeps can warn us about dangers that we don't see, but they don't actually protect us.

Whether your warning comes via beeps or your own observation, the next step is the same: You, as the driver, have to decide what to do about the warning. You must determine if the threat is valid and you must act, or if it is a warning about an acceptable risk—e.g., the car beeped because you passed a car in the slow lane. The beeps are useless if you just ignore them. The same is true of the mirrors: If you never check them, they will do you no good.

Feedback is like that. Feedback is information about a danger we are facing. It might be something we are aware of and paying attention to, or it might be something we have never

89

considered before. In either case, the feedback will do no good if we don't act on it. We must thoughtfully consider feedback we receive and determine what we will do about it.

This is especially true for feedback that we receive about what we don't see—our own hidden dangers. These are actions we take, or impacts we have, that we are unaware of. We might use a certain tone of voice when we are stressed. We might tend to react strongly to certain people. We might be inclined to forget agreements we've made or to focus on the wrong priorities. We might have an implicit bias that we are unaware of. In any case, by definition, we are unaware of these dangers.

When we receive feedback on our hidden dangers, it is easy to be defensive exactly because this information is unknown to us. We want to deny it, or at least justify it. But we must slow down in this moment and consider that this feedback about something we don't see might be a gift. We need to open it slowly and try it on. Ask ourselves the vital questions: "Could any part of this be true?" "What would the implications and dangers be if this were true?" If the one giving the feedback is a mentor or someone you trust, chances are, there's at least some truth to it. If you receive the feedback from someone with less positional power than you have in your organization, they are taking some risk in sharing it with you. It is very rare for someone to make up feedback out of nowhere. Perhaps we can observe ourselves with the feedback in mind. In any case, we must respond to it and apply it, or it is meaningless.

I doubt there are seat warmers in my future, but I am diligent in my use of mirrors to reveal hidden dangers, both in the car and in my life.

Make It Your Own

- Consider a time when feedback was instrumental in your changing your behavior. What did the feedback giver do or not do that allowed you to hear their information?

- What happens in a relationship and/or an organization when people are resistant to receiving information about the things they do not see about themselves? What about when those resisting are leaders?
- How can leaders establish an environment that will lead to a healthy culture of giving and receiving feedback?

Owning Your Shit (Primarily for White Folks)

Being a white, cis woman working in the field of social justice is not always easy or comfortable. And that is okay. Other people have felt unease and discomfort for ages; it's okay for me to feel a little now. When I am actively engaged with my colleagues, I am often aware of my whiteness in a way I don't have to be in the rest of my life. In my personal life, I can sometimes forget and enjoy the anonymity and privilege of being who I am without carrying the baggage of who I am. The fact that most of my life I *can* be unaware of my identity, and the social comfort that comes with, is a clue about privilege. I always strive to remember and understand the legacy of being a white, cis woman and the critical fact that our histories matter, both our personal backgrounds and the ways in which others who identify as we do have acted throughout history. In order to be a trustworthy partner, I need to continually practice awareness and ownership of my history, my identity, and my privilege.

My personal history is all the individual baggage I bring with me—things I learned growing up and absorbed about who I am and who others are by being in our culture and that continue to be reinforced in my adult life. Even if I've rejected early programming later in my life, I am probably still carrying those constructs around with me—beliefs, practices, and perspectives I've learned about myself and the world.

My identity history is both personal and much more broad. I was a child in a small town in New Hampshire and did not see a Black or brown person until I moved to California when I was seven. Being white was normal to me. Being straight was normal to me. Being cisgender was normal to me. Being a native English speaker was normal to me. Not having a disability was normal to me.

As I grew up and learned about privilege and oppression, my understanding of the world adjusted and expanded. I stand for and with others in strong solidarity now. However, my early learning did not just disappear because I changed my approach, my beliefs, and my ideas. Those early learnings may still show up and trip me up. I may not even realize something I am doing or saying is offensive or inappropriate.

To stand in true solidarity with others, I must be both vigilant and humble. I must be open not only to learning but to *actively* learning, and never reach a point where I think I know it all now. I must read and watch and, most of all, listen. I must be open to feedback. I must be ready to apologize— without making the conversation or situation about me.

I must be ready, at all times, to own my shit—my personal shit and my identity shit. And there's a lot of that, particularly in the area of racism and whiteness and, for cis men, maleness. I must acknowledge the ways in which a white supremacist system taught me to be racist. I'm not talking about overt racism here; I'm talking about the really deep and sometimes subtle beliefs that we, as part of our society, hold about things like who gets to talk, who decides, who leads, and much more. I must continue to work to be antiracist in thought and in action. I've been digging at this for more than twenty years, and I still have much, much more to unearth. I won't ever finish digging. But that doesn't mean I can give up or get a pass.

In particular, I must recognize and own my privilege and all the fruits thereof. And in that vein, I must be ready to ask myself, in a real way, "What am I willing to give up? What am I willing to risk?" in small moments of calling someone out or in big moments of showing up to significantly change the system.

Most of all, I must do all this in my day-to-day work and life. How do my actions undermine, or reinforce, racism? I have never been a racist à la the Ku Klux Klan, but I have been a participant in a white supremacist system that values white bodies most of all. We all have. I have not always been an active antiracist.

When this societal power and privilege couples with the power and privilege of being a manager, a great level of awareness is necessary. Your staff of color are going to be watching you to see if you know you are white. All of your staff will be watching to see if you act consistently and fairly. They will scrutinize your responses and your actions to see if you are replicating oppression without even knowing it.

Without this level of awareness, vigilance, and humility, we will get in the way of the mission and the movement. We will take up time and space when people have to explain to us or work around us. Worst of all, we will inevitably perpetuate the systems that created the society we live in.

White people have an important role in the social justice movement. We can often speak truth to power and peers and call out injustice, rather than waiting for others to do so. We can help other white people understand issues and implications in such a way that they may be more able to hear the information, because we are like them. It shouldn't and can't always fall to BIPOC people to help white folks "get it." We can use our power and privilege to move things forward. We can mentor, support, and work for BIPOC and then get out of the way and follow their lead. We can be allies and accomplices in the work that must be done. But as white people working for and with social justice, we must own our own shit, and our white shit in particular.

Make It Your Own

- How comfortable are you stating that you grew up in a white supremacist system (whatever value that system assigned to you)? Name the discomfort and fear that come with that acknowledgment.

• How does someone's personal and identity history impact the work?

• What norms did you grow up with, and how do they show up for you now?

······································

When a Man Talks . . .

When I was in college, I told my career counselor I wanted to be a writer. He was not an actual career counselor; he was a professor whose job required him to take on a certain number of students to counsel. He told me to go to a junior college and take a medical terminology class; then, he said, I would be able to get a writing job. Luckily, I knew enough to call bullshit on that advice!

Some years later, I applied to a graduate writing program. I submitted about thirty pages of a story about Noah's daughter-in-law as my writing sample. I was imagining writing a women's story from biblical times. This time, the male professor was even less helpful. He told me that my writing was good but that he thought the subject matter was ridiculous. He could not imagine anyone who would want to read that kind of story. (A few years later, *The Red Tent*, a biblical tale from a woman's perspective, sold more than three million copies. Obviously, an audience for that kind of story existed.) The horrible thing is that this time, I believed him. I put that file away and never wrote another word of that story.

Our society values the white male voice, which has traditionally been seen as the voice of reason, truth, importance, and morality. And men are often raised to be listened to and to listen to other men—and not so much to women.

Social justice spaces often have a female majority. And when men work in these spaces, they usually have the same values and commitment as their women partners. And yet some of the behaviors we learn in the greater culture seep into our work spaces. I am certainly not saying all men do all these things (but if they don't, it's almost always because they've worked on building awareness and becoming antisexist), nor am I saying that women do not also engage in some of these behaviors. I am saying that these are gendered actions that our culture has conditioned all of us to see as normal. I am saying that these things happen in our work spaces and that we need to notice and correct for them.

The following is not an exhaustive list; it is a list of male behaviors that either I or my clients have experienced directly:

- Men talk over and interrupt women.
- Men assume that they are right.
- Men repeat what women say as if it is their idea.
- Men explain things to women that don't need to be explained.
- Men talk more loudly.
- Men take up more space—physically and emotionally.
- Men harass and bully their colleagues.
- Men claim more expertise than women with similar experiences—or about uniquely women's experiences, such as childbirth.
- Men offer advice and try to fix something that a woman mentions—without receiving a request or permission to do so.
- Men negotiate for more money.
- Men don't apologize.
- Men call women "girls."

Men who do these things often do not even realize that they are doing them. They may or may not intend disrespect through their actions. And men who work in the field of social justice are usually shocked when someone calls them out on these behaviors. When a male leader engages in these actions, he is often *not* called out on them. Yet because of his power and authority as a leader, the impact of his actions will be intensified.

I once coached a man who was reprimanded for yelling at a female colleague. He swore up and down that the woman was making it up. "Were you ever exasperated with her? Did she frustrate you? Did you ever get sarcastic with her?" I asked. He answered yes to all these questions. I explained that often men take on an authoritative tone of voice without even knowing they are doing so. Their voice becomes stronger, maybe a little louder (but not technically yelling), and their words are more forceful and less neutral-sounding.

When this happens, many women will feel as if they have been yelled at or have gotten in trouble.

This is traditional cisgender dynamics at play. The man acts "alpha-masculine" to emphasize his rightness, and the woman interprets his actions as threatening. She may even cry, causing the man to then interpret her as manipulative.

This is also systemic sexism. When women apologize for interrupting and men don't. When women cede to a male voice. When men overrepresent their skills and women underrepresent them or are seen as arrogant. When men get to be assertive but women are viewed as aggressive. When the loudest voices in a discussion "win." When sexual harassment against women is still happening. When women are paid 50–80 percent (depending on racial pay gap factors) for doing the same work as men— which adds up to an average lifetime pay gap of $590,000!

Recognizing what's going on takes self-awareness. We must uncover and address the sexism in our workplaces, as well as racism and other oppressive practices that are normalized and replicated. Even a multiracial, LGBTQ+-friendly workplace may find that sexism has crept into its dynamics. And we must all be ready to name that bullshit!

Make It Your Own

- Have you ever witnessed anyone calling out sexist behavior in a workplace? How did people respond?
- When you have attended harassment trainings, have gendered dynamics been a part of the discussion?
- How you identify is one aspect of gendering at work. The other is how you act (e.g., gay men sometimes pride themselves on their "out" identity and still engage in many of the typically male practices listed in this section). Are any of your actions supporting culturally oppressive dynamics that lead to sexism in the workplace?
- How do racism and sexism reinforce each other in our society and in our workplaces?

CHAPTER 6:

HR AS A JUSTICE PARTNER

"Why would I ever take anything to HR? They're not going to be any help."

"HR works for management; they're as likely to fire me as help me."

"The worst part of having cancer was dealing with HR."

"If I took a complaint to HR, I might as well kiss my career goodbye."

These kinds of statements break my heart! My view of HR and its role is vastly different. But the fact that people are making these kinds of statements shows how many see HR as irrelevant at best and adversarial at worst. This perception must change. HR can be so much more than compliance driven. I know many HR professionals who chose this work to support employees.

HR can and should be the department or the person who paves the way forward for individuals and for the entire organization. HR can and should be a constructive liaison between management and staff, not a puppet to make things work for management. I consider HR to be in service to the organization, to the work, to the mission. AND, ultimately, it is happy, engaged, and respected employees who are going to not only get the work done but protect the agency.

Many small, grassroots organizations have no HR role. This is understandable; it is not the first role that organizations hire for. It is often not among the first ten roles that organizations hire for. But it should come soon after that, if not as an entire role in itself, then in the form of someone who can wear the independent, accessible, and supportive hat of human resources—someone to whom staff can bring problems and who is not "the boss."

HR is the function that can operationalize values—that is, make values a concrete part of day-to-day work practices. HR can protect employees and address concerns. HR can coordinate tangible benefits and facilitate benefits that make the organization user-friendly for staff. At its best, HR can be a guardian of culture and the voice of internal justice. Granted, historically and in many organizations, it has not always done so. In fact, it has often served as a very effective gatekeeper for maintaining oppression. But there is another way to do HR. HR can be reimagined and realigned to be of value and service. HR can be the partner of justice when the role is staffed by people who are committed to equity and who understand the power and the sacredness of the role.

The Wide Umbrella View of HR

Some HR professionals see their role as that of enforcers, making sure rules are followed and management is protected. Some see their role more as that of a "house mother," making sure each employee gets what they need and everyone gets along. Many of my colleagues in HR take on this role to support people but *also* recognize the importance of maintaining compliance. Even when you agree on the purpose, we all bring ourselves to the role, and that affects the experience of those with whom we work.

I work to address the challenges and cultures of social justice organizations, such as how to supervise in a style of partnership while still having clarity about roles and decision making and responsibilities, and how to meet contractual requirements and move the work forward. How do we unconsciously replicate, or consciously repudiate, external oppression and mainstream norms? How do we adapt, innovate, and partner to do the best work together? I recognize the importance of attending to compliance issues while keeping front and center a focus on people and partnership and justice. This is my approach, which is influenced by my training and experience in both HR and organizational development (OD).

I have taught graduate students at two universities. I taught a course called HR in a Nonprofit, and I bring my multifaceted and integrated approach to HR and OD to those classes and to my work. I have been amazed at the perspective that students bring to my class. So many people think of HR as only hiring, benefits, and people who deal with you when you're in trouble. Others say that HR is concerned only with management—the implication being that management comprises people "other" than the employees. My students expect the class to be dry and boring. It makes me sad and angry that this is what they have seen of HR.

When they leave the class eight weeks later, they have a much wider and deeper understanding of the possibilities for HR roles and how that role can support staff. If staff are engaged and happy, and if you focus on relationships, expectations, and feedback, you will be more likely to have an effective and successful organization. This is what I call the wide umbrella of HR. It covers a lot of territory.

Some people do lean toward the "police" side of HR. They see their role as enforcing laws and rules and upholding the status quo, which not only is a very limited view of HR but raises past and present concerns about how policing is practiced in this country, with its roots in slave catching.

It is a given that organizations must follow the law or they will jeopardize their very existence. That is the baseline. HR starts there, but it can and should go way beyond that. There is another side of HR, one that supports people and believes in worker and human rights. HR staff on this side also recognize that happy and engaged employees do not rush to sue their employers when problems occur. These professionals tend to bring creativity, joy, and a spirit of service to their work.

My view of HR is wide and deep. At its best, it can support staff in doing the important work of the organization by ensuring that everyone is safe, paid, and protected; that everyone's voice is heard; that roles, responsibilities, and goals are clear; that supervisors know how to support without being authoritarian or micromanaging; and that staff have a safe, effective, and objective way to work through problems. HR can serve as a guardian of culture, making sure that intentionality and strategy underlie the way things are done in the organization. HR can serve as a positive liaison between management and staff, without owing allegiance to either side. In its truest form, HR serves the mission and the values of the organization. While HR often reports to a director of finance or even directly to the executive director (ED), its true accountability partner is the organization itself, in service of the mission. This is not an easy path to tread. There were times when I was an HR director that I had had to tell my ED that she couldn't do something, or when I've needed to coach her about how she was handling an employee dispute. HR supports *all* the employees of an organization, no matter what their position.

In far too many nonprofits, no designated HR role exists. The ED or the chief financial officer (CFO) handles issues relevant to HR. But because HR is not their primary focus, it usually becomes a low priority, and the reality is that they often address compliance, pay, and benefits, and little else. Granted, those areas are important, but if that is all HR does, a lot is missing. This situation can also cause a significant conflict of interest if staff have concerns regarding their ED, CFO, or upper management.

When no designated HR role exists, what message does that send to the staff? While it is understandable that HR might not be among the first positions that an organization staffs, by the time twelve or more staff members are on board, this role becomes necessary. (This number is an approximation; some organizations need an HR presence when they have eight staff members, and others function fine until they have twenty or more.)

Ideally, an organization would invest in some kind of HR function from the beginning. If that is not feasible, here are a few of the signs that it might be time to hire a dedicated HR person:

- When your organization experiences a growing sense of "us versus them"
- When the ED or CFO spends more time than they want listening to problems or addressing staff concerns
- When conflict is erupting
- When staff are feeling unsupported and/or unsafe
- When protocols like job description updates, evaluations, and training are lagging or nonexistent
- When staff are feeling unheard and unappreciated
- When you find out that you have been out of compliance on a labor law you knew nothing about

For a small organization, it might not make sense to hire a full-time HR person, but it can be a good idea to assign the HR role to someone and get them support and training to do the job well. Someone safe and objective, to whom staff can bring problems. Lining up an HR consultant can also be an important step to assure you are meeting the needs of staff and the organization as a whole.

When strategically designed and staffed, the HR role can be both protective and proactive. HR can help to keep the focus on the work and the mission while providing clarity and safety. By serving as a thoughtful leader, the HR person can help the organization be true to its values and intention. Staff can feel supported, not policed. This is the role I strove to fill when I worked as an internal HR director. I held my wide-open umbrella over every aspect of the organization. One of my proudest moments in that role was when I knew that the umbrella was recognized during a staff recognition event. A board member whispered to me, "You serve as the heart of this organization."

Make It Your Own

- What roles have you seen HR play in various organizations?
- How can an intentional and strategic HR function in an organization add value to the work?
- How do you see HR being "guardians of culture," and who else plays that role?
- What message does it send when no HR function exists within an organization, especially a larger organization?

Transforming HR for Justice

This section was written by Rita Sever, a network member of RoadMap, a national collaboration of social justice consultants, with input from network members Mala Nagarajan, Terrill Thompson, Scott Lowther, and Emily Goldfarb. This statement is focused on a particular issue of concern in HR and is not intended to address or negate other forms of equal employment opportunity practices and inclusion.

HUMAN RESOURCES MANAGEMENT RUNS through every vein of an organization, either directly or indirectly. If an action touches or impacts the people in the organization, then HR is involved, from strategy to workforce planning to organizational culture to people development. Unfortunately, the dominant model, which too many mainstream HR professionals rely upon, focuses solely on the administration of recruiting, hiring, and onboarding staff. This approach is a lost opportunity for HR to play a productive role in creating equitable organizations.

Several studies—Daring to Lead (2011), The State of Diversity in Nonprofit and Foundation Leadership (2017), and Race to Lead: Confronting the Nonprofit Racial Leadership Gap (2019)—show the nonprofit sector is still predominantly white-led (more than 90 percent, in some studies), and that the root cause is systemic racial barriers. In addition, according to Top Nonprofits' March 8, 2018, article, "Where Are All the Women in Nonprofit Leadership?" while about 73 percent of nonprofit employees are women, only 45 percent of nonprofit CEO roles are held by women. When it comes to pay, women leaders in nonprofits earn just 66 percent of male salaries. HR management, if not done through an explicit lens of racial and gender justice, perpetuates these structural biases. That said, HR professionals are in an optimal position, through formal and informal roles and practices, to begin to dismantle systemic racial and gender barriers.

Background

The practice of HR, like the history of the United States, is rooted in an oppressive mainstream culture. HR is often, perhaps inadvertently, the method by which systemic racism and sexism are replicated and authorized in the workplace. HR has too often upheld a practice of meritocracy defined by white and dominant-culture measures. We cannot ignore that harassment, gender bias, and sexism exist and often thrive in nonprofits as well.

While HR is charged with compliance and protection, that cannot be viewed as a limited scope of work. Without a comprehensive and intentional commitment to employee engagement and satisfaction, an organization is more vulnerable to lawsuits and disruption. That commitment must acknowledge the veins of racism and sexism that snake through our organizations and actively work to repair those veins and build a system of racial and gender justice.

In order for HR to truly be a facilitative partner, its role and function must be redefined and reimagined. We can no longer be perceived as working for and protecting management. We must return to the original intention of HR, as a protector and supporter of employees. We must be recognized as a true partner to every employee.

Consider what it would mean to reclaim the broader understanding and practice of HR, which is designed to support the success and accountability of an organization's number-one asset: the people.

Human Resources as a Driver of Racial and Gender Justice

By bringing a focus of racial and gender justice to HR, we broaden that concept and the practice of HR to focus on the full recognition, participation, and valuing of every employee. HR can work to systematically eliminate the barriers that restrict employment opportunities and satisfaction, as well as to eliminate the present effects of past discrimination and practices. HR can demonstrate that EEO (equal employment opportunity) is more than a policy statement—it is an active practice that requires affirmative steps to ensure the full representation, at all levels, of qualified people of all backgrounds and identities.

HR can work in partnership with all employees to build organizations in which people work effectively and joyfully. When employees are connected and engaged and happy, they will be more likely to seek direct means of reconciliation and restoration when problems arise. And, most important, they are more likely to work collaboratively in service of the mission.

With every voice contributing and heard, with full participation and engagement, our organizations can be welcoming and more effective in serving their missions and in transforming our society.

Principles

Justice: Repairing practices that harm BIPOC or hinder their full participation in our organizations. Considering the impact of policies, practices, and decisions on women and people of color. Allowing every voice to be heard when decisions affecting staff are made. Paying careful attention to transparency of process and outcomes during any determination or adjustment of any compensation, benefits, perks, practices, flexibility, etc. Working actively to hire, promote, and retain BIPOC, women, gender-nonconforming people, trans and queer people, and people with disabilities.

Connection: Without a personal connection, change is fragile and tentative. We must bring our minds, our hearts, and our spirits to this work. Relationships are the strength and the vehicle for our work as social change organizations. Therefore, we must see, value, hear, and respond to every person in our organization and coordinate strategies for all components of staff, management, and boards to connect with each other. True connection requires self-awareness, self-management, empathy, and strong communication skills. Particularly for white leaders, men, and white staff, an intentional practice of reflection and consideration of the impacts of our action is critical to stop harming and start supporting women and our colleagues of color.

Clarity: Ensuring that expectations, feedback, and every other organizational dimension are understood and fully vetted in a manner that prioritizes mission and collaboration. Values do not thrive in an organization until understanding, clarity, and implementation exist throughout all levels of the organization.

Consistency: Analyzing policies, practices, procedures, and impacts to ensure that all staff are treated in a consistent and equitable manner across all levels and identities. This does not mean that all staff are necessarily treated exactly the same in every situation; it means that standards about and an understanding of when and how flexibility is appropriate and good are in place.

Learning: Lasting transformation happens when behavioral change is rooted in people's hearts, minds, and core values and when people are resourced with structural supports (e.g., training and development, organizational policies, changes in resource allocation). A clear commitment and accountability must be present. A commitment of resources to support individual and group learning not only supports the value of racial and gender justice but invests in staff to be stronger, more engaged, and more effective in their work with each other and in the world.

Sample Practices

The following are some key practices that can show good faith in starting to address past and current structural oppressions. This list is not exhaustive but demonstrates the breadth of the role that HR can play in building organizations' capacity to center racial and gender justice in their work.

Organizational Structures

1. The organization develops, displays, and enlivens its own statement of racial and gender justice, which is then touted from leadership to line staff and implemented throughout organizational practices and culture.

2. The organization analyzes and updates all policies and practices to remove those that have a disparate/adverse impact on marginalized communities, paying particular attention to race, gender, and disability.

3. The organization develops thoughtful, legal, fair, and creative benefits, such as help repaying student loans, support for current education, on-the-job training and coaching, training on hidden rules of advancement, paid parental leave, sabbaticals, and workable infant- and child-friendly policies.

4. The organization allocates resources to support its transition to an organization that centers on the value of racial and gender justice. This includes time, money, coaching, training, patience, and process.

5. The organization develops standards of supervision and leadership that distribute power and privilege across the organization and that don't replicate oppressive practices.

6. The organization creates and facilitates intentional space to help people talk about and process racism, sexism, ableism, classism, heterosexism, transphobia, gender conformity, etc., in its activities.

7. The organization gives attention to the components of a truly inclusive culture that build a sense of belonging.

8. The organization tells stories about its founding, history, and culture, including stories of inclusion and stories of failures—and the lessons it has learned from these events. Storytelling connects people and continues the learning and the conversations that need to happen.

People Development

1. All recruiters and interviewers are trained in and account for implicit bias. Racial and gender justice values are highlighted in recruitment and integrated into the interview process. Educational requirements should always include

"or equivalent" (unless licensing or funding prohibits doing so) to open the door to those who have not had the opportunity for higher education.

2. All managers are trained in effective supervision, which includes attention to power, privilege, and oppression. All supervisors are trained in giving and receiving feedback, in providing ongoing strength-based evaluations, and in having courageous conversations.

3. Self-awareness, self-management, and empathy are recognized as essential leadership skills and practices.

4. All staff are trained in implicit bias and recognition of unconscious practices, in conflict resolution (to help each voice be heard), and in having difficult conversations.

5. A coaching culture is established to support development and advancement of all staff.

Make It Your Own

- How is the following statement true or not true, based on your experience with HR? "HR is often, perhaps inadvertently, the method by which systemic racism and sexism are replicated and authorized."
- How are the five stated principles alive in your organization, or not?
- What impact would HR have in the larger world if it worked to disrupt mainstream replication of so-called meritocracy and standardized best practices, as this section suggests?

HR Stands Alone

A union campaign was in full swing when I joined my last organization as an HR director. I was shocked and offended when the union put out a flyer shortly after I arrived, saying something like, "Management tells you to go to HR for help. Anyone who has gone to HR knows it is scary and that they don't care about you." I took that statement personally and railed at the union for lying about me. I was particularly appalled at the idea that I could be scary. Me? I was quiet and calm and had never yelled at an employee in my life.

Two different people helped me to transform my reactions, and in doing so helped me to understand my role. The first was a dear friend who was helping me process my experience of my son's turning eighteen and separating from me. Kelly framed the union in this same context: "It doesn't really have anything to do with you. Teenagers need to separate to claim themselves as adults, and the staff need to have their own voice at the table. In both cases, it's about respect for them as independent adults." Okay—that helped me depersonalize the situation.

The second person was a mentor who had been the first one to point out to me that I was white. In this instance, Barbara told me, "It's not about you as a person. It's about the role of HR. You, holding that role, have power, and you, as a white woman, have a lot of power. The power can be scary. You need to figure out how you are going to use it." I have spent my entire career focused on that imperative.

In the beginning, it certainly didn't matter what I thought or even what I said. Staff had some initial interest in my feedback, but if I couldn't back up my words with actions, what difference did it make? Who cared if I was nice if they still couldn't pay the rent, or if they were being harassed? If staff did not feel cared for and supported, that was their experience. If staff perceived my team and me as biased or as a management tool, it didn't really matter if we weren't. If the perception was that HR was scary, HR was scary.

Over time, through my actions, people started to trust me and my team. I worked hard to be fair, to be supportive, and to create user-friendly policies and practices, like allowing parents to bring their baby to work policy, raising our entry wage, and creating a sick-leave donation plan—all more than twenty years ago, when such ideas were not the norm. Slowly, I built a better perception of HR.

But one day, a temporary employee on my team was rude to a staff member. She was representing HR, so her behavior was directly connected to my team and me. I could feel myself sliding back down the perception hill when I heard about the incident. I had to spend about twelve hours in meetings over three months to rebuild the trust of that individual staff member and her team, and even longer to rebuild trust with the union representatives. Even then, it was tentative. It was always tentative. And I had to live, and work, with that.

Staff need to see HR as fair, objective, and authentic—every minute. Without those characteristics, HR can do more harm than good. One of the worst situations I've seen was within an organization whose HR staff were seen as untrustworthy, gossipers, and people who took sides. No one would go to HR voluntarily, and if they had to, they were as quick and succinct as they could be. What a disaster. And then the HR staff wondered why no one liked them!

It is essential that whoever wears the HR hat, and in whatever manner, understands the importance of fairness, objectivity, and serving the organization. *This* is why I say that the role of HR is sacred—not because it is religious or spiritual, but because it deals with living, breathing, dreaming, daring, hopeful staff. Because the currency of HR is trust.

Being in HR can be lonely. You can't really be friends with anyone inside the organization. You can be friendly and connected, but if staff know you are friends with managers or individuals, your perceived objectivity is undermined, because at any moment, a situation could arise wherein you could be called on to investigate wrongdoing by your colleagues or friends. You need to find your friends elsewhere—and maintain confidentiality even when you are away from the organization. You don't know who knows whom, and you never want any doubt about where you stand.

Trust is essential for all leaders in an organization. All leaders need to be seen as neutral and supportive. HR creates and maintains policies. HR operationalizes culture. HR is privy to documented secrets of employees. HR guides managers in hiring and firing. HR is the bridge between management and non-management. The bar is high for HR. If HR is not a distinct island, its role is undermined. Perception matters as much as reality, if not more so, in how HR is known by staff. For all these reasons, HR stands alone.

Make It Your Own

- When and how does HR stand alone, and when and how must it join with others?
- How does the metaphor of an island with a bridge (or bridges) serve the function of HR? What other roles could be described that way?
- How is one's awareness of one's identity important in any role of power?

Connecting the Dots

Did you ever do connect-the-dots sheets when you were a kid? They were both sort of fun and sort of stupid. You could clearly see that the design was going to be a kangaroo, so there was no secret about the eventual outcome, but you also got a strange satisfaction from following the process and completing the picture.

In the world of HR, connecting the dots is both more difficult and much more important than those puzzles. It is the role of HR, along with management, to ensure consistency throughout the organization. HR is the monitor in this process. It's all about fairness and equity, and a key practice of both is consistency. Ask yourself the following:

- Are employees in the same situation being treated the same?
- Are positions paid in a truly equitable manner?
- Are evaluations done as objectively as possible, with an understanding of how bias plays out in this area?
- Are apples being compared to apples and not to pears or pickles?
- Is discrimination or bias slipping into the treatment of any category of employees?
- Do the same rules apply no matter who's following or not following them?
- Is the organization walking its talk?

It is up to HR to connect the dots. We do that by objectively looking at the data (hiring stats, retention patterns, turnover numbers, safety patterns, etc.) and by listening to concerns. Are there certain supervisors who trigger more grievances? Are there incidents of harassment that may not be directly connected, but then a pattern emerges? Are there inappropriate comments or teasing that don't bring complaints but still need to be stopped? We also need to observe from a microcosmic and a macrocosmic perspective. Are there areas of us-versus-them dynamics developing? Are people working in silos, disconnected from other departments or projects? Are certain employees expressing regular anger or upset? How is the morale overall? You can't control all of this, but noticing it is the first step; the second step is determining what's behind what you're noticing and how the organization can impact it.

A few examples might help explain further how this is an important area of attention for HR.

1. The Angry Employee

Jane is usually a very even-tempered employee who is always one of the first to volunteer to help when chairs need to be put away. Lately, though, you've noticed that she is often by herself, with her arms akimbo, and that the last time you asked her to help with the chairs, she said, "Do I have to?" You've also heard her snap at other staff members recently.

You decide to talk to Jane. "How are you doing?" you begin. It takes a little while for her to open up, but you simply ask a few more questions, all work related: "How is work going?" "Any problems that I should know about?" Maybe she never gives you more than one-word answers. Okay. You tell her, "Well, you know I'm here if I can help with anything."

Or maybe Jane tells you that her husband left her and that she is struggling financially. You can refer her to your employee assistance program and offer support.

Or maybe you learn that someone has been bullying Jane at work and that her supervisor refuses to intervene because the bully is the supervisor's top employee (or best friend!). That calls for an HR intervention.

2. The Flirty Employee

Last year, you heard that Vince made a slightly inappropriate, flirty comment to his coworker Zamira. You talked to Vince and made note of it. Last month, you received a complaint from an organizer that Vince had shared a couple of jokes that made her uncomfortable. She couldn't, or wouldn't, say what Vince did, and that made the situation hard to address, but you spoke to Vince and reminded him that he needed to be respectful to everyone he came in contact with. You made note of that too. You quietly watched Vince with other employees when you were in meetings together but saw nothing out of the ordinary. Now, you have just heard that a woman in another department reported feeling uncomfortable with some of Vince's comments about her body. When no one is paying attention and connecting the dots, these incidents could each be seen as an isolated incident. But now you see a pattern and you need to take stronger action to stop Vince from saying, or doing, inappropriate things.

3. Looking at the Big Picture

You look at your data and realize that your organization has a problem. Your leadership is all white, you hire mostly white people, and when you do hire nonwhite people, they tend not to last more than two years. You review their exit interviews and notice that they all spoke about feeling out of place, especially in leadership meetings. Maybe you even had a sense that this was happening, but now you see that it is a critical problem. You bring the data to the rest of the leadership team and, once they are on board, hire a consultant team with strong BIPOC leadership and expertise in HR with equity to help you address the recruitment, hiring, and retention problems.

One of the reasons I enjoyed the paper version of connecting the dots was the satisfaction I felt at the end, from seeing the big picture and knowing that I had made it visible. A similar satisfaction stems from connecting the dots in HR. You can show both successes and challenges and make them visible and actionable.

Make It Your Own

- What dots do you see in your organization that make you wonder if it contains a hidden picture? What dots do you see that you know need to be connected?
- When no HR person or department exists, who is responsible for connecting the dots? Or do they remain unconnected because of competing priorities? What steps can you take to ensure that some team is responsible for connecting the dots?

- Funders often don't want to fund operating expenses, especially those they might consider extra, like HR. What case would you make for the value that HR brings to an organization?

Infrastructure to Hold Up the Work

As I drove on the freeway in Northern California one day, I had a clear memory of driving there and seeing guardrails lying flat on the ground because the devastating fires that had recently ravaged the northern Bay Area had burned the wooden "feet" that held up the guardrails.

What are the posts that hold up the work of your organization? Administration as a whole is a big part of what holds most organizations together. Too often, the staff in administration are considered other or less than, instead of as key employees working behind the scenes. Today, I invite you to consider four key "feet" that hold up the work. These items are not particularly fun or pretty, but they are important and they keep the work moving. When these tasks are ignored or outdated, people get confused, systems fail, and the essential work gets bogged down.

1. Job Descriptions

Each position should have an up-to-date, accurate job description. This gives the staff member occupying the role a clear overview of their responsibilities. It gives the supervisor the same overview to facilitate conversations about tasks, outcomes, and accountability. When necessary, job descriptions are important to define physical requirements and useful in identifying comparable work, contrasts between positions, and the relationship between different roles.

2. Organizational Charts

An accurate and current organizational chart is important for understanding lines of authority and accountability, how positions compare to each other, how departments or programs relate, and the entire positional lay of the land. The lines of authority and accountability are not about command and control but about clarity. When people don't know who their supervisor is or how their work fits in to an organization, they can feel disconcerted and disincentivized. Even "flat" organizations must ensure that each staff member understands their relationship to other individuals and programs.

3. Policies

Organizations rely on their policies to make sure everyone is on the same page with "how we do things here." Up-to-date policies assure staff that their rights and responsibilities are clear and safe. It gives them a way to make sure they are protected and to process concerns, as well as a clear understanding of what is required of them as employees. If something goes wrong, everyone has a playbook for how to respond and, in times of liability, knows they made a good-faith effort to do the right thing.

4. Meetings

Many organizations have too many meetings, which cause staff to feel as if they bounce from one to the next, with no good outcomes. Other organizations have too few meetings, and staff feel as if they don't know what's going on and don't know anyone outside their own area. Good and thoughtful meetings can alleviate both of these extremes. Knowing the purpose of a meeting can help inform the timing, the participants, and the outcomes. Well-planned meetings keep communication flowing up and down and throughout the organization and, when done well, can facilitate decision making and processing, as well as connections.

Altogether, these four components can help hold up the work of the organization, keep people involved and informed, and reassure them about what they need to be doing and how they fit in. Make sure you spend some time, annually, checking on these important "feet" that can help hold up your organization and keep it safe, like guardrails should.

Make It Your Own

- What are some of the indications that an organization's infrastructure is not being supported? And what are some of the unintended outcomes of this scenario?
- Which of these four "feet" do you feel confident about in your organization? Are there any that need attention?
- Are there any gaps in understanding that your staff needs to acknowledge to do their work well and be on the same page?

Try Saying Yes

One of the things that HR is known for is saying no. "No matter what we want to do, they always say no, so I stopped asking," a manager told me. Employees have their own versions of these stories, but I hear them most from managers:

Can I make this employee exempt? No.

Can I extend this person's health insurance? No.

If I restructure the department, can I keep this staff member? No.

Can I fire this person? No.

That last one is the one that managers and HR get most frustrated about. The manager is finally ready to let someone go, and HR won't let them. And HR is frustrated that the manager didn't come to them earlier so they could have taken steps to make the situation clear to the employee. Without intermediary steps, the termination would seem to be coming out of nowhere, which would not be fair or defendable.

Managers too often sideline HR and act on their own. This pattern is dangerous and terrifies HR. HR must be more user-friendly and must be seen as a partner. In the corporate world, high-level strategic HR staff are known as "business partners." I propose that HR staff working in social justice position ourselves as "justice partners." But that is never going to happen if managers don't trust us and think we just say no.

One of the best questions I've learned to ask is from the book *Decisive*, by Chip Heath and Dan Heath: "Under what conditions would this answer make sense?" That question has helped me understand the parameters of a decision, as well as reframed the pro-con debate.

In a similar fashion, I've learned to respond to any well-intentioned HR question or idea with a pause and a reframe as I consider how it could be possible. In particular, I try to start my reframe as a "yes":

Can I make this employee exempt?
Yes, of course, if we make their job duties fit the requirements. Let's see what that would look like.

Can I extend this person's health insurance?
Yes, if we keep them employed for thirty hours per week or put them on a COBRA plan.

If I restructure the department, can I keep this staff member?
Yes, I'm sure we can find a way to make that work. Let's look at what you're trying to do.

Can I fire this person?
Yes. Not right now, but I can show you what you need to do to make that process less risky to you and the organization.

Let's also look at what's problematic about the work this person is doing and if there's another way to address this situation and make it work.

Leading with "yes" is a way to approach partnership. You and the person who comes to you for help are on the same side and want the same thing, but you, in HR, know the best pathway to get there and can help the other person figure it out. They may end up deciding that the "yes" is too complicated or against what they are trying to make happen, but there is a way, and we can show them. We can also help them think through the best way to get where they want to be, in terms of staffing and compliance.

This takes a shift in mindset—on the part of both HR and the manager. Both sides must actively recognize that they are on the same side—of the mission. And then HR must focus on the possibilities, not the limitations. The manager, for their part, must trust that HR has an important role in supporting the staff and in protecting the organization from liability, and that HR has big-picture staffing information that the manager may not know.

In no arena is this approach more important than that of policies and values. HR has a strong and unique role in operationalizing values. In themselves, values are important and can guide our work and our actions. But until they are codified and staff are held accountable to them, they are just ideas. Important ideas, but just ideas. When they become thoughtful, intentional policies, the organization is purposefully walking its talk. It may be doing that without policies, but that's either accidental or grassroots. A grassroots organization may exist for a long time with an organic approach and a trust of implied values and practices. But eventually, as staff numbers grow, an organization may hire someone who sees things differently—someone who has a different understanding of conflict resolution, transparency, or even racism. And then how do you address those issues if nothing is concrete? Staff can be held only to clear and distinct values, which are ideally translated into policies and practices.

It is in this step of crafting thoughtful, intentional, and actionable policies and practices that HR can be instrumental in operationalizing the values and approaches of a mission-driven organization. And this is where it is essential for HR to lead with "yes":

We want to make a policy that people have to talk to each other to solve their problems.
Yes! I love that idea. I will have to build in some caveats for when we don't want people to have to confront each other (in harassment scenarios, for example), but I will get right on that and have a draft for you within a week. Does that work?

We want to make all of our financial decisions in a transparent fashion, and we want staff to trust us on what we do need to keep to ourselves.
Okay. The value of transparency is part of who we are, so let's make it happen. We will need to protect people's private information (like individual salaries), and we'll have to find an objective way to encourage staff to trust us, but I think we can find a helpful way to think about it and word it. Let's put it on the leadership team meeting agenda.

We need to support Black Lives Matter as a movement. I think the first step is to add "racism" to our list of prohibited behaviors. And then I want to find a way to pay people of color more than we pay white folks.
I am 100 percent on board with supporting BLM. We will need to identify what we mean by "racism" in a concrete and explicit way (such as by forbidding the use of racially derogatory terms). We can certainly identify antiracism as a core value and then prohibit certain specific activities.

We can also build a process for who determines, and how they do so, what else might be racist and therefore not allowed. Let's talk about your intentions when you say you want to pay people of color more. We can't legally pay POC staff more than white staff to do the same job, but I have some ideas about how we could legally and ethically address your concerns.

In this manner, HR can practice saying yes and can increase trust and collegiality with other leaders. Over time, this approach can lead us to claim HR as a respected "justice partner" that can actively help to bend the arc of justice within an organization while others work to bend the arc externally.

Make It Your Own

- This approach could be seen as manipulative if the reframe were "Yes, but . . ." What is needed to make it more than that?
- How could you implement, as a long-term strategy, the idea of HR as a justice partner? What kinds of factors would undermine that strategy?
- When and how does it make sense for HR to be "at the table" where decisions are made, and when and how does it not?

CHAPTER 7:

HIRING FOR JUSTICE

One of the areas of leadership that most directly replicates inequity is hiring. When an organization follows traditional practices, it gets more of what it has hired in the past. Who gets hired, who doesn't get hired, and the often unexamined process that leads to those results have far-reaching consequences. The impact is only compounded when salaries, raises, and promotions occur in a routine and unexamined way.

Without training and guidance, people often end up hiring candidates who remind them of themselves earlier in their career. This might work out fine, but it also might lead to a homogenous workplace where people not only identify the same but think the same too. Organizations and hiring managers need to bring awareness and rigor to the process of hiring and onboarding. With attention and oversight, organizations can be more active in hiring a diverse team with all kinds of identities, styles, and ideas.

Watch Out for Mini-Me's

"She just felt like the right person."

"I went with my gut."

"I had a strong sense that she was the right candidate, and it's worked out great."

"Sometimes the intangibles are what make the difference; there's a certain level of intuition in hiring."

"I just thought he would fit in best with the team."

These are all comments I've heard from hiring managers when they were trying to defend why they picked a certain candidate over another qualified person. And they all could be signals of implicit bias at work.

I trust that we all intend to hire in a fair manner. In fact, we probably want to actively build a multiracial and otherwise diverse team. However, we also know that implicit bias is an inherent part of the process when we hire new staff. And without active awareness and pushback, that bias often wins out and the mainstream candidate gets the job (be they white/male/extroverted/straight/non-disabled/middle-class or whatever), even when we hoped it would go a different way.

One of the most basic, deep-rooted biases is the inclination to hire people just like us. We experience often unacknowledged comfort when we meet and interview people who are like us. This "likeness" might include race, gender, background, orientation, personality—it just "feels" right. Knowing about this tendency can reduce, although it won't eliminate, the tendency to hire mini-me's.

Phrases like the ones listed above are used to justify hiring decisions. And yet all of those responses need to be challenged, and the process that got us there needs to be disrupted. If someone cannot objectively name why they chose the candidate they chose, they need to reconsider their process with critical inquiry. If this happens often, the whole hiring process must change.

Some of the ways in which bias in hiring can be challenged—and, hopefully, disrupted—are:

- **Hiring by committee:** When there are three people on a hiring committee, it is less likely that one person will be able to unilaterally populate their team with mini-me's. Three is not too intimidating to the candidates, and an odd number avoids a tie. Ideally, the hiring team will consist of people with diverse identities, positions, powers, and roles. It is sometimes helpful to have a non-staff member on the team (such as a client, a volunteer, or a community member). It is important to specify at the outset of the hiring process how the committee will make its decisions. Is it a majority vote? Does the one who will supervise the person have the final decision? Or does the hiring manager need to get approval from HR or the ED before the hire happens?
- **Reviewing résumés with redacted names:** Some organizations redact names to ensure that the staff members making decisions about whom to interview do not see any names in their review of résumés or applications. This removes the potential bias of consciously or unconsciously assuming the race, ethnicity, or gender of the applicants from the screening process.
- **Removing school names:** Far too many people are impressed with elite schools, and when those schools are listed on a résumé, they almost automatically trigger a call for an interview. On the other end of the spectrum, reviewers often discount community-college or state-school achievements. Does it really matter where someone got their degree? Maybe in a few professions it does, but for most jobs, you want the person with the right skills and the right experience, and where they learned those things doesn't have a direct impact.
- **Removing addresses:** This, too, can be a dog whistle to signal wealth, race, or ethnicity. At best, it's distracting at the initial stage of hiring; at worst, it can be another area that invites bias.

- **Anonymous samples of work:** It is more difficult for biases to impact our decisions when we eliminate the opportunity to make assumptions. As a result, a few organizations have moved to having all candidates submit a sample of work (e.g., writing a grant, creating a curriculum) before they even review those candidates' résumés. One of the companies that conducted some of the abovementioned research has taken this idea a step further. GapJumpers is a new type of job board that allows employers to recruit applicants by posting projects for them to complete before the employers meet them. An applicant can view all the projects and choose which one sounds like the best fit for them, all without having to see or speak to an interviewer. Compared with standard résumé screening, using Gap-Jumpers increases minority and female applicants' chances of being offered a first-round job interview by about 40 percent, according to the company.

- **Rethinking first impressions:** In my own experience, when a hiring manager came to me about a decision, I would routinely ask, "How did you decide to hire this person?" If they answered with anything like the first comments in this section, I would continue to question them. "Who was your second choice? What was different about them? What made you more comfortable with this person? What was it about the other candidate that didn't work for you?" If the answers continued to be vague or comfort-driven, I would suggest another round of interviews. I would often directly name my concerns: "I am concerned that I don't hear any objective reason why you did not choose the person with a Latinx name."

- **Training staff on hiring and bias:** For the process of second-guessing "comfort" choices to be effective, we had to have a clear, organization-wide commitment to our hiring goals and a common language and understanding about bias. I also needed to ensure that the staff doing the hiring were trained in equal employment opportunity (EEO) laws and best practices to avoid discrimination, as well as its less blatant cousin, bias. I drilled them with the no-nos of considering (or even mentioning) marital status, ethnicity, disabilities, sexual orientation, gender expression, age, and so on during the hiring process.

- **Training for internal applicants:** We also noticed that current staff members were not being promoted as often as we would expect them to be. It turned out that the staff were assuming that the hiring managers knew their work and so they would go to interviews as if it were a mere formality. Managers were comparing them against external candidates who often could put on a good interview, although they didn't actually have the greater experience. So we offered training in preparing for and giving good interviews. (We knew they might use that to go somewhere else but still decided it was a good training to offer our staff.)

- **Not incentivizing referrals from current staff:** Although it is tempting to ask staff to bring new people to the organization and doing so is often a good sign of staff engagement and satisfaction, instituting referral bonuses or other rewards for hiring can backfire. The critical step here is to look at the demographics of your current staff. If they are authentically diverse, referral rewards might work well. But if they are homogenous, you run the risk of intensifying that tone in your hiring. This does not happen automatically, but monitor it and see how it plays out if you do opt to provide a referral bonus.

- **Wide recruitment:** The key to building a strong and inclusive staff is to recruit far and wide and bring in a wide range of applicants. Post on a variety of job boards, expand your geographic area of recruitment when possible, research new methods of recruitment and outreach, and build a long and varied list of contacts to share your openings with. Get the word out, and put in the time talking with people who know people you would be interested in hiring. Invest in long-term relationships. If you are a good employer doing good work, the applicants will come.

- **Monitoring stats:** No matter what you do to decrease bias and increase the representation of your staff, you need to test it and see who is being hired and who is being promoted. That's how you will determine whether your system is working or not.

Mini-me's are like junk food. Hiring them feels good in the moment, but later, we might regret it.

Make It Your Own

- What is the allure of hiring mini-me's, and what might lead to regret about that decision later?
- How does your hiring process work, and what might you like to change or try?
- How might our guts lead us to replicate the white supremacist practices of the dominant culture?

Do You Know Who You Are Looking For?

In my class on HR in nonprofits, I am often asked, "Should we hire for skills or for passion for the mission?" My answer is yes! These two approaches need not, and should not, be mutually exclusive. Of course you want someone committed to the mission, and of course you want someone who can do the job. I don't think candidates necessarily have to have done the exact job to be able to do the job. That strict limitation excludes a lot of people, especially as people grow into bigger jobs.

It can sometimes be tricky to determine exactly who you are looking for. You often have snippets of information: We want someone who can organize; we want someone who can get along with all kinds of people; we want someone who can be a good team player . . . Then there are the things you don't want: We don't want someone who is going to be intolerant; we don't want someone who is going to question everything we're doing; we don't want someone who is going to take long showers and hijack the only bathroom for hours on end! When I see job postings that are hyper specific about requirements, I know that this organization has had either a really good or a really bad experience with a staff member and that it's either trying to replicate that person or trying to find someone who is the opposite. You can find out a lot about an organization by the questions it asks in an interview. Figuring out what you need and then how to get that is a complicated, and somewhat mysterious, process. Traditional interviewing has been recognized as a rather ineffective manner of predicting success on the job. At most, it is said to offer a 55 percent accurate prediction of who will do well in a role. Investing time and preparation in your process can help to raise that rate of successful hiring.

Here's a brief overview of steps to take to try to find the right person for the job.

1. Analyze the job to determine the required skill set for each job.

> **a. First, review the most obvious requirements:** What skills and/or experience are needed to do the job? Any licenses or certification required?

> **b. Go beyond the usual:** Don't just think of overt qualification factors, like "two years of experience" or "skill with Excel." Dig deeper to consider who would likely be successful and who might be unsuccessful in the job. Watch out for factors that are often assumed to be required but may or may not be, such as asking for someone with a bachelor's degree, or "someone good with people," or

even someone "outgoing." A degree is not always required and may exclude a lot of people who did not have the opportunity to go to college. If you still think you'd like someone with a degree, at least consider adding "or equivalent experience," so if you find a perfect candidate without a degree, you can still hire them. "Good with people" is too vague; "outgoing" implies that only extroverts need apply, and that is rarely a true need for a job, unless the job is doing cold-call selling or something like that. (And, trust me, no introvert is going to apply for that job!)

c. Think about past successes: What kind of person is successful in this job? What is the most difficult part of this job?

d. Think about what didn't work: What would make an unsuccessful candidate? Why have people left this job in the past?

e. Think about the organization as a whole: What values support our mission? What is our culture? What skills do we want every employee to have? Make sure you think about these factors on a deep level, not in a trivial manner. Your culture is not "We all like to go out for a drink together on Friday evening"; it's more like "We give and take feedback across all positions" or "We respect our hierarchy."

2. Bring the mission into the interview: Ask a direct question that invites candidates to demonstrate their alignment with the mission of the organization, or to share their thinking about the history/systemic background that drives the mission.

3. Develop questions and/or projects that will elicit a match between identified skills and the candidates' history and skills. For the interview, aim for at least a few behavioral

questions that ask candidates to describe past experience, not theoretically but tangibly. For example: "Tell me about a time when you intervened in a conversation with a coworker about the value of your organization." CNBC shared a great question that Fractured Atlas, a nonprofit tech company supporting artists, uses to enliven its value of inclusivity: "Without using the word 'different,' what's your definition of diversity?" During a second interview, the company asks, "What specifically did you do to advance justice in your last job?"

For a sample project, if you decide to require one either before or after the interview, select an actual skill needed on the job and ask the candidate to demonstrate it. (Important caveat: If you ask them to produce a project like a grant proposal, do not use it if you do not hire the person!)

4. Bring an equity lens to the interview process. Assume that bias is in the room, and be alert for it. Review your questions for wording that centers on dominant-culture norms. Ask yourself, "What long-term community relationships do we need to invest in to recruit qualified candidates?"

Thinking critically and creatively in this way will help you develop questions that might help you get to know your candidates better and, hopefully, improve the odds of your finding a successful match.

Make It Your Own

- How realistic is it to pause and consider all this before moving into actively filling an empty position? What factors work against your taking that time?
- What message do you send to current staff when you do take the time to dig more deeply into how to get the right person?

- What have you seen happen, in this organization or elsewhere, when there was a rush to just "get somebody"?

Affirmative Hiring

An executive director once complained to me that she tried to hire a multiracial team, but the only people applying for her jobs were white lesbians. Now, obviously, white lesbians can be great candidates and good staff—that is not the issue. When an organization is trying to build a global majority team, it needs representation from all kinds of people.

In order to build that kind of team, you need to look at your hiring practices, your language, your culture, and your reputation. How are you known in your community? Have BIPOC been hired and left? Why? Building a truly inclusive and diverse staff takes time, attention, and commitment.

Affirmative action is one practice that can help predominantly white-run organizations start the process of expanding their demographics. An affirmative action plan is a public and written commitment to eliminating barriers that restrict employment opportunities and acknowledging the present effects of past discrimination. It calls on organizations to recognize that EEO may require affirmative steps to ensure the full representation of qualified people of all backgrounds.

While the language and the practice of affirmative action may feel dated, the process of developing a plan can unearth problems and force a specific strategy to be more inclusive and welcoming. Many people assume that affirmative action is illegal. Even when it is, that usually applies only to public entities. I can't comment on your specific locale's laws, but I can remind you that, barring specific state or local ordinances, affirmative action hiring is legal in the United States and has been since the 1960s. In fact, if an organization has a contract with the federal government, it may even be required to have a written affirmative action plan.

The process will include an objective review of the demographics of staff and who is not included. It will look at numbers in specific positions, on teams, and at levels of leadership. This is all important information. Once that information is known, your leadership team can make a strategic plan about how it can more deliberately grow into an organization that represents your community and/or the global community. This process will undoubtedly challenge assumptions and attitudes and practices. This can be more than an exercise; it can be a litmus test for your values.

Quotas are illegal, but goals are not. Discrimination is illegal, but inclusion is not. You cannot hire someone simply because you want to have a person with that specific identity on your staff. But you can and should make sure your recruitment is wide and seen by different eyes than the ones that have always seen your offerings, if those offerings have led to a white staff or white leadership.

As important as recruitment, if not more so, is how you welcome and include people once they begin working for you. How do you (individually and as an entire organization) show up when you hire people? Are you walking your talk and open to learning and responding if you get feedback that something is inappropriate or too mainstream? Find out why BIPOC have left. Did you do exit interviews? What did they say when they decided to move on? Do research. Read. Study. Learn.

And keep at it. Time, attention, commitment, and perseverance are essential. It won't happen overnight if you are a predominantly white organization, in demographics and/or in thought and practice, but looking closely and thoughtfully making a plan, perhaps with help, will lead to a varied applicant pool and, ideally, a more representative staff with the experience and skills needed to achieve your organization's mission.

Make It Your Own

- What kind of baggage does affirmative action carry for some?
- How would you answer people who complain that affirmative action programs are simply reverse discrimination?
- What are the challenges of moving toward more representative staffing?

Team Input on Hiring

Naomi was the executive director of an organization focused on youth programs. When it came time to hire a director for the after-school program, Naomi wanted to involve the team in that decision, so she sent her top two candidates to a meeting with the after-school team. Her directions to the team: Just meet the candidates and let me know what you think.

The answer came back loud and clear: We love Jasmyn, and we hate Rodney. You've got to hire Jasmyn. So Naomi hired Jasmyn, even though Rodney had a lot more experience and was clearly the stronger candidate when she sent him and Jasmyn to meet the team.

Was that the right decision? I don't know—and neither do you. Maybe. Maybe Jasmyn had great interpersonal skills and Rodney looked good only on paper. Maybe Jasmyn had innovative ideas about revamping the program. Maybe Rodney said something inappropriate and didn't seem like he would relate to kids. But it could also have been true that Jasmyn had recently been in a line-staff position and therefore really understood and related to the staff but had no preparation for leading the team. Maybe Rodney wasn't great with kids himself but knew after-school programming in and out and was a good leader. Maybe Rodney was nervous meeting the team and came across as awkward. We don't know. Since the team lacked clear directions, it could have been a popularity contest, for all we know.

It's good to get input from a team, when possible, before hiring a leader for that team. But the input should come from a designated member of the hiring team or should be very specific after a structured meeting. A meet-and-greet is simply not effective. What can staff learn from that? Mainly, they will learn how good the candidate is at making small talk.

Most of all, the team should not make the final decision, except in rare circumstances, such as a work collective. In that case, the decision would be the result of a structured interview process, with all members voting. And in that case, all the team members would be trained about the job, the process, and the criteria.

In other team environments, staff can provide input, but they should not make the decision. Even if they make a great choice, they're setting up weird dynamics for when their new boss starts their job—a *we hired you; we can unhire you* kind of thinking.

The hiring manager should conduct a regular interview process, perhaps with a member of the team on the hiring committee (and respecting confidentiality in that role). Then, once they select the top two or three candidates, they either send those people to meet the team in a structured way, or initiate a group interview process with prepared questions and a recommendation sheet. In either case, the team understands that they are providing input and understand how the final decision will be made. After the meeting, team members are asked to submit their ranked choices and their reasons for such rankings. This can happen individually or as a group decision. The comments are just as important as the rankings and can include the pros and cons of each candidate.

As it turned out, Naomi's desire to involve her team backfired because she had to fire Jasmyn within six months, and the team felt disrespected and betrayed by the entire process.

We know that it is not easy to predict who will be successful in any given job, but rarely is the basis for that success a popularity contest.

Make It Your Own

• What could go wrong with a popularity contest?
• There is wisdom in groups, and then there is groupthink. What factors would indicate that team wisdom, not groupthink, is emerging?
• What can be gained by involving a team in hiring their leader? What can be lost?

Compensate More Justly

When I was first doing diversity work, more than twenty years ago, we held an annual retreat for our diversity committee. At one of these retreats, I organized a soccer game. Without at first naming out loud what I was doing, I divided the staff into two teams. I assigned the white committee members to one team and the BIPOC to the other. Then we played the game on a hill so that white people had to struggle to get the ball uphill while the ball would easily roll downhill for the other team so they could score goals with little effort. I also appointed a Black woman as the ref, and she would arbitrarily call out "foul" for the white team and give the other team a break whenever she could. Then we debriefed. Even though this was the diversity team and you would think the lesson was fairly obvious, I was amazed how a few of our white members could not let go of "It wasn't fair!" even when we explicitly pointed out what we were doing, by saying, "Yes, you're right, and that's a tiny taste of what our colleagues live with every day in the real world." Feeling it, even in a short-term and playful lived experience, was much stronger than simply talking about it.

All these years later, the playing field is still far from level. In the most recent studies, women still lag far behind men in terms of income. According to the 2020 National Partnership for Women and Families (NPWF), Asian American women earn 90 cents compared with a white man's dollar, white women earn 79 cents, Black women earn 65 cents, Native women earn 57 cents, and Latina women earn 54 cents. The difference adds up in a striking manner; the NPWF figures that this additional money could pay for four to twenty months of health insurance for women. In addition, a 2019 Yale University study found that Black households have $10 for every $100 a white household has.

No one organization can right the wrongs of our past or fix the lasting imbalances that come out of that history. It takes a movement and a lot of consistent action to begin to adjust our financial imbalance as a country and as a sector. But there are a few things we can do to contribute to the process.

The first step is to recognize that we have a long way to go. This is what the numbers look like in a society in which it is *already* illegal to pay women differently than men and *already* illegal to pay based on race, ethnicity, or any other protected class. These pay and wealth gaps result from a terrain in which we theoretically pay equal wages for equal work.

Although we may be paying in a legally equal manner, we must recognize that it does not play out as equal results. Focusing on equity, instead of equality, moves us from acting like there is an equal playing field to recognizing the impact of past practices. When we think about equity, we need to factor in both history and current realities, as we determine salary ranges. We can't do that on an individual or identity basis, as that would be discriminatory, but we can start to think about equity in terms of our practices surrounding compensation.

The most obvious place to start is to stop using across-the-board percentile increases when we figure raises. When we give everyone 3 percent, the top wage earners get more money than the entry-level workers—even though it looks fair from a certain perspective and is technically equal. If you reframe this scenario from percentile-based "equal treatment" to naming the results, and one employee gets a $600 raise while another gets a $4,000 raise, this perspective is clearly not fair or equitable. This notion is even more relevant when we apply those percentages to retirement funding; 3 percent of $120,000 is obviously a lot more than 3 percent of $60,000—and then the money goes toward investments that make the "rich" richer. The fact that most retirement benefits are structured as matching programs exacerbates the situation further, because people don't contribute to retirement accounts when they are having trouble making ends meet.

So we need to think about our values and the outcomes when we consider these practices, and not just repeat routine compensation habits. We must be fair and objective, but we do not need to do things the way they have always been done. So, instead of a 3 percent, across-the-board raise, maybe we offer 5/4/3 percent raises and give the entry-level jobs the largest percentage. Do this by job classification, not by individuals. Yes, this approach might be a disincentive for the top earners, but if the policy is aligned with the organization's values, leaders should support it.

The wealth gap has a different impact when we look at retirement accounts, because traditional plans allow those with more money to retire with savings and income, while lower-income staff end up with nothing. There are specific rules about employer contributions to retirement accounts, so the challenge is to think creatively about how they can be done more equitably while following the rules. Can they be funded through a reverse-percentage amount, a flat dollar amount, or some other creative and more just factor? When I last ran a retirement account, we wanted to encourage entry-level staff to simply participate in the account so they could see the magic of compounding interest. So we did a yearlong education campaign to encourage people to put anything into their retirement account—even a dollar per payday. To give them an additional incentive, we put 3 percent of the total payroll into the retirement bank. Knowing that some staff would not participate, we used that pool of money to invite people in by promising to equally divide up whatever was not committed to individuals who invested, even if it was just a few dollars. So if we had ended up with $10,000 that was not committed and we had one hundred participants, then everyone who participated got another $100—even if they contributed only $50. It worked! We convinced twenty-five people who had never contributed to a retirement account to give it a try. At the end of the year, they got the "extra" money and saw (and felt) how investing worked, and then they told others about it.

In terms of pay, equitable practices can also be implemented more creatively, while remaining fair and legal. The criteria for any compensation decisions must be objective and defensible, not arbitrary. If people know what is being paid (read: valued) and why, they more readily accept what otherwise could appear to be random decisions that value some jobs (or people) over others.

One way to be transparent about compensation decisions is to start with a base salary for every employee (e.g., $50,000 per year), then add money to that amount, based on objective factors like supervision duties, public representation duties (serving on municipal committees, for example), and specific skills that the organization wants to encourage all staff to share (e.g., nonviolent communication training). Income can be added for volunteering to participate in certain committees or for optional projects. A colleague extends the inclusivity of this approach by allowing staff to determine the payment factors beyond the base pay.

A full compensation package also includes what an organization pays for benefits. Creativity about more equitable benefits is also important, if the creativity is objective and implemented consistently among all employees. For example, you could institute a benefit to contribute toward student-loan repayment for first-generation graduates, or develop tuition reimbursement plans for people going back to school in an area relevant to their work.

Remember that these factors need to be applied fairly and cannot discriminate against any of the protected classes—in other words, you cannot pay BIPOC more or men less. They must be identity-neutral policies that are applied fairly and consistently. By rethinking mainstream compensation policies, you can transition from technically treating people equally to achieving real-world results. These steps are necessary to get us to a place of equity, one where pay has the same impact—not just the same number.

The move from equality to equity ideally involves a further step of liberation, wherein past injustices are acknowledged. In the arc toward liberation, a liberation compensation plan would somehow not only level the playing field financially but redistribute wealth and build a safety net of benefits for *everyone*. That is probably beyond the scope of one organization, but it is an important vision for the movement toward social justice.

Make It Your Own

- How realistic or unrealistic is it to think of one organization bending the arc from equality to equity to liberation?
- How does it help for people to "feel" injustice, instead of just "knowing" it?
- Can you think of a personal instance when you were told something was "fair" but from your perspective was far from it? Can you think of a policy that tries to be fair but doesn't succeed? Brainstorm how that policy could be reworked to be more fair.
- What could liberation look like in the field of compensation?

"There's Your Desk" Is Not Enough: Onboarding New Staff

When Beatriz started her last job, her supervisor was on vacation. HR welcomed her and walked her through her hiring paperwork. A coworker then walked her to her desk and told her, "Um, I guess you can read the employee handbook and get settled in. Anthony should be back tomorrow."

Not a good start! When Anthony did return from vacation, he spent an hour with her on the first day, giving her an overview of her job, and then ran off to a meeting. As he left, he said, "Ask your coworkers for help if you need it. I'm sure you'll figure it all out."

Beatriz is smart and good at what she does, so she did figure it out eventually. But this lack of a welcome left a bad taste in her mouth. She felt disrespected and in turn did not have much respect for her job. When a new opportunity came up a year later, she did not hesitate to leave the organization, with little warning.

Don't be like Anthony. Plan to spend time with your new staff when they come on board—not just the first day, but every day for the first week or two. It doesn't have to be a long meeting, but half an hour to an hour each day will make a world of difference. Once you're through the first two weeks, don't abandon the new hires. Set up regular meetings every week for a month or so, and then at least monthly after that. Help set up policies so that all supervisors model best practices for onboarding.

Here's a template of what you can discuss with them over the initial two weeks. This will help new employees to feel welcome and, just as important, will set them up for success—which will also make you look good.

Onboarding Template for New Hire

First two weeks: half an hour to one hour per day with supervisor. Make sure every meeting is a two-way conversation.

Week One

Day One: Welcome

- Start with introductions/chatting.
- Show office/desk space.
- Complete hiring paperwork.
- Say you're glad the new hire is here.
- Explain the onboarding process.
- Encourage questions and observations.
- Ask a few questions (e.g., "What led you to this job at this point in your life?").

Day Two: Job Description

- Provide general overview.
- Explain how new hire's job supports the mission.
- Unpack bullet points one by one and discuss why they matter.
- Ask questions to invite new hire into the conversation: "Any questions so far?" "Which part of the job do you think you'll enjoy most?" "What might be challenging or confusing for you?"

Day Three: Grounding in the Mission

- Explain mission, vision, values.
- Share organization's and mission's history.
- Tell stories (e.g., founder story, hero story, crisis story).
- Ask new hire something about how they see themselves contributing to the work of the organization.

Day Four: Understand Other People's Jobs

- Set up a meeting for them with each of the new hire's essential team members for fifteen to twenty minutes to meet them and understand each job. The new staff member can learn how their job fits with and impacts the other staff members' jobs, and current staff members can gain understanding about how the new staff member fits into the team.

- Have new hire ask questions (e.g., "How does my job support yours, and vice versa?" "What's the best that can happen if all goes well?").
- Ask if they have any questions or concerns after hearing those perspectives on their job.

Day Five: Success Factors

- Discuss with new hire what it means to work together on this team.
- Explain how you want them to tell you if they disagree with you.
- Explain what to do if they make a mistake.
- Describe your working style.
- Tell them your style for giving and receiving feedback.
- Teach them the importance of making clear agreements with you and their team.
- Talk about what to do when one of you realizes that you can't honor an agreement.
- Ask, "What will make this a successful job, from your perspective?"
- Be sure to also congratulate new hire on getting through their first week and repeat that you're glad to have them aboard.

Week Two

Day Six: Deal Breakers

- Explain the other side of success factors.
- Explain what is not acceptable—for the organization and for you.
- Explain what will get them in trouble.

- Explain traps/problem areas to be wary of.
- Ask them what their deal breakers are—what might make them want to leave?

Day Seven: Learning Styles
- Ask how they learn.
- Ask how they do their best work.
- Ask when they feel most comfortable/confident in their work.
- Talk about your learning/work style.

Day Eight: Check In
- Introduce new hire to the structure of your regular supervision meetings.
- Tell them you will take notes during meetings to help keep track of your agreements and projects.
- Tell them how you expect them to prepare and show up for the meeting. What will you cover? How will you use your time together?
- Determine the schedule of your regular meetings.
- Make a plan together about how to address questions that come up in between regular meetings.
- Invite them to talk about how it is going: What's working so far? What's not working? What do they need more information about? What are their top priorities for the rest of this week?
- If you use a form to prepare for your regular one-on-one meeting, share it with them.
- Ask if there's anything else they want to be a part of these regular meetings.

Day Nine: Evaluation Process
- Review the evaluation process and form with new hire.
- Share an understanding about the criteria on which they will be rated.

- Tell them what you'll be looking for in each area.
- Tell them when the evaluation will happen.
- Tell them that tomorrow you will ask them to give you some feedback about your work so far as a supervisor and about the organization as a whole. Tell them they have a valuable perspective as a new staff member and that you really want to hear what they have to say. (And make sure you do!)

Day Ten: Ask for Feedback

- Ask new hire how your supervision has worked so far.
- Ask them to tell you what they'd like you to stop, start, or keep doing.
- Ask them if they have any questions or observations about the teamwork or the work of the organization.
- Ask them to tell you what they still need to learn to feel as if they are fully functioning as part of the team.
- Ask them how you can best support them in their work.

Make It Your Own

- How would management's involvement in onboarding produce a better experience for new and incumbent staff?
- This all takes time and preparation from managers. What would get in the way and make this seem less important?
- Studies show that onboarding makes a tremendous difference for new staff. Share stories, your own or gathered online, of bad onboarding. What were the results?

CHAPTER 8:

HOLDING ACCOUNTABILITY

M any people can be good and supportive supervisors when all is going well. What happens, though, when things stop going well? When the work is not being done? When poor performance emerges? When your values are being undermined?

Because people who care about social justice care about people, this can be a confusing situation for some leaders. They really care about their staff. They want to be supportive, and they want to be nice. They don't want to hurt anyone's feelings. As a result, they sometimes fail to hold people accountable. Maybe they try to coach and persuade people to do a better job, or maybe they try moving responsibilities around. Occasionally, they get so frustrated that they suddenly fire the person, with no warning or process.

This scenario leads to problems throughout the organization, because the message to staff is, *You don't really have to do good work* or *Watch out, you can be fired at any time*. Neither of these messages is good for morale or performance.

Supervisors at every level must learn how to calmly and straightforwardly hold people accountable, which includes understanding the importance of clarity, process, consistency, and feedback.

I want to be clear that I am not determining what people need to be held accountable to or even what the process must look like. I understand that unquestioned standards can lead to biased results. Vague standards like "professionalism" can be used as weapons against BIPOC, who may have an approach and values that are different than what dominant, mainstream culture considers professional. Expectations must be fair, clear, and understood. Accountability is not about micromanaging, and it is not about replicating white, middle-class systems. It is about supporting staff to fulfill the mission.

It's About Clarity

When my granddaughter was four, she had a very serious conversation with her grandfather in which she commented, "Everyone has their eyes in front of their head, except mommies also have eyes in the back of their head."

This is the start of accountability, knowing that someone will know whether you do what you are supposed to do. By the time we get to work, however, our concept of accountability is usually more developed and internal. Most people hold themselves accountable for doing the right thing.

For a supervisor, therefore, it can be confusing when people don't hold themselves accountable, when they don't do what they should do or agreed to do, or don't meet a certain deadline. Then people want to know, "How do I hold them accountable?"

In my work with supervisors, I find that two missing ingredients are often required before we can even discuss that accountability question.

1. Are you absolutely clear that you both understood and agreed to the same thing? Were your expectations clear? Did you specify relevant time factors? Was the method of completion apparent? In short, were you on the same page about the expected accountability, or did you make

assumptions about what "common sense" results, deadlines, and communication would look like in this situation?

2. Did you speak to the person when the action was not completed as expected? Did you ask them about the report on the very day it was due? Did you let them know right away that the work was not done in the manner you expected?

Too often, one or both of these components is missing—at least for a time. And then suddenly (at least, it seems sudden to the employee) it's a big deal and the supervisor is really upset about something being tardy, or not completed, or done in a way that worked for the employee but is not what the supervisor expected.

It starts with you. As soon as you realize something is not completed at the time or in the manner you expected it to be, you must say something. Calmly. Directly. In a neutral tone that does not convey upset:

"Where is the report that was due today?"

"I expected the project to be done by now."

"This is not done as thoroughly as I would like."

Address the issue right away, and proceed from there. The start of holding someone accountable is making your expectations clear and then addressing them right away when they are not met.

You don't want staff to feel like you have eyes in the back of your head, but you do want them to understand that you expect them to follow through when you make a plan with them.

Make It Your Own

- What is the culture of accountability in your organization? Is it consistent throughout the organization?
- What is the difference between holding staff accountable and micromanaging?

- How does accountability become internalized, and how does it not become internalized?

....

Success as Motivation

I feel a little thrill of excitement and pride when I see the happy explosion of fireworks on my Fitbit when I accomplish a fitness goal. This could be for working out for thirty minutes, reaching my designated step count for the day, or moving at least 250 steps per hour between nine and five o'clock. It's a little embarrassing how much satisfaction those electronic blips give me, but they actually motivate me, and I figure if it works, use it! Most days I reach at least one of those goals, and often all three. And I celebrate each with a moment of graphic joy and internal pride.

Compare this with the experience of my colleague Maria, who recently completed a huge project. She had spent months working on the annual event for her organization, attending to countless details. For weeks, all she could talk about was her stress and worry over this event. No matter what we were talking about, she would suddenly grab her phone and jot down something she remembered she had to do. Then, finally, the event happened and by all accounts was a great success. I talked to Maria the next day and asked how she felt. "Okay. It's done. Now I need to catch up on all my other work," she said. No fireworks for her! No basking in her success. She reached this milestone and then looked up to see what she had to do next.

Some of her reaction is undoubtedly a personality trait. I do tend to value celebration, and Maria is more stoic in her work ethic. However, part of it is also the perpetual focus in many (most?) work cultures on what is still pending. Rarely do we stop and acknowledge what has been accomplished. I asked Maria if anyone had thanked her or acknowledged her work. "No," she replied, with an awkward combination of hurt and a why-would-they attitude.

Not only is acknowledging hard work, completion, and success kind and appropriate, it is also motivating. And, even more important, lack of acknowledgment and appreciation can be demotivating. If I feel rewarded by little graphic fireworks, imagine how I respond when someone tells me my work matters to them!

As a supervisor, you are the primary person from whom your staff need recognition. If you don't give it, they probably won't get it. Here are a few ideas to consider:

- Take a few minutes to identify benchmarks or milestones with each staff member. For some jobs, these will be project-based; for others, they may be time-based.
- When a milestone is reached, recognize it and acknowledge the success. Pause for a moment before tackling the next looming project. (If the milestone is missed, notice and address that also.)
- Occasionally, celebrate a big accomplishment or milestone. The celebration might involve balloons and treats, or it might be a simple, sincere thank-you email.
- For the times when success is a change in behavior, establish tiny steps forward and celebrate them. (This is what my Fitbit does for me.)
- Periodically, look at what you and your staff have accomplished, instead of looking only at the mountain of work in front of you.

You also set an example and influence the culture of a team. When you acknowledge success, you encourage your staff to recognize their own, and others', successes. Over time, this approach will build a more positive and cohesive team.

My Fitbit is simply a tool. If a little celebration encourages me to be more active, then why not use it? If a little acknowledgment of success motivates more success, why not use that?

Make It Your Own

- Is your organizational focus always on what must be done, or do you take time to celebrate wins as you go along? Between "often" and "never" on the celebration spectrum, where does your organization fall?
- What happens individually, and to the culture, when no one acknowledges accomplishments?
- What is the ultimate success that your staff aim for? Is success clearly defined or a vague, "someday" goal? How do these perceptions of success inspire the work?
- Who tends to receive the most and least recognition in your organization? What patterns occur in terms of recognition and who receives it in terms of race, gender, class, position, and other identities?

Accountability Tools

I don't want to micromanage anyone, and I know you don't either. Accountability is not about micromanaging or hand holding; it is about outcomes. It is about managing the work. I am not talking about productivity above all else, or about tracking tasks. I am certainly not suggesting you treat people as cogs in a machine. Accountability is about making sure the work that your organization values gets done in a manner that works for your organization. It is about your responsibility as a supervisor.

When I coach managers who are queasy about holding people accountable, I sometimes take the position of a donor. I would be quite upset if I were a donor to your organization and I found out you didn't care if the work that I was contributing to was not happening. You owe it to me and every other stakeholder to spend funds in service of the mission.

I know you care about your staff, and I do too. I want you to treat your staff well and pay them well. But I also expect you to guide the work forward. That is your job as a manager.

A large measure of accountability is clarity—clarity about what needs to happen, how it needs to happen, why it needs to happen, and what will happen if it doesn't happen. The most direct way to get there is by practicing these basic steps:

Basic Steps of Accountability

1. Schedule regular one-on-one meetings and make them a priority.

2. Every conversation is a two-way conversation. Listen at least as much as you talk.

3. Clarify expectations.

4. Practice making clear agreements.

5. Support your staff in learning and developing.

6. Acknowledge what is working.

7. Address what is not working. Look for the breakdown together. This includes making sure the workflow is clear and that the problem does not lie in the division of labor or in a structural snag. (If it does, resolve that!)

8. If the problem lies with the staff member, make a plan with them on how to improve. Follow up on this plan.

When Expectations Are Not Met:

You have six choices when expectations are not met. Only a couple of them really work, but those are often the ones that managers avoid the most.

1. **Ignore it:** The first choice is to ignore the problem and hope the staff will recognize it and change their behavior.

This rarely works, in part because they don't know it's a problem. If it were a problem, their supervisor would talk to them, right?

2. **Make it okay:** Lower your expectations, change the agreement, do it for them, own the problem, etc. This, unfortunately, is often seen as a viable choice. Supervisors decide it is easier just to do a task themselves or assign it to someone else, without any consequences or adjustments to the employee who did not do what they were supposed to do. Or they take back ownership of the task and lead the staff member through the situation step by step (which might be appropriate with a new staff member who needs training, but *not* if the person was hired for this level of work and is not doing it).

3. **Keep giving feedback and asking for change:** This is a good choice when the problem first shows up. Give clear feedback and tell them what must change. But if this is all that you do, and nothing changes, then don't expect it to work the 5th, 12th, or 20th time you do the same thing.

4. **Have a hard conversation:** This is really the only appropriate response when the staff member knows what to do, is just not doing it, and has not responded to feedback. This hard conversation can be calm, respectful, and supportive, but it does not avoid the situation. The supervisor names the problem and then helps the employee move forward. This might include helping them own the problem and/or clarifying your expectations, why it matters, or how to do it.

5. **Coach the staff member on development if/when they are ready:** This is a partner of number four. If the supervisor realizes that the staff member wants to do the task

and is willing to learn, the right choice might be to coach them in a developmental way (not just directing them step by step but helping them learn and grow). They must be ready to participate in the mentoring, though.

6. **If the behavior is a deal breaker, let the staff member know that it must change:** You may also move to a performance improvement plan (PIP) or discipline. This is not an immediate response, and no one is eager to go in this direction, but at some point, it may be necessary. This approach will hopefully get the attention of the staff member and they will step up. If they don't, this could be the step before termination. Remember that even this step (and termination, if it comes to that) can and should still be done respectfully and supportively. There simply comes a time when you must acknowledge that someone's employment isn't working and that this might not be the right job for that person.

Before the conversation:

When you decide you need to have that hard conversation, here are a few things to remember. The first set is to help you coach yourself to have the hard conversation; the second set is for your approach during the conversation.

Keep these ideas in mind as you approach the conversation:

- It's about the mission!
- You are not doing this *to* them.
- This is a consequence; it is not coming out of nowhere.
- Take time to prepare for these conversations. If this is a hard conversation for you, coach yourself to be strong and clear. Know your bottom line ("I want to see a detailed work plan by next Friday").
- Remember that this is their change to make. You can, and should, help and support them, but it is their problem to fix.

- *And* people can change only what they understand. Are your expectations (and reasoning) clear?

During the conversation:
Watch and manage your own reactions. It will distract the employee if you are crying or nervous or apologetic.

- Silence is a powerful tool. Sometimes when you ask, "What happened?" it's good to simply wait for an answer. And wait some more. Do not start suggesting answers to the employee, like "Maybe you have too much on your plate?"
- Speak like a partner. This is not about getting someone in trouble. You are giving the person information they need to be successful.
- Use "I" statements, not "you" statements. Starting with "You . . ." tends to cause defensiveness.
- Give clear, objective feedback about what is not working and why. State the problem and focus on moving forward.
- After you give concise feedback, invite the employee into the conversation. Be curious. Listen to their input, and consider their perspective and their concerns. Ask them if they are aware of any other contributing factors.
- If necessary, go back to basics. Ground the conversation in the mission and their job description. Underline why it matters. Make sure your expectations are clear.
- Help them "own" the problem. Ask them what they need to do. Give them a chance to fix it.
- Make clear agreements about next steps.
- The next step may be a PIP, discipline, or termination.

This is one of the most challenging, and the most basic, responsibilities of supervising someone. You are not their parent. Their feelings and their perspective matter, but they are not your only concern. Your job is to ensure that the organization achieves its mission.

The process of accountability is not magical. And it is not significantly different from what you do all the time as a supervisor. Your work is to set the staff you supervise up for success. Sometimes that success is harder won than at other times or for other people. It is worth the effort to make sure the staff member understands and has the tools to be successful. And if they can't be successful at your organization, let them move on and find a place where they can be.

Make It Your Own

- What makes "accountability" a bad word in some circles?
- How does the idea of thinking about the donor help or hurt the process of accountability for you?
- When does it make sense to look at structural factors for performance while still supporting the staff member to be accountable to their commitments?
- Have you seen other managers do the accountability dance in a way that works? What did they do?

Some Good Coaching Questions to Support Accountability

- What are you specifically going to do, and when will you do it?
- Do we have an agreement?
- Tell me what you'll do so we can make sure we're on the same page.
- What steps will you take from here?
- What are the deliverables for our next meeting?
- What piece of this will you own?
- How will you respond if things go off course?
- Look at your schedule and your current commitments; when can you fit this work in?
- How long do you think this will take?
- What obstacles might stop you from completing your agreement?
- What will you do if you run into problems?
- What are you responsible for? Are there any parts of that agreement that are outside your control?

Some Questions If It Didn't Happen

- We had an agreement. What happened?
- What can you do differently next time?
- When there is a pattern of dropped agreements:
- Did you keep the agreement? (Yes/no answer. When a pattern develops, it can be helpful to make this a simple one-word answer to make the lack of follow-through clear instead of rushing into the reasons why it did not happen.)
- What led you to not follow through on our agreement?
- Which of those events that led to you not keeping the agreement were under your control?

Every Which Way

Once, when my husband was playing with my niece, I suddenly heard her raise her five-year-old voice as she said quite clearly, "That is inappropriate, Uncle Mark!" Everyone in the room looked over to see what he had done. It turned out that he hadn't rolled her ball back the way she wanted him to.

What I appreciated about her reaction was that she dealt with her own problem. She spoke up and told her uncle what she expected and that he had not done it the right way. She held him accountable.

That is the place we want to get to as an organization, wherein every staff member holds every other staff member accountable for their agreements and shared work. Of course we want this to happen in a respectful and appropriate manner, based on shared understanding of the work (not just opinions), and generally not spoken about loudly in front of other people. What we want to avoid is a cycle in which every misstep is brought to the supervisors because people are afraid of holding each other accountable.

Ideally, accountability is part of the culture. People aren't afraid to go directly to their team member and address problems, misunderstandings, or priorities or check on deadlines. They feel safe calling their supervisor on dropping the ball on an important issue. Every issue does not need to go through "the boss." It's the way everyone works together, and it goes every which way—up, down, sideways, and diagonally, as necessary.

This approach does not replace the accountability that a supervisor has. This is about directly addressing problems that are impacting their own work, when possible. If people are trained in how to do this and the organization has a deep culture of respect, this should be the way the team works together. The managers will hold the big picture of the work progress and will be available if something or someone is not approachable in this direct manner.

When the direct approach doesn't work, the supervisor steps in to either facilitate the conversation or take it over, as is necessary and appropriate. This might happen when someone displays harassing behavior, with a bully who won't listen, when people refuse to hear their peer's concerns, or when emotional manipulation or intimidation makes direct confrontation unhelpful or downright dangerous. It would also need to happen if some staff got themselves involved in other people's work in a way that was not relevant or helpful.

For an organization to reach this point requires intentionality and commitment. People must be trained and coached and supported to have direct, and sometimes uncomfortable, conversations with each other—although if they are truly afraid to meet with someone, they should seek support and help from their supervisor. People must also be trained, coached, and supported to receive and respond to these conversations. Supervisors especially must be trained to give clear feedback and to listen to feedback from their team members. They must recognize that they too need to be accountable for keeping their agreements and deadlines. This takes a lot of work and a lot of humility. It must be seen as service to the mission and one of the costs of working together effectively.

In the organizations where this happens, a tangible feeling of respect and progress exists. People don't have to walk on eggshells because they know they can have difficult conversations with each other if they need to. They know that people will most likely keep their agreements, and if not, that they can talk to others about it. Most of all, they know the work is moving forward and that everyone is behind it.

It takes effort and sometimes courage, but accountability every which way can strengthen a healthy organization.

Make It Your Own

- What gets in the way of peers holding each other accountable?
- If one supervisor reacted badly to an accountability conversation from their staff, their reaction would have a widespread impact on the entire organization. Why? And how could that be remedied if it happened?
- How does a culture of accountability free staff to be more productive?
- What are the qualities that make a manager approachable?

You Can Decide, but You Might Decide Wrong!

I was playing PLAYMOBIL with my granddaughter one day, when I found myself getting frustrated that she was telling me exactly what to do with my "people." It was a camping scene, so I would say, "I'm going out for a hike," as I walked my person across the carpet.

"No, she doesn't want to hike; she wants to go swimming," my granddaughter would reply.

So, the next time we played with those figures, I asked ahead of time, "Can I decide what they'll do this time?"

My granddaughter replied, "You can decide, but you might decide wrong."

Okay—fair enough. At least I knew where I stood!

The only consequences in this scenario were that I felt a little frustrated in the midst of my joyful play. But think about how this plays out when you pretend to delegate to your staff. You tell them to do something or make a decision, and then, after the fact, you say, "No. You shouldn't have done it that way." The consequences when that happens are disengagement and a growing sense of mistrust between you and your staff member. You told them to do something. They did it.

Then they "got in trouble." At the least, they will second-guess their performance the next time; at the most, they will wait for you to micromanage them and not show any initiative—and eventually they will find another job.

Do not read this to mean that you must let your staff make the decisions and that you don't get to train them or help them learn from mistakes. Just be clear. Are you okay with whatever they decide? (If the answer is no, set some limits so you both understand the parameters of their work.)

- How much do they get to do or decide on their own?
- When do you want to weigh in on a decision?
- Can they ask you for help if they're not sure what to do?
- Do they need to do something the same way you would do it?
- Do you want them to make a plan and run it by you before they act?
- What outcome are you looking for?

Let them know, ahead of time, what limits, judgment points, and areas of control they have (and don't have). Tell them you will help them learn what they need to learn but that you are going to start out with small steps and then increase their responsibilities over time. Set benchmarks and check-in points (regular meetings) so that you both feel safe. Don't just pretend to delegate and then let them know that they decided wrong!

Make It Your Own

- Why do people resist delegating? What would need to be in place to make delegating more successful?
- In order for delegation to be successful, the supervisor needs to be ready to delegate and the staff member needs to be ready to accept the delegation. How do you know if/when both of those components are in place?

- What happens to the work, the staff member, and ultimately the organization when a supervisor holds on to too much work and refuses to delegate?

Delegation Questions for the Supervisor

How important is this project?
- What's the worst that could happen if someone else handled it?
- What's the best that could happen?

Is the task part of this staff member's job (or could it be)?
- Can you picture them doing this on their own?
- Is it relevant to their priorities and their role, or are you just wanting to get it off your plate?

Do you think they're ready to take it on?
- Do they have the skills?
- Can they learn the skills?
- Are they already overwhelmed?
- Do they want to learn this?
- Have they demonstrated the ability to learn and grow in responsibility in the past?

Do you have time to dedicate to this?
- Can you prioritize teaching while they get up to speed?
- Is it worth the investment of time to help them learn this?
- Can you be available for questions and support?
- Will you resent them for interrupting your work when they have questions or need guidance?

Evaluation Trauma

I have a colleague, Janice, who was scheduled to receive her evaluation. Janice had excelled in her work and moved up her chosen career ladder swiftly and steadily. She had no reason to think her evaluation would be a problem, but she felt sick with worry. I asked her the next day how it had gone. "Fine. It was good, actually," she said in a dull voice. I raised my eyebrows at the incongruity between her words and her expression. She explained, "I realized that I was traumatized early in my career when I got an unexpected and horrible review. I can't believe that still comes up ten years later."

No matter what the content of an evaluation, its delivery should never cause trauma to the recipient. I've identified four ways in which even a fairly good review can become problematic. And they are all under *your* control as the supervisor.

1. **Surprise/unfair:** When I train supervisors on how to write and deliver evaluations, I always stress that the golden rule is "No surprises." If something is important enough to come up in an evaluation, the staff member should know it is of concern and should have been given a chance to correct it. If they haven't, that means you have not been fair and the staff member is going to feel blindsided and betrayed. They should know ahead of time, based on their job description, onboarding, and ongoing supervision meetings, on what criteria their work is evaluated.

2. **One-way conversation:** The most important part of any evaluation process is the conversation with the staff member. (Although, having worked in HR, I do understand that the conversation needs to be documented in their file. Hence, the evaluation form.) And conversation, by definition, is two people talking. If you just read off a list of problems (or even successes), there is no conversation. It needs to be a genuine two-way discussion. This is what

moves the performance forward. Invite the staff member to respond to the feedback and to make a plan for next steps. (Some people will need time to respond in this way. You might schedule this meeting a day later.)

3. **Tone/delivery:** If your tone is punitive, that will be the impact of the evaluation, even if the words themselves are neutral. If you make broad pronouncements, speak in a condescending manner, or present yourself as the only person who has input in this situation, the staff member will leave the meeting feeling demeaned and disengaged. If you show up and it is obvious that you have not prepared for the conversation, the staff member will feel devalued—even if what you say is all good.

4. **Overreaction:** If a staff member has an emotional reaction to the evaluation and the supervisor responds quickly or harshly or joins in the emotional upset, the whole conversation can go awry. The focus is off the feedback, and now defenses are up, both parties feel stressed, and the discussion can quickly move to an adversarial situation, when it should never be that way.

Don't do any of these things. Take time to review the time period that the review covers, and note successes and concerns. Think about how you will deliver the information—especially about your concerns. Invite the staff member into the conversation early and often, and listen to them. (Ideally, they will have had an opportunity to give you their thoughts ahead of time, but whether they have or not, listen.) If emotions arise, take a few breaths, pause for a moment, and then continue. If the emotions are interfering with the conversation (e.g., sobbing or yelling—yours or theirs), take a short break. This could be a few minutes or a couple of days, but make sure you continue the conversation. Otherwise, let the person have their feelings and move on. Plan for the new year together. Create actionable goals that support the mission and fit the job, hopefully with input and agreement from the staff member. And practice so that your tone and delivery are calm, supportive, and encouraging. If you know your face "gives you away," find a way for your approach and your face to be positive.

It is true that you cannot control how someone responds to your feedback but you can control how you present your feedback. You can offer feedback in a way that gives it a greater chance of being heard and considered. I also want to acknowledge that I don't know the details of Janice's evaluation years ago. Maybe her supervisor would say, "My feedback led to her success." Even if that were true, the delivery did not have to be traumatic. The same information could have been delivered calmly, fairly, and conversationally.

No one deserves to feel haunted by an evaluation for ten years. Janice does not deserve to feel nervous when she is doing great work. This is an example of how incredibly important your role is and how you can impact your staff in a direct and positive way.

Make It Your Own

- What is it about tone that can ruin a conversation? What are your experiences with being on the receiving end of a conversation when the other person is using a judgmental or condescending tone?
- How do people respond when they feel treated unfairly? Does that usually lead to improved performance?
- What does lead to improved performance, in your experience?

What Makes an Evaluation Fair and Equitable?

Every HR professional has faced this moment: A manager comes to you, exasperated and angry. They are ready to fire someone—right now! You have them sit down while you look at the employee's file, and, lo and behold, you find nothing but good things in there. Every evaluation says that the person walked on water. There is not one hint of a problem, so you have to tell the manager, "No, you can't fire them right now."

That is why evaluations matter and why HR wants you to do them. They want a record of both problems and successes, so any actions, positive or negative, will have justification in writing. I don't think the evaluation must be a specific form or an annual ordeal, but it must be fair, it must be in writing, and it must happen on a consistent basis—generally, annually or quarterly. Sometimes the best evaluations are simply memos of a conversation that happened between a manager and an employee about what was working and what wasn't, and listing goals and priorities for the next year. That works for me—*if* it is done impartially and the employee believes it was done equitably.

Two things are required for any kind of evaluation process to be considered fair: procedural justice and outcome justice. Especially for organizations working for justice in the world, if these ingredients are not in place, you can't expect staff to line up for their evaluations—no matter how user-friendly you try to make them.

Procedural justice means that staff trust that the process was fair. They trust that the supervisors are trained and are "rating" in a consistent manner. They trust that apples are compared to apples and that the same standards and criteria apply to all employees. They trust that "above average" means the same thing across the board. Ideally, the staff has a role in designing the system so that they are in alignment with what is being assessed and how it is rated. This is why creating an evaluation system is much more complicated than simply cutting and pasting a form from another organization.

Outcome justice means that staff can see the rationale of where people were rated—who got raises, who got promotions, etc. (Don't think for a minute that staff don't compare their evaluations. It is human nature to be curious. You should never share anyone else's information, but if someone wants to share their own information, they can.) If it turns out that the ED's best friend got the only raise, that is going to undermine the process. Or if it turns out that the only people being promoted are white, or straight, or men, etc., that will be noticed.

When a process is deemed procedurally fair and the outcome just, evaluations can be a workable tool. The best process focuses on the conversation, not the form. Evaluations are a process for stepping back and looking at the big picture. They may or may not lead to raises. There are valid reasons to disconnect the two events.

Some organizations are abandoning evaluations completely. I'm okay with that if conversations between a manager and each staff member to talk about what's working and what's not working still happen on a regular basis. They also need to periodically step back, look backward and forward at the big picture and the work, and document that conversation in a consistent and accessible manner, like an HR file!

Even worse than my initial example of someone coming to HR ready to terminate someone is when a manager comes to HR to promote someone and HR has to ask, "Why this person and not that person?" because there is nothing in the file to tell them how either of the staff members are doing in their jobs. It is therefore hard to justify why one person would be promoted and not the other.

It's not about the file, but it's not *not* about the file either.

Make It Your Own

- How has it come to be that supervisors and staff both hate evaluations?

- Have you ever had an evaluation process that helped you improve your performance? What made it work?
- How do procedural justice and outcome justice play out in the larger world, e.g., in police and court proceedings?

"We Never Fire Anyone"

You know what pushes my buttons? When I see a parent using empty threats. I don't mean threats of violence or danger; I mean threats like "If you don't clean up your room, you're not going to get a birthday party," or "Santa won't come if you fight with your sister." Bullshit! I know you're bullshitting, and so does your kid, or they will after a few years. You *know* you're going to give them a birthday party, because you've already sent the invitations. And we all know that Santa always comes, if you celebrate that kind of thing.

I am *not* equating parenting with supervision. That would be a false and dangerous analogy. I am using the example to emphasize the vacuity of empty threats. So don't give your staff empty threats either. Actually, termination isn't and shouldn't be a threat; I think it's a logical consequence that, in most cases, would follow other efforts to improve performance. And I don't think it should happen lightly or easily. If terminating staff ever becomes easy, it's time to stop being a manager. You always want to recognize the person, not just the position. You want to remember that firing someone will impact their life.

However, if you let those humane considerations stop you from ever terminating an employee, then not only are you keeping a poor performer on staff, you are also sending a clear message to every staff member that it doesn't matter how well or how badly you do your job, you will all be treated the same. That is a huge disincentive. Retaining a poor performer in their role, and sending that message to the rest of your staff, ultimately undermines the mission.

I don't want you to fire anyone without good reason or as your first reaction to a problem (unless it's a doozy of a problem!), but I do want you to recognize that sometimes firing a staff member is necessary.

When is it necessary? When someone has done something egregious, when poor performance has not improved after numerous attempts and chances to help the person improve, or when someone is acting consistently in a way that negatively impacts the morale and teamwork of the staff (and won't change). When these issues and steps are documented, open the door and say goodbye. Do it fairly and do it with compassion, but don't be afraid to say goodbye when it's time to let someone go. You're not doing the organization or the staff member any favors by keeping the person on. Ideally, they will move on to another job where they can be successful and happy.

When I hear a manager say, "We never fire anyone here," I know that means there is dysfunction at work. It's not because every single employee has been a stellar performer or has immediately stepped up and changed their ways when problems arise. (Okay—maybe if the organization is brand new, that could be possible, but it's generally not.) The dysfunction might be the result of reorganizing around someone whom the organization should terminate, so that they can lay them off instead. Or they make it miserable for the person so they'll quit. As a management philosophy, it is not a healthy option, and the message you are sending is that performance doesn't matter.

I often receive calls from a manager asking for advice about how to improve performance. I ask them to tell me what they have tried up to this point. Sometimes they have done everything they should have done: provided clear expectations, feedback, coaching, chances, warnings, etc. But when I say, "It sounds like you might be moving toward termination," they say, "Oh, no, we don't want to do that." That option should never be the first thing on the table, but at some point, the manager and the organization must decide what the deal breakers are. What is bad enough that it won't be tolerated? Start with the obvious things, and go from there: You would fire someone for assaulting someone. You would fire someone for embezzling. You would fire someone for not ever showing up to work. What else?

Once you have a sense of what these deal breakers are, you have a path to discipline and, if necessary, termination. Save discipline and termination for actions or repeating patterns that are truly deal breakers; otherwise, don't go there. If you're not prepared to follow it through to termination, don't go down the discipline road. The only two logical ends of the discipline road are improvement or termination. At that point, there is no "never mind—good enough." The time for good enough is before you start down that road.

It's not a threat—it's a consequence. And it's never a good idea to set up a consequence if you're not prepared to see it through.

Make It Your Own

- When people who are not doing their jobs are ignored and kept on indefinitely, what impact does that have on strong performers?
- What are the across-the-board deal breakers for your organization or for you?
- When organizations have a "we don't fire anyone" mindset, what are they hoping to achieve? What are they hoping to avoid?

The Challenges with Flat

Many staff working in social justice organizations are at least somewhat resistant to hierarchy. They are fighting against oppression in the world, and they don't want to give anyone inside the organization the power to oppress anyone. I get that. I don't want anyone to have the means, opportunity, or power to oppress employees in an organization either. Hierarchies are also often equated with bureaucracies.

These staff often want to flatten the organization. They want to work in teams and have everyone vote on everything and have all staff members be responsible for themselves. Great! Except, in my experience, it doesn't usually work like that. Or it might work like that for a while, and it might work like that for most people, but sooner or later someone ends up being a jerk or simply not following through on their agreements or work, and then it gets messy quickly. The staff member is not being responsible for herself, so who is going to hold her accountable? That is when the flat organization becomes clunky and sometimes ineffective. Maybe they figure out who will talk to the wayward staff member. Great. And maybe that even works. Even better. But what if it doesn't work? And what about next time? The process to move someone out of a flat organization is cumbersome and often moves very slowly.

I am not saying that flat is bad. I am saying that totally flat structures can pose challenges to organizations. I am all for staff holding themselves and their coworkers accountable. But there needs to be some system (or people) in place to step in when that doesn't work. It can be minimal, but I do believe that some system of accountability and decision making helps an organization to run more smoothly.

When severe resistance to hierarchy occurs, the process of decision making also gets awkward. Who is the decision maker in this situation? How many meetings will an organization need to hold to render a decision? Who will be in those meetings? If the organization is only four to six people, maybe that can work, but when there are thirty or more . . . Does everyone really have to learn everything about everything in order to make good decisions? Can't there be specialists? Do meetings end up taking up everyone's time?

There are also problems when an organization talks the flat talk and encourages staff to offer input and have a buy-in on decisions, but what about when they don't care about some decisions or don't know enough about the topic to offer knowledgeable input? Then the situation gets messy again. Or if the staff offers input but then the "real" deciders decide something different, pushback, if not revolution, will happen.

Things work better when everyone is clear on what is necessary to be an effective organization that can make timely decisions and act quickly, when necessary. How will decisions about accountability or new positions be made? An organization run by cooperative teams or democracy can work. As long as the way decisions will be made is clear and everyone is on the same page, mostly flat can work. But totally flat too often ends in chaos.

Make It Your Own

- When and how is your organization like a bureaucracy, and how is it different?
- What would need to be in place in order for a flat organization not to devolve into chaos? Is it still flat with those conditions in place?
- What successes and problems could result from an organization run by a system of teams?

CHAPTER 9:

CULTURE—WALKING THE TALK

The culture of an organization is similar to an individual's personality, in that it tells you a lot about who they are. It drives how they show up and how they act. It can enhance their work or diminish it. An organization's culture can be aligned with its mission, or it can undermine the organization. It can be intentional, or it can be accidental. Without intentional focus, an organization will still develop a culture, but it will be haphazard at best.

When I use the term "culture," I mean the way things are done in an organization. It covers policies, practices, and organizational structure, but even more, culture is about how people act together and how and why organizations have the policies, practices, and structure they have. "Culture" includes the organization's values, beliefs, assumptions, theory of change, and interpersonal relationships. What is tolerated and what is not. What is rewarded. The spoken and unspoken rules and expectations. How conflict is handled. Who's hired. Who's fired. Who's promoted. Who has power and how they use it. What people talk about and what they ignore. What stories are passed on to new staff. Some aspects of culture are named, and some are not. Culture is what people tell each other about when their friends are hired or are considering applying for a job at the organization: "You should know that . . ." Culture is the fabric that sews the organization together. Sometimes it is beautiful and coherent, and sometimes it is a messy patchwork that clashes and hurts to look at.

In the support of justice, an organization must develop a culture that not only supports the external work but actively fosters internal justice. This takes time, energy, focus, and leadership. It takes a careful review of what the organization has been encouraging, rewarding, and valuing. And an even more thoughtful analysis looks at what has unintentionally been tolerated, replicated, and ignored.

The strongest organizations build cultures that center the work, monitor fairness, and support the staff. They build a culture of respect wherein every staff member is seen and included. They encourage innovation but never lose their focus. They are clear on their values and how those values show up—and they do not tolerate actions that damage those values.

There is no one-size-fits-all culture for organizations that center on justice, but there are common elements among them, perhaps the most important of which is that they walk their talk by building a culture aligned with their mission and values.

Culture Happens

I was buying a few pieces of furniture to update our living room. I went to my usual Costco and picked out the pieces I wanted. When it came time to make my purchases, I found a worker who walked with me to the specific pieces and told me to take a photo of the description code and show it to the checker. Then he explained how Costco would charge me for the furniture, and how someone would then meet me out front with my items. He also apologized that they did not have one piece in stock, but he called another nearby Costco, which did have it, so he asked them to hold it for me. The checker was friendly, the person who met me out front helped me load my car, and I went on my way.

Different story at the other Costco. I couldn't find anyone to help me. I wandered around the furniture area, but no one came to help. I went to the help desk, stood in line for several minutes, and then was told to go stand in another line. They said, "Go stand in the furniture area, and someone will help you." Another fifteen minutes. Finally, someone came, gave me a card, and said when I paid for my item, someone would meet me at the door. I paid and waited at the door. Fifteen more minutes. In frustration, I went back to the furniture area, and there they were, *not* where they had told me to wait. They rolled the piece out to my car, but I had to ask them to help me load it.

Same company, different cultures. This comes down to the manager. Somehow, the manager at the first Costco had instilled a value of service and friendliness in the staff. The second, not so much. And yes, you shop at Costco not for the service but for the prices, but when you can get both, what a difference it makes.

The point is that culture happens whether or not anyone is intentionally guiding or monitoring it. Patterns develop. Behaviors and attitudes spread. Culture can be defined and intentional, accidental and amorphous, or a combination of both.

Culture can be described as "the way we do things around here," and that is a valid summary, but it does not convey the importance of culture. The culture of an organization is what people experience every day that they work in (or visit) an organization. It is a communal recognition of what is valued and what isn't. Think of all those companies we heard about in the wake of the #MeToo movement. They all had harassment policies, I'm sure. But the culture did not enliven any sense of safety for women and gender-nonconforming people. The documents do not make the culture; the behavior of the staff makes the culture—especially the behavior of the leaders. So when a leader harasses someone and nothing happens, everyone knows it—both the abusers and the abused. That culture does not respect staff or safety. When a known bully is promoted, instead of being reprimanded, that tells staff what is valued. When gossip runs amok and leaders take part in it, then that too is the culture. When meetings routinely start late and no one even notices, or when jokes are made at clients' or members' expense, that becomes normal. When corners are cut, when no BIPOC are hired, when microaggressions are ignored, all of these become "the way we do things around here." These are examples of culture "just happening," of bad behavior being tolerated and thereafter becoming the norm.

Of course, good culture can "just happen" too. People can be kind to each other. Staff can give their all to the mission. Leadership can make equity a reality in the organization. Members can be held front and center in all the work. Workers can be respected and valued. But when culture just happens, it can change quickly, because it tends to be personality driven. As long as there are good leaders, it works. Sometimes one person can leave an organization, and the whole culture changes.

The alternative is for an organization to intentionally build, enliven, and monitor their staff and hold them accountable to the kind of culture that the organization needs—the kind of culture that supports the work, the staff, and the leaders and that is aligned with the mission.

Culture happens whether anyone is paying attention to it or not. But how much better it is to pay attention and actively work to build a culture that is aligned with your mission and your values. Then you're walking the talk, and people will feel it.

Make It Your Own

- What is rewarded in your organization? (Not just what you say you reward or what should be rewarded based on policies, but what is actually rewarded?)

- Are there any toxic behaviors that your organization ignores or overlooks?
- Describe the ideal culture for an organization like yours.

Culture Invigorates Values—or Not

People were dying every week, sometimes every day. When I worked at Face to Face, an AIDS service organization, during the height of the AIDS epidemic, tears were frequent. But so was laughter. Laughter and tears were both part of our culture. Grief and playfulness.

I was the sixth person hired, and when I left, nine years later, there were fifty employees. During those years, I worked with a staff who were passionate about their work. One of the results of that passion was that together we built a culture that was very intentional in supporting the difficult work. Our executive director was integral to building that culture.

We played games. We laughed together. We cried together. We expressed our rage about the national response to the epidemic. We not only allowed feelings but made a place for them. We found some therapists to hold a monthly clinical support group to help staff process their work and their losses. And the group was open to every staff member, not just clinicians. We were informal. We welcomed authenticity. I could address the bittersweet pain of my youngest child heading off to kindergarten, as well as the challenges of work. We told each other stories—about our work and our lives. We took half a day off each month to do something not work-related together. We addressed problems. The ED wrote each of us a silly poem and awarded us a homemade medal on our work anniversary. This was part of appreciating the work and the people. We didn't do everything right, for sure. We blundered, but we also cleaned up the best we could when we did blunder. Together, we built an intentional culture that supported and enhanced our difficult work.

Culture in an established organization is kind of like gravity—it keeps pulling practices to the way things are and have been. It is a very powerful force. Being strategic and creating a culture that aligns with and supports the mission requires constant care, intentionality, and commitment. We must focus on both the way we do things and why we do them that way.

Culture is influenced from the top down and from the bottom up. In fact, one of the key elements of an intentional culture is the alignment that exists up and down the organization. One of the most confusing situations for staff is when an organization has stated values but does not live them. This can feel crazy-making. For example, teamwork is a stated value within an organization, but the individual achievers are the ones who are promoted, perhaps even when they are known to be backstabbers. Or an organization says it values straightforward communication but labels people "complainers" if they challenge a policy or practice. The organization says it values direct problem solving, but staff members talk behind people's backs and nothing happens.

At its best, culture is aligned with the mission, vision, and values of an organization and reinforces the theory of change. At its worst, it undermines those elements. Marc Koenig, an author at Nonprofit Hub, suggests we think of culture as a garden: "How you care for the garden affects the quality of your produce. Your culture determines how you can make an impact on the world."

Leaders' actions have a big impact on culture. Our policies, procedures, practices, and rituals; the physical layout we create in work spaces; and the stories we tell all impact culture. Do we tell stories about the early days, when "all hands on deck" was the prevailing practice? What's rewarded? Who gets hired and promoted? Do people communicate directly? Do we laugh in our meetings?

Culture can change, but it usually does not do so quickly or easily. Cultures tend to evolve, rather than change abruptly.

It isn't a matter of simply deciding, *Let's center racial justice now*. The members of an organization have to look at what they consciously value and unconsciously practice. They must recognize what it does just because it has always been done, and how that impacts people and the work.

A few common nonprofit practices that are often unexamined and therefore replicated are that nonprofit staff are paid less than for-profit counterparts, nonprofit work is overwhelming, leaders are predominantly white, and conflict is avoided. Ask yourself, "How does our culture continue those practices or counteract them?"

In order to change culture, an organization must take a multilevel approach and build a process to involve staff and leadership (and perhaps other stakeholders) in deep discussions about unconscious practices, hidden rules, and unrecognized assumptions. Then it takes time to consider what culture would best support the work and how to bridge any gaps between that culture and your current one. This is not a quick fix, but it can be invaluable in both living your values and in retaining staff.

At Face to Face, we valued life, we honored death, we embraced authenticity, and we recognized the power of fun to connect us and support the emotionally difficult work. We enlivened those values in our culture, and the result was profound.

Make It Your Own

- Think of a business that everyone knows, like Walmart or Bank of America. From what you know and experience of those companies' culture, what do you surmise their values to be?
- How does thinking of an organization's culture as a garden make the concept more accessible? How might it be distracting?
- When and why would it be worth the time and effort to reimagine an organization's culture?

A Culture of Respect: The Seeing Triangle

I've been married forever. Happily so. At one point in the forever, I came home from a therapy session and told my husband, "We need to fight more." We weren't one of those couples who proudly proclaim that they never have fights. We had them, but they were relatively rare. And that was the problem. I realized that we were both avoiding fighting. In my case, if I thought about saying something that I knew would make Mark unhappy/sad/disappointed/angry, I would play it out in my mind first. I'll say this, he'll say that, I'll say this . . . and then we'll both be upset and it won't make any difference. And I was right in one sense: that it probably would play out that way most of the time.

But I missed two important points in my rush to avoid fighting. One: I didn't give either of us a chance to see how an argument would actually play out; either one of us could have reacted differently at any given point. Two, and even more important for us, as it turned out: The one with the concern did not get to be seen in their upset or concern. And sometimes, maybe most times, that is actually what people need. It was certainly what we needed.

This is true in our personal relationships and at work. People need to be seen. They also need to see each other and need to see themselves. These three practices make up the seeing triangle. When all three components are in place, you magically have a culture of respect. And when a fully functioning culture of respect exists, people feel safe being who they are, speaking their truth, and doing the work of the organization and the work needed to maintain relationships in support of the work. Within a culture of respect, if people don't feel safe or respected, they know they can ask for help to address what is causing their unease.

Seeing Self

When self-awareness (see chapter 5) is a shared value and a commitment of the entire organization, it becomes a component of a culture of respect. When this happens, it becomes an expectation that staff will actively practice self-reflection, self-awareness, and self-management. The practice is discussed, invited, modeled, and addressed.

This practice is about understanding who we are and how we show up. We won't—we can't—always do this 100 percent. Not recognizing our own hidden dangers and forgetfulness are part of our human experience, but within this practice, we pay attention to recognizing our own assets, challenges, and hidden dangers.

When people are aware of their own strengths and recognize when someone else could probably do a task or a project better than they could, they are seeing themselves—recognizing their challenges and both owning and actively addressing them. Being aware of hidden dangers—our so-called blind spots. This is tricky, because by definition we can't see what is hidden unless we look for it. But we can anticipate some of these blind spots. For example, I know that I have a tendency to wait until the last minute to meet a deadline. So, in anticipation of this habit, I would delegate the oversight of deadlines to my assistant, because she would help me address the issue. Being self-aware also acknowledges that you may not have intended harm, but your actions still might have caused harm.

The other way we can practice seeing ourselves is by inviting feedback and considering it when we get it. Feedback can help us feel safe and effective if it is done well and if we let ourselves learn from it.

This seeing of self is demonstrated by practicing self-reflection, recognizing our own challenges and hidden dangers, being open to feedback, and acknowledging our impact on other people. This is especially true in regard to considerations of race, gender, power, authority, and privilege.

This mode of seeing is so critical that the other two modes of seeing lose authenticity if this is not in place. If someone has little or no self-awareness, it is harder to trust their ability to see others and be seen.

Key questions of seeing self include:

- What am I assuming or interpreting?
- What's my part here?
- Am I considering feedback?
- Do I need to clean anything up?

Seeing Others

Seeing others is about recognizing and accepting your coworkers as individuals, appreciating their work, and collaborating in support of your common goals. This seeing comes down to knowing that your coworkers are more than cogs in a machine. It involves knowing them as people—not in a prying way, but in a connective way. None of this is personal; it's about that key question—How can I help this person be successful so we can move the work forward?—and seeing what they need, hearing what they need, and responding to what they need, to the extent to which that makes sense for each person's job.

Enacting this aspect of seeing requires listening and lots of authentic two-way conversations. It requires a level of trust so that each staff member trusts that everyone is there for the success of the organization. Start with that assumption—and if it's proven to be untrue, address it at that point.

On an organizational level, this aspect of seeing others translates into clear expectations about how people will treat each other—expectations like zero tolerance on bullying and harassment, which in turn makes space for healthy boundaries and good mutual intentions. It means having no gossiping policies and practices. In an effort for every person to be seen, organizations make a point of training staff to facilitate meetings so that introverts are not overlooked and extroverts don't routinely dominate decision making. To support people who process more slowly, staff share agendas ahead of time and supervisors give people who need it a heads-up when they will be expected to offer ideas, e.g., "When we meet tomorrow, I'd like to hear three ideas you have about your goals."

At their best, teams that are committed to seeing everyone will hold a series of meetings to help the team develop their own agreements about what they need to do their best work together—agreements such as how they will address conflict, when and how they will communicate with each other, how they will give each other the benefit of the doubt, how their shared space will be used and cleaned. These agreements can be the touchstones that guide an intentional culture.

This is not about everyone needing to be friends or even liking each other. It is about seeing each other and trying not to get in each other's way by supporting each other's success.

Key questions of seeing others include:

- How is this action impacting the work?
- What does this person need to be successful?
- Are we ignoring anything that makes people feel unseen?
- How are my team members seeing (or not seeing) each other?

Being Seen

The third component of the seeing triangle is being seen—making sure that everyone knows they are seen, respected, and appreciated, and that people let themselves be seen. It is not about being exposed but about being known, and therefore vulnerable.

When we feel invisible, we react, even if the "not seeing" is only a perception. Perception usually speaks louder than reality. And when it is true that we are unseen, it is infuriating. In many cases, this is when people sue—when they feel unseen and unheard. The results can be malpractice suits, corporate-liability actions, police-misconduct complaints, and wrongful-termination suits, among others. Then, when that invisibility has been systematically institutionalized, it becomes larger and it becomes about justice. That's when people join together and demand to be seen, via Critical Mass bicycle rides, Black Lives Matter, #MeToo, and so on.

This feeling of being unseen impacts our work relationships too. If someone was harassed in their last job (seen as an object, not a person), they are not going to instantly respect their boss. If you are a white person supervising a BIPOC, don't be surprised if you have to earn trust. If you are a man supervising a woman, be thoughtful about how things might be interpreted by a woman and how you are taking up space.

At work, people feel unseen when the quiet, consistently effective employees get no attention. They get overlooked while others get recognition, praise, and maybe even raises and promotions. The loudest and most insistent voices in the room drown them out. People who don't play well with others get promoted. People are not performing, or coworkers have to pick up their slack, but they suffer no consequences. People start to wonder, *Why am I working so hard?* They feel invisible, and they feel angry.

On the other hand, we know that giving people an opportunity to be seen and heard makes all the difference. In his book *Blink*, Malcolm Gladwell tells us that doctors who had never been sued spent three minutes longer with each patient than those who had been sued (18.3 minutes, versus fifteen minutes). They were more likely to talk people through the visit and engage in active listening, and they were far more likely to laugh and be funny. This is not about medicine; it is about human nature. It is about people's feeling seen.

Being seen requires that you show up authentically. Let yourself be seen—mostly in your work, but also as an individual (though only to a point where you feel comfortable and you are not distracting from the work)—so that you can connect on a human level. If you are a supervisor, honor your regular meetings. (I know I'm a broken record about this.) Let yourself be seen as the decider when you are. Being seen also means you have to speak up if you need something, whether you are a supervisor or not. You may or may not get what you request, but if you don't speak up, you have little chance of getting it. Respect is different for different people. If most people are okay with the office jokester teasing them but you don't like it, you need to let the offending person know or find help to do so.

This too is part of being seen—talking to people about your boundaries, concerns, and requests, especially when things come up and you are tempted to turn against people in response. Maybe they don't know what you need; it doesn't mean their actions are okay, but a culture of respect involves a joint commitment to trying to work things out, in service of the mission.

This component is twofold: making sure you listen and respond if someone tells you they feel unseen, and being seen yourself. If someone tells you that they are feeling unseen, believe them. They might not say it in those words. It may come out as "You're not hearing me," "You don't respect me," "Why do you even ask for my input?" or even "Whatever" when you ask them for their input. What they are saying is, *I do not feel seen.*

Key questions of being seen include:

- Am I showing up authentically?
- Am I owning my responsibilities?
- Am I letting people know I see them?
- Is anyone telling me that they need to be seen?

When we can build departments/programs/work groups that build an active practice of seeing self, seeing others, and being seen, we have a culture of respect. It's the sweet spot in the middle of the three seeing circles. That's what we're going for. That's what we're leading for. And it is up to all of us— leadership and each team member. A successful team has to function in all three areas. This is a huge part of any culture—are these things at play, or are their opposites at play? Is the culture one of not seeing self, not being seen, not seeing others?

When my husband and I started fighting more, it was awkward and a little silly at first, but we quickly learned that for us, fighting was an enactment of the seeing triangle. We had to see ourselves to recognize the upset or concern, we had to be seen when we raised the issue, and we had to see the other past the discomfort of fighting. If this triangle can help a couple who have been together forever, imagine what it can do for your team.

Make It Your Own

* Do you do anything individually to practice self-awareness?
* What do you do, as a team or organization, to support the practice of seeing your coworkers and/or community members?
* What do you need in order to be seen, or what makes you feel seen?
* What are the signs of a culture of *not* seeing self, *not* being seen, *not* seeing others?

Pen or Pencil Culture?

We were traveling and sat down with our cups of coffee (him) and tea (me) to do our crossword puzzle. The pencil had fallen out of the book, and we couldn't find a replacement pencil, so we grabbed a pen and started in. Between the two of us, we can usually complete a puzzle in thirty to forty minutes.

However, within five minutes, I called it. "Let's stop. This isn't fun." Because we had only a pen, we were afraid to commit. When we have a pencil, we can try out words and adjust and adapt as we need to. We work fast and cooperatively—and the work is fun and challenging. We can think outside the box, with no concerns or ramifications. But with a pen, none of that happened. We wrote only when we were absolutely sure, and even then, we were hesitant. As a result, the time felt totally product focused and my brain froze. I didn't let myself play or enjoy the process, because if I was wrong, it wouldn't work. I would be in trouble because the puzzle would be a mess!

So, I ask you, are you a pen or pencil culture?

Pencil Culture

- It is clear when there is a specific way that things need to be done and when there is room for innovation.
- Staff are encouraged to try out ideas and strategies. Supervisors tell staff what outcome they are looking for and let them figure out how to get there.
- When someone makes a mistake or a strategy doesn't work, they are asked, "What would you do differently next time?" or "What did you learn?"
- It is a practice to watch for joy and engagement in the work and highlight that activity.
- Managers are clear that they do not have all the answers and that they want to hear other ideas.

Pen Culture

- Work is expected to be done in the same way every time. There's a right way and a wrong way.
- If someone has a question, they'll be told what to do.
- Managers share their knowledge and experience and expect staff to learn from it.
- One of the unofficial mottos is "If it ain't broke, don't fix it." Staff have literally heard this said.
- Management determines who can do what based on people's skills and experience, not their enthusiasm.
- When someone makes a mistake, they are asked, "So, what happened and whose fault was it?"

I am assuming that staff know how to do their job. When staff are new or in learning/training mode, the management style might require a more nuanced approach. And, no doubt, some jobs require a more pen style of management—e.g., firefighting. Other jobs seem designed for pencil-style management—e.g., marketing. I am thinking about the approach of individual managers and the culture of supervision in an organization. What is the preferred style of supervision in this organization? How are managers expected to show up for staff? What are the expectations of managers across the organization? How does leadership respond to mistakes and messes? Finally, the most critical question to consider is whether the pen or pencil culture aligns with your values and your mission. In a broad sense, strong pen cultures tend to replicate white supremacy values of perfection, one right way, and either/or thinking.

If a pencil culture would work better for your organization but you have a lot of pen supervisors, the transition can be difficult. Each supervisor can take a few baby steps at a time, and the organization can be intentional in its approach to shifting this aspect of its culture.

Steps to Embrace a Pencil Culture

1. Practice asking, "How much trouble could this one assignment/task cause the organization? Do we have wiggle room/time to try something new?"

2. When people make a mistake, remember that you can't change the past but the past can inform the future. So focus on the future when you debrief with your staff.

3. How might innovation help your team? Ask yourself, "Even if it ain't broke, how could it be improved?" What if someone else could imagine improvements that you can't from your perspective?

4. Observe how work is different when people are engaged and enthusiastic. Just notice.

5. Find one area where you don't know everything. Sincerely ask your staff for input in that area, just to experience that process with them. (Don't be surprised if they are slow to offer ideas, since this is a new venture for them too.)

On the other hand, in some cultures, managers can be too flexible and adapt for any reason. If you show signs of this kind of culture, consider these steps.

Steps to Move Toward a Pen Culture

1. Be clear with your staff when a protocol must be followed without exception—e.g., safety procedures.

2. If you have staff members who innovate too much (perhaps in a way that makes their coworkers' jobs more difficult), explain your concerns to them. Teach them to say to you and their team members, "I have some ideas. Is this negotiable?" before they change things.

3. Make sure that this culture is not a by-product of a conflict-avoidant culture that avoids hard conversations and therefore tolerates constant change and/or lack of performance and calls those issues "creativity" to disguise them.

4. Sometimes managers do have the experience and answers that people need to honor. Own it.

5. If the same mistakes keep happening, or when the same person makes them over and over again, the focus on the future may be premature. You may first have to acknowledge what went wrong and have the person take responsibility for that.

A little wiggle room can be a good thing. Managing in pencil can give your staff room to make mistakes, try things out, think outside the box, and create engagement and fun among your team. What is a six-letter word that allows for possibilities? P-e-n-c-i-l.

Make It Your Own

• When have you felt constricted or afraid of "getting in trouble?" How did that feeling impact your actions?

• Do you tend to be a pen or a pencil supervisor? How does it make sense for you, your team, and the work? When might the other option make sense?

• Is there a place for innovation in your work area? If so, can you identify how an innovation practice might work for your team?

Is Pretending Undermining Your Culture?

When I was working in my "regular" jobs, before I became a consultant, I experienced occasional periods of discontent. I would start to feel restless and think that maybe the grass was greener on the other side of the fence, so I would start to look around at other opportunities. I would give myself a week or so to do this, while I kept working. At the end of the week, I would ask myself, "What are you going to do?" Year after year, I would decide, "This is still the right place for me." I would stop looking and double down on the work I had in front of me. It was not the organization's problem to fix; it was mine.

It is not the organization's job to make any individual happy. Leaders and staff can work to create good work cultures and support staff to be engaged and productive, but the bottom line is the mission—not individual happiness. Sometimes that line gets blurry and individuals expect organizations to make their job better for them, or to take care of their need for more time off, or even to fire someone they don't want to work with. When individual needs get enmeshed with organizational practices, a good culture can be undermined. But that undermining can be hard to spot when people are not overtly doing anything wrong.

For any kind of problem, whether it is conflict, unhappiness, confusion, or whatever, there are really only three choices: accept it, change it, or leave. And each path has a healthy way to go through it or a pretend way to proceed. The more a culture tolerates pretend choices, the more unhealthy it will be.

When staff are upset, it is important for them to recognize the three options and then to make a decision. It does not have to be an immediate decision, and it does not have to be a final decision, but when the problem is intruding on the work, they need to address their concern. If you are helping your staff through a problem or a decision, help them see their choices and then help them take that path cleanly. If they do not take the path cleanly, it gets messy, as they may (perhaps inadvertently) simply pretend to have made a choice. As an organization, and as a leader, you must name and stop any undermining to protect the culture.

Let's look at the three paths and consider what a clean path looks like and what pretending looks like.

Really Accept It	*Pretend-Accept It*
This is the decision to accept the situation the way it is. Maybe you are choosing your battles and decide this is not worth any extra effort at this time. Really accepting it means you take a deep breath and do what you need to do to show up at work and do your best, given the situation as it is. You truly let the situation go.	Fake accepting it would mean that you decide not to try to change anything but you are still unhappy and you let people know it, one way or another. Often this shows up as frequent complaining, sarcasm, eye rolling, or constant grumpiness. You hang on to your dissatisfaction.
This is where I ended up many times in my past jobs. I would look around and quickly realize that my job offered me exactly what I was looking for (or much of it, anyway). I would decide to accept it. And that meant that I rechose my job and gave it my all.	In my job situation, I would have stopped looking for a job every day, but I would not actively choose to stay. I might have ignored the parts of my job I didn't like or stopped returning calls. I might have taken excessive time off.
It may be that you work with someone who annoys you. Accepting the situation means that you don't try to change the person and you don't work around the person—you accept the situation as it is, because there are enough other positives in the job, and then you deal with your annoyance on your own.	With the annoying person, you wouldn't do anything to change the situation, but you would complain about this person to other staff members. You might make snide, passive-aggressive, or sarcastic comments every time you felt annoyed, e.g., "I'm so glad you could grace me with five minutes of your precious time." Or if they asked you if everything was okay, you'd answer, "I'm fine," and then not talk to them for a week.

Really Change It	*Pretend-Change It*
If you really want to change something, you figure out what you need to be different. You recognize what your part in the situation is, what someone else's part in the situation is, and what you're going to do about it. You have difficult conversations when necessary. You own your truth and your experiences. You change what you can change in the situation and ask others to change in a way that will make the situation better.	Fake change would focus completely on someone else while not considering your own part of the situation. You might address the situation by blaming others and/or threatening to leave or stop attending meetings if the other person didn't change. You would act as if the organization owed you happiness.
So, if I were really unhappy with something about my job, I would spend time figuring out what was contributing to this discontent and take action to address that. For instance, if I were bored, I might ask to change my role. If I felt like I was being treated unfairly, I would talk to someone who could help me. And if I had a conflict with a coworker, I would address it. I would carefully consider first what *needed* to be different in order for me to accept the situation, and then what I *wanted* to be different to make the situation perfect.	In my job situation, I would not change positions but would let people know that I had thought about leaving and had decided to stay. I might even hint that I wanted another job, but I would wait for it to happen without taking any action myself. And if I had a conflict with a coworker, I might start avoiding that person. If the coworker asked what was going on, I might ignore them, or deny that anything was wrong, or tell them to figure it out on their own.
With the annoying person, you might say something like, "I find it hard to stay present when you	With the annoying person, you might agree to both make some changes, but then you

(continued on next page)

(continued from previous page)

Really Change It	Pretend-Change It
repeatedly look at your phone during our meetings. What would make it possible for you to be fully attentive during our meetings? I am willing to meet at a different time or for a shorter duration, but I really need you to put your phone away during our time together." Or you could see if you could get out of that meeting and find someone else, who wasn't distracted by the phone use, to host it.	would wait for the other person to change first. You might just work around the person and act like that was an acceptable change. Or you might make it a bigger issue and state at a staff meeting, "Millennials are so rude. You guys need to get off your phones and act like grownups while you're at work."

(Notice you don't say that the other person is wrong or bad for doing that; you simply own that the situation didn't work for *you*.)

If you could not change the situation (since even when you take all the right steps, maybe multiple times, it might not change), you would decide if you were unhappy enough to leave.

Really Leave	*Pretend-Leave*
Leaving means that you accept that the situation is not working for you and that you are responsible for taking care of yourself. If you could not accept the situation the way it was and could not change it, or if the change did not result in the outcome you hoped for, you would accept that it was time for you to go. You would gracefully announce that you had decided to move on and would make a transition plan with your team.	Pretend-leaving is staying in the job but disengaging. You don't actually leave but you stop working so hard and begin to "phone it in." You hang on just for a paycheck. You no longer care about the mission, your work, or your team—and it shows. You might even think, *If they don't like it, they can fire me.* Meanwhile, you complain and blame and make everyone else unhappy too, and/or make global statements and undermine the situation: "This place is a mess. I'm leaving." You might even start rallying your coworkers to back you up, thereby splitting the team and making it about you—not the work.

All three of these paths have a clean, healthy, self-directed process, or they have a blaming, negative, and toxic process in which it only appears that people are doing their work. When a culture tolerates this kind of undermining, whether it is intentional or not, toxicity can spread rapidly and make the whole organization sick.

Make It Your Own

- What would be necessary for a culture to insist on healthy choices from all staff members?
- What is the impact on coworkers and the organization when people adopt a "pretend" style of action?
- What does it look like when people feel as if the organization owes them more than they are receiving? How does it impact the culture and the work when it becomes about an individual's satisfaction?
- What other actions would you add to the category that I call "pretend" and label as toxic? How can they be addressed, or, even better, prevented?

Support Through Hard Times

We all have hard times. My brother died suddenly in 2016 and I was devastated. Returning to work, I noticed that I was easily distracted and sometimes felt waves of grief. If I had returned to a workplace with coworkers around and no one knew or cared about my personal loss, it would have been even harder.

We also face common hard times now and then. This was the case after 9/11, during the COVID-19 pandemic, and in our collective witnessing of the murders of Black people like George Floyd and Breonna Taylor and countless others over the years. It also happens when a natural disaster strikes or when a staff member dies or is severely ill or injured.

While it is absolutely true that we have a job to do when we are at work, that does not mean that we are emotionless robots doing the work. Therefore, thoughtful leaders who support a people-centered culture have a tricky job of balancing support for individuals (or teams) facing difficult times with getting work done. Here are a few tips to help you balance those needs in difficult times:

1. **Watch your assumptions:** You don't know how people react to situations. You don't know how your team feels. You can't always interpret how people act as a clear indication of their feelings. Some people wear their emotions publicly, and some people keep their feelings private, so don't assume you know.

2. **Don't make absolute statements:** Speak thoughtfully and carefully. Say, "Many people may be feeling sad this week," versus, "We are all devastated" or, "We're ready to move on now."

3. **Recognize individual pain. Be kind:** This is a time to see and hear individuals and to meet pain with kindness, without making promises. Say, "This seems like a hard time for you right now. What do you need?" In the case of individual loss, this kind of question can make a tremendous difference. In times of mutual loss, it can be supportive and grounding. Model kindness and balance by taking care, while also getting work done.

4. **Double down on your mission:** Whatever the focus of your work, highlight the importance and the impact of your work, connecting it with what is hard at this moment: "Our clients are counting on us more than ever." "We cannot forget the value of our collective work."

5. Encourage people to find meaning in their work: Remind people to focus on what they can do. Encourage them to do their work well to feel pride in their work, to make a difference in the world, and to support their coworkers.

6. Remind people, when necessary, that this is a workplace: I strongly encourage support and time to process, but that cannot supersede the work of your organization. After a certain time period, or after time off, if people are at work, they need to be able to work.

7. Make room for shared grief and pain to be expressed: Ignoring pain or rage or grief does not work and does not help the organization. These feelings are impacting the work, and ignoring them will not make them go away. People will not be able to move forward without somehow having their feelings honored. See them, hear them, acknowledge them. This is especially true when the grief is large and mutual—i.e., when a specific act of violence against Black people takes place and the trauma of that practice is vivid. Host a facilitated meeting to help people express their feelings. The feelings cannot dominate the workplace, but ignoring them will force them underground and lead to more upheaval in the long run.

The balance, as always, is to model a professional and kind relationship while never forgetting that your work is critical. We all face hard times—as individuals and as teams. One role of an effective supervisor in a caring culture is to acknowledge the painful times while not letting them hijack the work. When we are able to do that, we build stronger bonds to face the work ahead.

Make It Your Own

- What are some examples of what you individually need and have appreciated when you have faced hard times?
- There are two extremes in tough times. One extreme thinks, *We are here to work. Nothing else matters, so don't mention it.* The other extreme thinks, *We need to give our staff time to express every feeling and process endlessly to come out on the other side.* Where do you fall on the spectrum, and where does your organization fall on the spectrum? What actions does that lead you to take as a supervisor?
- What can the organization do as a whole to support the tough times while not throwing away the work?

Zero-Tolerance Culture re: Harassment

Some cisgender men may have been surprised when the #MeToo movement caused an outpouring of sexual-harassment accusations. Women were not. Trans and gender-nonconforming people were not. We knew it was real; we knew harassment happens *all the time*, and we all knew that it could happen to us or that it *had* happened to us.

Employers in California with five or more employees must provide one hour of harassment training to staff within six months of hiring and then another training every two years. Those with fifty or more employees are required to provide two hours of harassment training in the same time frames. Unfortunately, for too many organizations this has become simply one more HR requirement. The overriding message has been *Get the compliance box checked.*

Leadership has too often been asleep at the wheel. Even at nonprofits and other progressive organizations, other things have often seemed more important, and leaders have looked the other way. The leaders skip the trainings or look at their phone throughout the whole training. They reinforce the culture that makes harassment an HR issue. It's not—it's a leadership issue and a respect issue.

It's all about respect. It's about helping your employees recognize that their experience is not the same as that of someone who is different from them. It's about providing a workplace that provides a culture of respect, safety, engagement, and growth for people. All people. Not just cisgender men. Not just white folks. Not just the majority—whatever the majority is for that particular work group.

Not until our workplace cultures dig into what respect looks like for the people who work in those cultures can we start to move beyond this messy and hurtful place as a society. This takes time, attention, conversations, and action. Leaders' actions are some of the strongest factors in building the culture of an organization. And nowhere is this more true than in the area of harassment, respect, and treatment of staff. Until leaders can model respectful interactions and humility in the face of someone's alternate view of reality, the problems will just keep coming.

I have seen this change happen. I have seen the pro forma training and that culture change when a leader steps up. When a leader asks, out loud, "How can I do this better?" and then listens sincerely to the answers. When a leader seeks coaching because they recognize that the staff is not trusting them. Things shift when a leader speaks up about their own concerns regarding harassing behavior. *Then* they get the attention of staff. *Then* you start having real conversations. *Then* the culture starts to change because staff see, and feel, that this is different. That this matters.

Here are ten things leaders can do to instill a culture of respect:

1. Don't reward the bullies.

2. Walk the talk. If you say you have a zero-tolerance policy for harassment and discrimination, show it. Don't make exceptions, and don't look the other way.

3. Make sure your harassment policy is clearly written, available, and followed.

4. Believe people. This doesn't mean you don't investigate and don't listen to the accused's side of the story, but at the least, suspend your disbelief when you hear a complaint.

5. Institute conflict-resolution policies and train people on them (not so people have to address their harassers, but so they know they are respected and empowered to address problems).

6. Conduct in-person trainings (or conversations after online trainings) to underline that this is not just a "check the box" issue—it is real and important.

7. Train your supervisors. Make sure they have the tools to supervise in a clear, engaging, supportive, and accountable manner, without resorting to intimidation and autocracy.

8. Give managers and HR the autonomy and authority to confront disrespectful and inappropriate behavior long before it becomes illegal harassment.

9. Recognize and name the value of inclusion, and train people not just to tolerate others but to value and include all critical voices in decision making. Recognize this as a value-added proposition. Model it.

10. Say "good morning." Say "thank you." Say "please" and "excuse me" and "How are you?" Be human together.

Yes, some of this takes time and money. (And some of it doesn't.) Know that any money you invest in this will save you lots more in the long run—and sometimes in the short run too. Staff who feel respected and safe are more effective in their work. Also remember that harassment lawsuits are terribly inconvenient and much more expensive than anything on this list! And the value of building a culture of respect that makes all employees feel valued, engaged, and included? Priceless.

Make It Your Own

• How have you, as a leader, shown your staff that you take the issue of harassment seriously? How might you have inadvertently indicated that this was a "check the box" issue?

• What does respect look like to you? Specifically, what do you need to see to know that you are respected and in a safe place? Ask other people this question too, and listen carefully to what is important to them.

• Which of the ten action items listed above resonates most with you, and what can you do about it?

A Culture of Inclusion

I was doing a training at a foundation. Staff were involved in small group discussions, and as I waited for them to finish, I walked around, listening to and observing how engaged people were. Everyone I saw was actively participating in their group, so I let my mind wander. It was then that I noticed something that made me feel a little uncomfortable. I saw high heels. A lot of high heels. Every woman in the room had them on. I had not worn high heels in more than thirty years—and even then, I wore them only to weddings. I realized I did not fit in. I did not belong. I didn't have to fit in; I was there as a trainer, not as an employee. But it made me think about what it would have been like to be an employee. The high-heel thing would have been obvious to me every day I showed up to work. Perhaps I would have shifted the dress code to flats and other comfortable shoes, but I doubt it. Most likely, my discomfort would have led to self-consciousness and uncertainty. And I imagined that for every woman in this room to be in high heels, others must have noticed this workplace norm and adapted their own needs to fit in.

It made me think about how people must feel excluded based on other normative practices, and even more so when the exclusion is based on identity. How does it feel when no one in leadership looks like you? When you are the only trans person in the entire organization? One of only a few BIPOC staff? In those cases, the discomfort could be excruciating.

I cannot speak to the discomfort of that level of exclusion. I can attest briefly to a few things that have been proven to help build a truly inclusive workforce. Most organizations profess to value inclusion, but too many of those same organizations do little more than write the sentence "We value diversity." And then the leaders are frustrated and dumbfounded when their token hires do not work out.

Inclusion is about belonging, not just being tolerated. It is about being welcomed for who you are and how you show up—not just in theory, but in reality. But in order to be that kind of welcoming organization, we have to look closely at what we consider normal and routine. Are our practices based on patriarchal, white, middle-class, heterosexual, Christian norms? Most likely they are, if we have not actively reviewed and updated them. To do that, we must look at our practices, our policies, our assumptions, and, perhaps most of all, our hidden rules. Together, that will tell us how we show up.

But that still isn't enough, because if we are all white leaders looking at our norms, they will seem normal. If we are all men reviewing the dress code, high heels might seem normal. If everyone in leadership is a Christian, when planning a holiday party we might forget that we have people of other faiths working at, or visiting, our organization. If we're all straight or cisgender, we might have no idea how our use of pronouns or our friendly personal chitchat (which may seem barely personal to us) could be creating a heteronormative and possibly transphobic environment. *Nope, no problems here—not from our perspective.* We may need help to look beyond ourselves.

To be truly inclusive, look at these areas:

Voices

We must accept pushback and styles that are dramatically different from those we may be used to. These may include body language, volume, various ways of sharing information, basic assumptions, and approaches to the work, as well as strong opposition to the way things have been done. To become an inclusive organization requires more than just an intention to do so; it most likely means staff must be trained in how to listen, how to communicate in a truly respectful manner (not just based on the norm), and how to sit with discomfort and ambiguity.

Demographics of Staff and Leadership

Ask yourself these questions: What does our staff look like? Do we all look the same, love the same, gender the same, use our bodies the same? Staff representation matters, but leadership representation does even more so. A leadership team needs to demonstrate representation of its community and its members. Again, doing so requires more than intention. At every level of hiring, building a multirepresentative staff takes active recruitment, openness, welcoming, and listening.

Turnover

Who leaves? Who stays? And why? If BIPOC are hired and leave within a year or two but white folks stay longer, something is not working. Go back to square one, and get help looking at what is driving people away. Sure, you'll notice some unrelated turnover, but if a pattern emerges, it matters. And even when you consider the "unrelated" turnover, are you sure? Why did the people who left decide to take other jobs, or decide this was the year to go back to school?

What Is Said

What is said in the room when BIPOC are present and when they are not? Are mocking or stereotypical jokes told? Are micro- or macroaggressive comments made, in public or in private, and how are they responded to? If people recognize them but no one speaks up, does it matter that they recognized them? Do people make random comments about identity factors or tease about specific traits? And what do the newest staff members say? If they tell you something was offensive, believe them, even if you don't see it. Be ready to learn.

Hidden Rules

What are the rules that no one talks about? They might be about speaking up, clothing, socializing during nonwork time, jokes, who goes to meetings, what holidays staff celebrate, how much personal information people share, or what constitutes an acceptable work conversation. For example, there might be hidden rules like the following: Talking about Christmas is okay, but talking about Ramadan is considered exclusionary. Talking about menopause is accepted, but a trans man talking about his hormones is considered private. Singing rock or pop songs is celebrated, and hip-hop is denigrated. These hidden rules normalize the dominant culture and identities while marginalizing staff who do not share those norms. These people might even be told, "Leave your personal life at home," while others flaunt it and the organization doesn't even recognize that contrast as a disconnect. If we don't uncover and recognize our hidden rules, we cannot be truly welcoming to people who don't know or agree with them.

Training and Facilitation

If an organization has not been inclusive, turning that around will take some time, attention, and action. That will include some specific trainings and, most likely, some facilitated groups to look at the organization's norms and history. White people may feel uncomfortable and even unwelcome and not know how to handle those feelings. Make a group for that, and support it with a trained facilitator who will help them process what comes up, without having BIPOC do the training on the fly. Likewise, the BIPOC staff might want their own identity group to process what is going on, as well as other identity groups, as appropriate. The idea is not to encase the differences but to give them voice in a safe place from which the members of the different groups can then come back together.

This is about more than giving people a seat at the table. It is about developing an organization that welcomes each person and encourages all of us to be authentically who we are. That allows us to show up in all our truth and glory. The truth is, I would not accept a job where I was expected to wear high heels every day. I would exclude myself from that workplace. Whom are your hidden rules excluding? How are you replicating a culture that invites some people in and tells other people that they are not welcome? Diversity is a start, but without inclusivity, it is at best window dressing.

Make It Your Own

- What does it mean to belong? How does belonging or not belonging impact morale, performance, and teamwork?
- Of the areas listed, what do you do as an organization well, and what do you need to work on?
- Can you think of aspects of your workplace culture that you've never thought about because they just seem normal to you?

- What are examples of hidden rules that might trip up a new staff member?

Culture Snapshot

The following checklists are some indicators of toxic and healthy cultures. Culture is rarely going to be completely toxic or healthy, nor will it be static. Culture is always a work in progress. The point is to pay attention, monitor, and respond in order to build an intentional culture, and not just to let unhealthy culture happen or healthy culture slip away. These checklists can help you recognize the strengths and challenges of your organization's culture.

	Toxic Behaviors	Often	Sometimes	Never
1.	People gossip about each other.			
2.	Staff who call out sexist, racist, or ableist language are labeled complainers.			
3.	Managers act in a "my way or the highway" manner.			
4.	Information is hoarded, not shared.			
5.	Absenteeism and/or turnover rates are high.			
6.	Overwhelm is constant and normal. Workaholics are celebrated.			
7.	Some people are treated better than others, including some who get perks or special favors.			
8.	Supervision is seen as problematic or at best irrelevant.			
9.	Equity is referenced as a concept but not a real concern, or people put air quotes around anything referencing equity or inclusion.			

(continued on next page)

(continued from previous page)

	Toxic Behaviors	Often	Sometimes	Never
10.	Staff cheat or lie on grants and/or government reports. (Exaggerations and made-up data count.)			
11.	"Jokes" are made about race, gender, ethnicity, sexual orientation, etc.			
12.	Negative language focusing on what is not working is common.			
13.	One or more staff members are afraid of other staff.			
14.	Innovation is discouraged.			
15.	Behaviors outside white, middle-class, dominant practice are seen as suspect.			
16.	Mansplaining or whitesplaining is acceptable behavior.			
17.	People avoid giving feedback and/or having hard conversations.			
18.	People vent to a third party and never take their concerns directly to the source of their upset.			
19.	Staff are expected to go to their supervisor first, no matter the situation.			
20.	Staff are expected to fully handle any issues with coworkers on their own, and/or their supervisor isn't available, no matter the situation.			
21.	Staff feel unappreciated and unrecognized.			
22.	White leaders (and other leaders) demonstrate little awareness of the manifestations of white-supremacist culture on the organization.			

Toxic Behaviors		Often	Sometimes	Never
23.	Leaders show little self-awareness about how they show up.			
24.	Tough but important conversations stop when anyone cries or says they feel "unsafe" (though they might only be feeling uncomfortable).			
25.	Microaggressions are ignored or tolerated.			

Healthy Behaviors		Often	Sometimes	Never
1.	Microaggressions are addressed promptly and directly.			
2.	Every staff member is clear on their role and responsibilities.			
3.	Actions, decisions, and activities are aligned with the organization's values.			
4.	Staff at every level are held accountable in a fair, consistent, and respectable manner.			
5.	People feel valued and supported by their supervisors and their coworkers.			
6.	People's workloads are manageable most of the time, even if they are large or occasionally intense. Agency leaders take vacations and model work-life balance.			
7.	People work well together across departments and groups, sharing information and strategies.			

(continued on next page)

(continued from previous page)

Healthy Behaviors	Often	Sometimes	Never
8. Any known incidences of unfair work conditions (e.g., discriminatory policies/wage gaps) have been quickly addressed.			
9. Policies, procedures, practices, and the org chart are clear, understandable, and updated regularly.			
10. Employees have a way to suggest ideas and register complaints not just through their supervisor.			
11. A trusted HR department or person (who is not the ED or CFO) is available.			
12. Some kind of wellness/happiness/ morale committee is in place.			
13. Unsafe conditions are addressed immediately, including harassment and bullying.			
14. Racism and other isms are discussed, and power, equity, and inclusion are topics of real concern, conversation, and practice.			
15. Supervision training is ongoing, and a clear standard of supervision that all leaders are expected to practice is in place.			
16. The mission is referred to often.			
17. A multiracial team addresses equity concerns and keeps the internal justice work moving forward.			

	Healthy Behaviors	Often	Sometimes	Never
18.	Individual and agency training is ongoing and relevant, and includes topics such as communication, conflict resolution, equity practices, etc.			
19.	Hard conversations are normalized, and conflict is surfaced when it impacts the work.			
20.	Employees feel seen and heard.			
21.	When mistakes happen, the emphasis is on learning, not blaming.			
22.	Transparency is valued and practiced.			
23.	All staff members understand the difference between comfort and safety and push themselves beyond comfort when they need to.			
24.	Absenteeism, turnover, complaints, and other data are monitored and analyzed, and any unhealthy patterns are addressed.			
25.	Exit interviews occur in a fair and thoughtful manner, with a trusted staff person or external consultant (not the supervisor).			

CHAPTER 10:

ISSUES OF POWER AND PRIVILEGE

Issues of power and privilege are like a river running through every organization: Who has power and privilege? Who has always had it? And how do they use it? It is important to recognize that these issues are always at play—whether they are acknowledged or not. When they are unacknowledged, the river is flowing underground or rerouted, but it does not go away. As with any concern, you can't deal with it until you recognize it and address it.

Leaders, especially leaders who have not only positional power but also privilege based on historic and current oppression, must be especially vigilant about how we are and have been at least part of the problem. We must recognize our own history, our intentional and unintentional use of privilege, our comfort with replicating systems of oppression, and our discomfort when these concerns are identified directly. This is true even when we are fully committed to the values of justice and equity.

It is not just white men who have learned mainstream leadership practices. All leaders must learn to monitor our language, our ideas, our approaches, our actions, and our defenses so we do not hinder progress toward social justice and equity. We must listen, learn, and act to remove barriers and build bridges. We must recognize that we will no doubt have to disrupt the status quo to promote equity. Sometimes our most important action will be to acknowledge who we are and how we show up. Sometimes it will be to simply get out of the way. We must be partners and followers and leaders to keep the river clean and flowing and working for everyone.

Let's Talk About White Do-Gooders (Primarily for White Folks)

There is a certain kind of movie that is marketed as a feel-good movie; one that purports to be about someone making the world a better place. *The Help*, *Green Book*, and *The Blind Side* were advertised as such. They invite us to want to live in that world. At least, that is the message for white folks, because the films magnify and glorify the white savior. Without the white protagonist, all would be lost, or at least the same as it was before. But because the white hero appeared, they tackled racism and made the world better. Hooray for them! Hooray for us! Because we all know we would do that if we were in their shoes, right?

But really? Would we? Do we? And, even more important, wouldn't it be better to address the systemic problems so there would be no need for white saviors in the first place? Because the truth of those movies is that the savior has to be a white person. The system is so entrenched and messed up that until a white person sees it and points it out, nothing changes. It's not that the people in the stories didn't realize the problems and try to address them directly. They were just not in a position to do so, because they didn't have the societal power.

The problem is not the white heroes. The problem has two parts: 1) the need for the white hero, and 2) the message that it sends to the rest of us white do-gooders (and I use that term with great love and respect and identification).

The need for the white hero stems from the fact that the system is so racist that it is not until a white person steps up and says, "Hey, that's not fair" that anyone hears or sees it—even though people have been screaming to us about the problem for a few hundred years.

The movies uncover and celebrate these heroes. I am not disputing that they are heroes; often, they risked something to fulfill that role, although sometimes it was just a little discomfort, such as giving an unpopular speech or losing a friend or two. However, the risks do not compare to the constant risks that the BIPOC in the films face.

But what message do these movies send to those watching these movies? There is the blatant feel-good message that standing up for what is right is good. But there is also an underlying message that the situation is normal and that a savior is necessary. Without a savior, these people are lost. Because these movies do not usually address the system that led to the situation in the movie, the unspoken message is *These poor people. If only there were enough saviors to go around.* And under *that* is the racist message that that's just the way it is. "These poor people" can't help it. They just aren't as smart, clever, brave, or sophisticated as the rest of us. If they were, they would have done this on their own. But they can't be the heroes in these films. The situation needed a white person to fix it, and in taking a stand, the white person becomes the bravest, most clever, most evolved, and most celebrated character in the movie (even if what they do or say is the same as or much less than what the BIPOC characters have been doing for years). These movies normalize us/them thinking. *They* are not like us. *They* are different. *We* are the good people. *We* are necessary for the world to be a better place.

This kind of thinking is deeply buried in nonprofit work that started out primarily as charity work: *We* are doing good for *others.* "Ladies who lunch" help the downtrodden or the disadvantaged. Even in the civil rights movement in the 1960s, we good white folks wanted to help. We wanted to change. We wanted to support. But we too often still wanted to lead. We wanted to tell people what to do and how to thrive. We wanted to help people assimilate and fit in. Give the disadvantaged a chance to succeed. We were well intentioned but still not addressing the systems of racism and greed that are designed to keep certain groups down and to keep white people up. This is part of the dynamic that leads to 90 percent of nonprofits being led by white people, even while we speak often of justice and equity.

Social justice organizations see the plan differently and work to support people to claim their power and demand their rights. The work is imbued with the notion that this will improve the world for all of us, not just "them." The changes will look very different for sure. We white folks will most likely need to give something back so others get more that is due to them. But with that shift, the world will be better for all of us.

The challenge for we white folks working in social justice organizations is to find our place as partners, not as helpers, do-gooders, or heroes. Both inside the organization and outside in the world, we must constantly check ourselves: What is my motivation? Is this about me or about the work? What is my role here? How can I best help my staff succeed? How can I step back so the voices, needs, and power of those most impacted are centered?

We must imagine ourselves not reaching down to help but as partners walking with and reporting to leaders. Even when we are the putative leaders, we must still work with humility and camaraderie. The challenge for do-gooders is to be partners, not saviors.

Make It Your Own

- What are the associations that come up with the term "white savior," and how do you react to the term?

- Historically, "ladies who lunch" were rich socialites who donated their time and/or money to help the less fortunate. What is the modern-day equivalent?
- What does it mean to be a partner, and how is that different from a do-gooder?

What Are You Willing to Give Up? (For White Leaders)

The term "white privilege" has gained significant traction over the years since Peggy McIntosh wrote about it, in 1988. In social justice work, it is understood and appreciated as a fundamental truth. It is called out and acknowledged by white folks, including me, as a sign of our awareness.

Recognizing the impact of privilege is an important start. We can't dismantle the system until we acknowledge it. Often we start at one area of injustice and then begin connecting the dots—incarceration, pay rates, homeownership, police brutality, health outcomes, school discipline, immigration—but mere recognition is not enough.

I have struggled with the follow-up to recognizing white privilege. What am I willing to give up? Once you acknowledge that you have gained through white privilege and others have lost because of it, then what? Wouldn't giving up some of the privilege be the logical result of such recognition? Sometimes, understanding how the overall movement to equity benefits all of us is even more challenging. In the intersectionality of oppression (a term coined by Kimberlé Crenshaw in 1989), we all have something to gain by dismantling injustice—the benefit of living in a rich, full, just society that works for everyone.

It is easier to give up privilege at a conceptual level and more challenging to make it concrete. I don't need to talk first or offer the solution or claim the higher ground. I am good with BIPOC having power and leading. I am certainly good with not just establishing fair housing, hiring, and financial rules but leveling the playing field. I am good with affirmative action, health care for all, and reprioritizing spending to stop police brutality. I recognize that dismantling oppression of any kind can help weaken other kinds of oppression. When we undermine racism, we disempower sexism. It is all connected. We are all connected.

It is important to ask yourself, "How does any of this impact me personally? The feminist movement recognized that the personal is political. What I do and what I have and how I show up are political acts. What I talk about is a political act. Who I talk to matters. So what do I do personally, and within my role, to respond to my privilege?" We most likely donate to organizations we support, but that is not enough.

Am I willing to give up something real? Am I willing to earn less so others can earn more? Am I willing to calculate the financial success that has come to me from my first-rate schools and my private college education? Can I make ethical decisions about how and where I spend my money? Can I start a scholarship? Can I donate until it hurts? At work, can I give up my position of power after mentoring someone to take my place? Even better, can I mentor twenty people to take jobs like mine? Am I willing to take a 1 percent raise so someone else can get a 5 percent raise, and to recognize that things are fairer that way? Can I risk discomfort or even alienation by speaking up about injustice, bias, and privilege? How about giving up being right or unquestioned? Am I willing to put myself in uncomfortable situations and do my work differently? Can I do my own internal work to shift into a liberation mindset, instead of a short-term, narrow view that is the lens of the dominant system? This is the mindset that has trained us and wants us to see justice as a zero-sum game, instead of the long-term, broader view that recognizes the benefits to all of us of a more just society. Can we look through an intersectionality lens to see how our holding on to privilege in one area validates other oppressions? For example, when we hold on to racist privilege, we make class oppression worse. And when feminism actively excludes Black and/or queer feminist voices, we make patriarchy stronger.

In social justice circles, we like to say that equal rights for others does not mean fewer rights for you; it's not a pie. And that is certainly true in terms of rights. But in the case of fairness, equity, and reparations, sometimes there is less pie for us. And, even more important, sometimes there *should be* less pie for us. In getting less pie, however, we all get more justice.

Make It Your Own

- When does social justice require dividing the pie?
- How else can we white leaders make the personal political in a way that would make a difference?
- In your organization, are there any assets or power that could, at least theoretically, be redistributed?
- How is intersectionality addressed in your organization?

I Could Not Be Complicit (For White Leaders)

I recently accepted a friend request from an old acquaintance on Facebook. Yesterday, there it was—he posted a version of "All Lives Matter." I yelled at my phone for several minutes and then scrolled on down. Hours later, I woke up in the middle of the night, realizing, *In that moment when I scrolled down my Facebook page, I became complicit.* I got up and posted a reply to him first thing the next morning.

I am not proud of this. It was a relatively small act with few consequences in a great big system. And it took me twelve hours! I even realize that the post was more for me than for him. I don't think my post will teach my Facebook friend anything that activists have not been proclaiming for years, but to be who I think I am, I could not be complicit.

I don't pretend to have all the answers. Many people live and work in this area of justice, and I pay attention to and try to learn from them and apply my learnings to my work and life. But I have a responsibility to use my voice. So here are a few reminders about supervision and racial injustice, particularly right now, and particularly for white folks.

Don't Expect Appreciation
Maybe you've been working as a partner. Maybe you've been talking the talk and walking the walk. Good. But don't expect appreciation from BIPOC. Don't make it about you.

Remember That Inviting People to the Table Is Not Enough
First of all, it is not our table. In some areas, it has taken a big push to simply get the table to be inclusive. Now, hopefully, there is representation at the table. That is not enough, though.

Listen and Believe
We must listen and believe what we are told. Don't shut down any voices; don't talk over them; don't dispute what they say; don't just nod and move on.

Contain Your Defensiveness
If you have done any work in this area, you might be tempted to feel slightly superior to others, who are just waking up. It's easy to feel defensive and want to claim what you've done and what you've learned, but now is not the time. Take it in. Hear it. Hear it again, if necessary. Sit with it. Push down the defensiveness, and repeat the phrase "just listen" to yourself as often as necessary.

Recognize Trauma—Make Room
Know that times of blatant racist actions in the world might be exhausting and traumatic for BIPOC. Those responses

might show up later, anytime, or all the time. The body keeps track, and people might need some time to process and tend to self-care. Be generous; be flexible.

Don't Assume You Know; Assume You Don't Know
White people can never know.

Own Your Whiteness and All the Baggage It Carries
Our white ancestors did some terrible, terrible things. Some white people continue to do terrible things in our name. We may be actively working to be thoughtful antiracists, or we may be unaware of our society's racist history. Either way, we must recognize and acknowledge not only our privilege but the baggage that comes with our history.

Don't Fall into a Dichotomy—About Yourself or Others
Sometimes I find myself wanting to label things and people, including me, either good or bad. I want to be a "good white person," but that is distracting and not helpful. It feeds into a dichotomy that makes racism personal, instead of seeing the larger picture of systemic and historical concerns. It also lets people off the hook and puts others on it. There is no hook—there is only antiracist thought and action to lead us where we need to go.

Don't Take It Personally
Don't be surprised or offended if you are considered a white person—you are. Of course we want to be seen as individuals, and we will be, but it takes some time to build that trust with BIPOC. And without trust, there can be little individualism or relationships.

Notice When You Have a Racist Thought
Racist thoughts and reactions will spring up within us—thoughts like *Oh, he's so articulate* or *Maybe I should cross the road* or

Can we just get back to normal now? Notice them, address them (either internally or externally, if you said something racist out loud), and move on. When we deny that we ever have racist thoughts, we continue to deny the existence of the white supremacist system that has trained our minds in certain stereotypes and reactions. And we will be more likely to believe a passing thought or act on it if we are not able to clearly pause and recognize it as racist.

Don't Be Complicit

Speak up. Don't ignore racist, sexist, or other hateful comments. Disrupt the system when it is unfair and racist. Question practices that do things the way "they have always been done before."

I am not an expert; I am a learner. I hope to be an ally and a partner. And that requires me to continually ask myself, "How do my life and my work help to end racial injustice?"

Make It Your Own

- How does complicity show up in organizations? What is the impact on the complicit one and on others?
- How do the issues and concerns of racial injustice impact the role of supervision and leadership?
- Most of the time, a supervisor's work is about directing or influencing others' behaviors. What challenges do being in a listening and learning mode present for supervisors?

Insubordination and Other Dated Concepts

"But I'm not really a supervisor!" "I don't want to be ordering people around." "It's not up to me to tell them what to do."

These are a few of the concerns I hear when I meet resistance in a supervisory training. The word "supervision" has a lot of ugly and battered baggage attached to it. Some organizations try to work around the word and the position. There

are organizations that built a more democratic and flat structure. When that works, it can be powerful. But often there
is unacknowledged confusion in those designs and I find it
works until there are problems. Then it can get even messier
and, sometimes, more debilitating to the person who has been
identified as part of what is not working.

The style of supervision I teach and coach is one of partnership. The idea is that people have different roles in an organization but no one is better than anyone else. It is built on
respect and appreciation and self-awareness. The supervisors
have different responsibilities and decision-making authority
as part of their role, but it is about the mission and getting the
work done. Not about power and ego.

While we cannot and must not eradicate the history of these
concepts, we can reimagine them. We can do our work in a way
that reflects our values of equity, collaboration, and respect for
each person. In this framework, the role of a supervisor is still
important to moving the work forward. Structure is important
for clarity. And commitment to the mission becomes the driving force that ties it all together. While I have reimagined the
word supervisor to encompass all of these things, some people
might choose to throw the term out and call people in this role
a "lead partner" or another term. Just make sure the role itself
is clear, even if the terminology is new.

In this framework of collaboration and respect, we can
imagine and create an updated concept of some of the baggage
we carry. This is a total shift in approach rather than "spin"
or "doublespeak"; this is not about creating new words to
hide the same old power structure. Here's my initial repacking
of some of the problematic words.

Reimagining Problem Words	
Insubordination	Lack of cooperation
Authority	Responsibility
Obey	Collaborate
Ordering	Directing or guiding
Hierarchy	Structure
Rewards	Equity
Threat	Consequence
Boss	Team leader
Manage	Coordinate

Some will think that words don't matter. And that is certainly true if it is just about the words. If a manager uses this language but still acts authoritarian and superior, then that is worse than using the traditional language. (And vice versa: Some managers use the traditional language and work in a collaborative manner.) But when the words can shift our understanding and then our actions, they can open the door to a whole new way of working together.

Make It Your Own

- What happens organizationally when supervisors are ambivalent about their role and resistant to the responsibilities of that role?
- Can you recall a time when a change of words led to a shift in behavior? What was that process like to perceive and respond to something differently because of that change in framing? Or what was it like to observe if you were not the one shifting?
- How might the words on the right side of the chart shift one's approach to supervision?

- What words would you substitute in your reimagining of these words?

....

Strong Teams Require Pushback

The movie *Bohemian Rhapsody* was based on the real-life Freddy Mercury and his band, Queen. It portrays Mercury crawling back to Queen after messing up his life. He makes a heartfelt plea to his bandmates to forgive him. They basically ask him, "Why should we?" and he makes a passionate speech about teamwork, saying something like, "Without you guys to bounce ideas off and get pushback from, I wasn't as good. And you aren't either."

In this way, Queen embodies the idea of synergy: The four musicians were more together than you would expect from the simple addition of the four of them as individuals. Together they created something bigger and better. I started thinking about the role of a supervisor in the process of being stronger together. How can a supervisor support the kind of pushback that leads to synergistic results?

1. **Keep the mission/purpose of the team in the forefront at all times:** The team must be aligned in service to a common purpose and goal. If there are silos in which departments work disconnected from other staff or individuals who do the same, then the focus is going to be diluted and energy will quickly dissipate.

2. **Create ground rules and hold staff accountable to them:** Every member of a strong team must feel safe to be who they are and to fully contribute to the team. In order to do this, the supervisor must work with the team to create, maintain, and enforce ground rules and behavioral standards. These rules aren't simply about being "nice" to each other; they are about respect, listening, participation, equity, and

a focus on the work. They keep challenges from being personal and stop gossip from dividing the team.

3. **Be prepared to take risks:** Risk taking is essential for innovation and synergy. The risk taking is in the area of trying out new ideas and ways of doing things and it is also in personal risk taking. In order for a team to fully collaborate, each member must be free to speak up, suggest sometimes far-out ideas, push back, and be personally authentic and vulnerable with each other. Risk taking may not always be comfortable, but it should be safe.

4. **Listen and consider:** Because being the one to speak up and offer convergent ideas can be risky, team members must listen to one another respectfully and consider one another's ideas, especially when they are new or they don't agree with them. This is where it becomes safe, or not, for people to be heard. Voices that are not usually heard will test the waters and see if they will be heard. These might be people with less power in the organization, underrepresented community members, people who have been systemically oppressed in our society, and/or people with innovative ideas.

5. **Normalize pushback—with yourself and with each other:** As a supervisor, you need to model pushing back against ideas and performance and sometimes even individuals when necessary to keep the team moving forward. You also need to model responding appropriately when team members push back against you. If the members of the team see you acting defensive and/or shutting down the conversation when there is pushback against your ideas or plans, then the whole concept is dead in the water.

6. **Recognize that conflict is a vital component of strong teamwork:** This is not easy or pleasant, but it is true. Strong teams

must sometimes engage in spirited debate and fierce conversations. This does not mean personal attacks or fighting is required or okay. But it does mean that teams don't shut down when there is a hard decision to make or people have different ideas about how to proceed. They talk it through. Sometimes passionately and always directly. And when the decision is made by the team, or by you as the leader, people accept it and move on. This means that you support the team in having hard conversations. You train them on how to address problems in a respectful manner. And you uncover conflict that is in the room but not being talked about.

This is not easy stuff, but bit by bit you can lead your team from basic functioning to thriving as a collaborative, synergistic group. Together, you will be champions!

Make It Your Own

- What stops direct and hard conversations from happening on your team? What would make it safe for you and your team to have hard and honest conversations?
- What, if anything, makes you nervous about the idea of uncovering conflict that is not being talked about? What would be the advantage of having the disagreement out in the open? What is the cost of its being underground?
- How have the voices of oppressed people often not been heard, even when they are "invited to the table"?

Sticks and Stones

There's an old saying, "Sticks and stones may break my bones, but words will never hurt me." While intended to help children shake off verbal bullying, this is a lie. Words have tremendous power to hurt. Name calling, shaming, stereotyping, microaggressions, and blatant epithets all have the power to cause drastic and long-term damage, never mind the words that make oppressive and exclusive policies and laws.

In a work environment, we must pay attention to words. Words can cause harm and trauma and poison interpersonal dynamics. They can directly and indirectly interfere with people's ability to do their work. They can also be grounds for legal action. Discrimination lawsuits have included "random comments" to demonstrate that a certain organization's culture tolerated hateful or discriminatory speech.

Language can be disruptive to staff, and therefore the work, in several ways. Here are a few areas to watch for:

1. **Microaggressions:** Merriam-Webster defines microaggression as "a comment or action that subtly and often unconsciously or unintentionally expresses a prejudiced attitude toward a member of a marginalized group (such as a racial minority)." If your staff are predominantly white, these kinds of words and actions probably show up during work, and people might use terms that target members of other marginalized groups. It is part of the dominant culture to use microaggressive comments, but we need to hear and respond to them. A few examples include comments on Black people's hair; gendered language, like calling women "girls" or telling someone to "man up"; and terms that make light of someone's identity, such as "that's so gay" or calling people "Grandma" or "tranny" or "crazy" or "lame."

2. **'Splaining:** This is the practice of speaking with unearned authority. People speak as experts on any and every subject without considering the experience or actual expertise in the room. This kind of speech is condescending, disrespectful, and extremely irritating. And it can be even more offensive when a person *not* in an identified group explains (often in depth) to people *in* an identified group how something that applies to the identified group works. It could be

a man explaining about the glass ceiling (or childbirth) to a woman, a white person describing racism to a BIPOC, or a straight person pontificating about gay dating.

3. **Talking over people/minimizing:** This is a common practice of the dominant group; it involves literally interrupting and talking over less represented staff and/or dismissing or minimizing their ideas. This can happen in one-on-one meetings and in group settings.

4. **Defensiveness:** A practice, often unintentional, that a person challenged about doing or saying something will immediately move to. The person often proceeds to take up time and space justifying their actions, instead of listening and learning.

5. **Intention:** A form of defensiveness, this is the phrase we know and love/hate (depending on whether we are using it or receiving it): "That's not what I meant" (often followed by "You're misinterpreting what I said"). You said what you said. It landed how it landed. Intention does not equal, or always mitigate, impact. This is a critical lesson to learn and relearn. This is not to say that there is no time and place to learn about the impact of our intentions, but using intention as an excuse and then wanting to move on without hearing and learning is inappropriate. It is the difference between "That's not what I meant; stop picking apart my words" and "That's not what I meant. I'm sorry. Thank you for calling me on it."

6. **Gaslighting:** A kind of psychological manipulation in which a person or a group sows seeds of doubt that cause an individual or a group to question their own experience or perception. It might be negative gossip or negative job commentary based on nothing objective. It can arise from

an individual's action or from deeply embedded systems of bias. Gaslighting happens over time and creates a pattern of distrust and division.

We like to think these behaviors don't happen in enlightened spaces, but they do, though ideally not as much as they occur in mainstream culture. Still, these are practices to which we must be alert, and we must stop and course-correct when we do any of them or witness any of them happening.

Whenever any of these practices show up at work, those impacted by such words and actions have traditionally been expected to basically "grin and bear it," to respond politely, or to choose their battles. This kind of expectation has resulted in significant emotional labor expended in the workplace. "Emotional labor" is the term that sociologist Arlie Russel coined in 1983 to describe the experience of needing to appear happy and content at work, no matter how someone is feeling. The terminology has been expanded to include a wide variety of social and interpersonal work that must be done, especially by BIPOC, to take care of their colleagues—for example, in response to someone saying, "I didn't mean it that way." In this context, emotional labor has been a tool of oppression, because the focus has been on making the perpetrators feel okay at the expense of the harmed.

An organization must recognize and address all of these practices in order to support justice. Its initial response to identifying these practices may be to institute some staff training, but at some point, the idea that these practices will not stand needs to be defined clearly.

At work, identifying what kinds of behaviors are acceptable and what kinds are not is often important. Harassment is an example of unacceptable behavior. There are policies against it, and managers know they must address it. These kinds of spoken behaviors need to be treated in the same manner. They are not illegal, but they are harmful and inappropriate.

Even when the offending person means well and did not intend to cause harm, do not let the rationale minimize these actions. They do not fit the organization's mission; it undermines teamwork and interferes with the work it is trying to accomplish.

Sticks and stones may break my bones, and words will *also* hurt me, and hurt my organization's mission.

Make It Your Own

* What are the consequences for staff when any of these language affronts are tolerated?
* What is the impact on an organization when leaders participate in any of these practices?
* What are the conditions under which the targets of microaggressions and other disrespectful actions would feel empowered to speak up?
* What could a leader do to bring a team together after an incident of hurtful words or implicit bias?

Being "the Man"

My father was a postal worker. When I was ten, he was elected president of his local union. I remember the pride I felt upon seeing his picture in the paper as he was sworn in. Many years later, I was shocked and perplexed when I found myself on the management side of a table while negotiating with a union. Since we were a nonprofit working to fight poverty, I didn't understand. How could we be on opposite sides? Weren't we all on the same side? It wasn't as if we were dealing with deep pockets or harsh working conditions.

It was humbling to realize that to the union representatives, and, to some extent, the staff, we were part of the problem. We were "the Man." We, the executive and other directors, had chosen to work there to fight the Man. Now we were being painted in the same brushstroke. Once, during negotiations, when we were discussing health insurance benefits, I became exasperated with the assumptions the union was making about health insurance and money. They acted as if we had just picked an insurance plan out of thin air. (This was pre–Affordable Care Act.) I knew I had spoken to at least three brokers and looked at countless plans, trying to find the best option for our staff. The union reps did not want to hear this. They insisted that we were paying too much money for the insurance, and while I agreed that it was too expensive, there was not much we could do about it. In my frustration, I blurted out, "You know, we don't even have to offer health insurance. It's not a required benefit."

The union jumped on my comment and told staff that I had threatened to eliminate health insurance. I learned my lesson. It wasn't true that I had threatened to take away our employees' health insurance, but it wasn't untrue either. I had the power, and I had mentioned that possibility. I worked hard to win trust and work collaboratively with the union. All of us on the negotiating team did.

But we had to learn that we were not individuals at the table. We were not Rita and Ofelia and Helga; we were HR, the program director, and the executive director. And we were them and the staff were us. When I realized this and more clearly identified my role, I could be more effective in working to support the staff—even as they pushed against us as the problem. We knew we were not entirely the problem, but we were the problem inasmuch as we were the administrators who did not give staff what they wanted and needed, even if we had good reasons for our decisions, based on the constraints on the organization.

This dynamic plays out in many different organizations; it is not just about unions. Every manager, every supervisor, every director is sometimes seen as other. That comes with the power dynamics involved in supporting an organization.

A flatter organization can mitigate some of that tension but rarely eliminates it. It is a difficult part of working in management and/or administration.

Unspoken assumptions are always at play in the workplace, and this is an area where they often find a foothold. The assumption that management is other. The assumption that administration does not care about the mission or the line staff. The assumption that any hierarchy is bad. The assumption that an organization should be a democracy.

This last assumption can lead to big upsets when it is not named and clarified. If you are a democracy and decisions are made by consensus or by a majority vote among every staff member, great! Name it and live it. But if you operate under a different set of circumstances, you also need to name and live that. The biggest problems occur when staff think they have an equal voice and vote but don't. So name that. It may be that the directors will always have the final say, but more likely it depends on the situation, the timing, and the impact. Name that also.

Be clear every single time: "I am inviting your input on our strategic plan. We want all staff to be part of the process. The board and the directors will determine the final plan." Also clarify this expectation at the team level and even at the one-on-one level: "I want to hear your ideas about the marketing plan; we'll discuss, and then you will make the final decision about which way we'll proceed." Or, "This is an all-hands-on-deck decision. We will not leave this topic until we have reached consensus with every single staff member."

Being perceived as the Man is not fun. But knowing your role and your purpose will help you navigate this territory. In the end, I found that the view from the management side of the table had a different perspective, but we were all facing the same landscape.

Make It Your Own

- What can management do to mitigate the power dynamics that sometimes put them at odds with staff?
- When is it necessary for a select few to make an organizational decision, and when is it simply habit or tradition?
- What other kinds of assumptions about decision making need to be named in order for the process to work most effectively?

....

Deer in the Headlights

Here's a quick nature lesson from a deer biologist: "A deer's vision is optimized for very low light. When it is caught in a road by a headlight beam, the deer cannot see at all, and it freezes. It doesn't know what to do, so it does nothing."

We have all had moments like that, where we freeze up and don't know what to say or do. Often, this happens in response to something unexpected or something that shines light on our hidden assumptions. Or it might be a challenge to a decision you've made, or being called on an inappropriate comment, or even being asked to own the history of your people.

Usually when we freeze up, it is embarrassing or ineffective, but there may be times when it's healthy. When it comes to being confronted about privileges or oppressive practices, it might sometimes be the best we can do.

Too often, we err on the side of overreacting. Cases where white people are called out on racism sometimes result in over-explaining, hyper defensiveness, hysteria, or tears. The same can happen when men are called out on sexism, or heterosexuals are called out on heteronormative practices and other challenges to oppressive power. In those kinds of situations, it might be good if we could simply follow the example of a deer

233

in the headlights. Just freeze. Don't say or do anything right away. Take a few breaths and then listen. Even better would be to listen, apologize, and commit to doing better (assuming we know what we did that was inappropriate).

This is an important step, and it is crucial that we learn to listen to and believe those who do not and have not had power. We must listen and believe in order to understand, learn, and grow.

But then what? What happens to what we wanted to say, or to our explanations, or what we hear in our heads later? If we just freeze, listen, and then move on, we might not learn as well as we should. There must be a systematic way for white folks and others with systemic privilege to process our learned behaviors and our programmed reactions. And while we may understand the need to silence the mainstream, dominant voices that have held the power forever, we do not want to model silencing, *and* it doesn't work to support change in the long run. It is a sometimes inconvenient reality that if anyone does not feel heard, it is hard for them to move forward. And when people are not able to move forward, they sometimes start to feel mistreated themselves. People who feel victimized do not become partners.

It is certainly more important that we listen first. I am also not suggesting that those we have offended need to then listen to us. (Sometimes that is helpful for specific situations, but for generic, everyday acts of oppression and disrespect, that places additional demands on those who have been offended—e.g., BIPOC.)

However, I believe every organization needs to find a way for these voices to be expressed safely and effectively. Without an avenue for expression, these swallowed feelings can turn rancid and undermine the good work of the organization. There needs to be a safe space in which to process old beliefs and unjust conditioning, and to ask more questions to deepen understanding of what is offensive/stereotyping/disrespectful and of how privilege played into those contentious situations. Without that space, fully moving into partnership is difficult. This is not the job of BIPOC or other staff from marginalized groups to teach. Most often, the teaching will happen in affinity groups facilitated by a trained consultant (i.e., white caucuses). It could also theoretically happen with a trusted mentor, a coach, or an employee assistance program (EAP), as long as those individuals are trained and skilled in this process.

Even with these kinds of supports, not every staff member will learn and grow and become a partner for justice. That is where behavioral norms must be clear and enforced, when necessary. Most likely, a person who does not want to learn and grow in this manner will self-select out, but if not, they must understand what is acceptable and what is not—and then be held accountable.

Acting up and making it about me as a white or straight person does not serve social justice. But staying stuck as a deer in the headlights doesn't either.

Make It Your Own

- It is only when a deer's eyes become adjusted to the light that it can move. What is the correlation to that when someone with power is challenged and freezes?
- When an organization is focused on being led by the global majority, what are the advantages and disadvantages of giving white folks a place to process their feelings?
- What responses to being called out would demonstrate that a privileged person is indeed a partner for justice?

Disrupting Sexism

Seventy-three percent of nonprofit employees are women, but only 45 percent of CEOs are women. And in big-buck nonprofits, only 21 percent of CEOs are women.

Sexism is still alive and well within the dynamic halls of our institutions. Men carry their privilege with them. And women often carry out learned and stereotypical roles, even as we recognize and fight them. Even as we welcome nonbinary folks and work to empower women in the world. Even as we acknowledge intersectionality and raise up possibilities for a better way of working together.

Twelve Things Organizations Can Do to Disrupt Sexism at Work

1. Offer training to all staff in communication, conflict resolution, assertiveness, and leadership. Offer trainings on patriarchal gender-binary communication dynamics, such as male-dominant or male-centered communication, learned helplessness, harassment, and (over) apologizing.

2. Develop a leadership training and pipeline; this does not have to be open only to women, but it cannot be open only to men. And it cannot be available only to those whom managers recommend, because managers often see the stereotypical leadership skills of cis men and do not see the equivalent and different skills in women or non-gender-conforming folks.

3. Define leadership in a way that looks beyond assertiveness, charisma, and decisiveness and includes empathy, compassion, listening, mentoring, and equity.

4. Identify sexist actions like mansplaining, interrupting, discounting, and self-promotion—and build agreements about how to respond when they happen.

5. Review your compensation policies and ensure that job comparability is broadly defined and pay is not tilted in favor of higher negotiated salaries.

6. Offer robust and paid parental leaves.

7. Offer post-training affinity groups to talk about and address sexist patterns. Each group should be facilitated by someone who has participated in such groups or trainings about sexism in the past. (It is better if this facilitator is not from leadership.) Allow people to self-select the group that reflects their identity, gender experiences, and sense of safety in the world. This is especially important for trans and nonbinary people; they may choose to make a third group. Often for instance, trans men do not feel safe in a group of cis men because of past experiences and continuing gender norms and transphobic attitudes. These spaces create time and space for sexist patterns and attitudes to be explored in a safe way that honors experiences and allows vulnerability. These groups might bring up discomfort, but they shouldn't feel unsafe.

8. Offer support for advanced learning related to people's work. This could be tuition reimbursement, time off, or support for paying off student loans.

9. Do not make men the enemy or silence them. Emphasize the need to move away from certain typical male behaviors and to create more awareness of the socially dominant culture of male privilege and its harms. Moving into more equitable listening and communication styles is not the same as silencing certain staff members (though in the initial learning process, many men may feel silenced if they are not dominating conversations or are spending periods of time just listening). Men need to recognize their

privilege and realize the harms they may have caused with their conditioned dominance of conversations or spaces, or with subtly objectifying or belittling views of women, in order to stop causing harm and build truly collaborative work spaces.

10. Build a board that mirrors the demographics of the organization or those it serves.

11. Address any concerns about intimidation, bullying, or harassment immediately, fairly, and strongly.

12. Create an intersectionality team that can facilitate training, implementation, dispute resolution, and dynamic visions of future possibilities.

We know that we don't work in a black-white or male-female world, yet we often carry those learned dichotomies within us. It is important for everyone to understand how these replicated patterns of communication and behaviors hurt people and productivity. Creating time and space for this work not only will show an organization's commitment to an internally just workforce but will improve communication, teamwork, and collaboration. This work is ultimately about supporting the mission. Working together, we can unlearn and relearn how to work together in a better way as we create a better world together.

Make It Your Own

- What is the difference between silencing and holding accountable in a work setting?
- How have you personally experienced, and/or responded to, sexism in the workplace?
- How else do gender norms show up at work and what can be done to respond to them?

CHAPTER 11:

MISSES AND MESSES

W hile categorizing all nonprofits or all social justice organizations under a unified identity is impossible, certain
themes do emerge. Some themes are strengths that illuminate
the work. The themes of being mission-focused, being led by
caring people, and being supportive of staff are assets that
feed organizations. This collaborative approach to work and
its focus on the big picture help move the work forward across
the sector. And its shared commitment to justice, equity, and
inclusion makes these organizations beacons for our society.

There are also themes that can impede the work, that can
cause confusion, and that can push dedicated people out the
door. This chapter looks at some of the ways in which organizations can miss the mark with their attention or create messes
with unintended consequences. The actions are almost always
well intended. Leaders might be trying to create efficiency or
working to build a culture of care. They might take steps to
support a staff member in a difficult situation or find a way
to make a job work for an individual. They might be starting
to understand their own complicity in perpetuating systems of
oppression. But good intentions do not always lead to good
results. Sometimes they lead to misses and messes, and leaders

for justice must look ahead and avoid the easy solution, which will cause more trouble in the long run. And when there is a mess, it needs to be cleaned up.

One Supervisor per Person, Please!

Mia was hired as a part-time canvasser for a voting rights organization. Her duties included going out into the community and distributing information, registering voters, and organizing information sessions. A year later, when the organization was hiring a part-time administrative assistant, they offered the job to Mia. The people there knew her, liked her, and were aware that she needed benefits. There's already a problem here, but the hiring process (or lack thereof) is not the topic of this section (see chapter 7 for more about hiring). Here, I want to talk about what happened when this organization brought Mia into the new job and assigned her a second supervisor for her administrative work.

Mia's original supervisor knew little about the administrative requirements of the job and, frankly, didn't care much about them. Her new supervisor cared a great deal about them and was ready to train Mia and oversee her work. I see how it seems like a good idea for both people to have supervised Mia. As it turned out, she was a great canvasser; she was not a great administrative assistant. Her new supervisor quickly became frustrated and took steps to discipline Mia. Meanwhile, her first supervisor was recommending Mia for a raise. Mia didn't know if she was coming or going.

I have seen countless iterations of this two-supervisor dance, and I have rarely seen it work. Even when the incumbent in the two positions is an ace employee doing great work on both jobs, confusion about priorities and deadlines and who's in charge remains. I strongly recommend one supervisor per person—one supervisor who has the full range of duties and responsibilities and decision-making authority that a supervisor normally holds. This does not preclude someone else's having oversight over a part of the employee's job, however. This second person can be designated as a project partner or a job lead. This gives the employee direction and support in the second area of the job but does not confuse the role and responsibility of the supervisor. Here's the relevant role for each person and the distinction in duties that makes sense to me:

Comparing Roles

Supervisor	*Project Partner (PP)*
Relationship building	Relationship building
Direction of work; how it supports the mission	Day-to-day oversight of specific area
Establish priorities	On-the-job training
Meet on a regular basis	Meet informally as needed
Convene meeting with employee and PP three to four times per year and as necessary to confirm agreement on priorities and goals and to ensure that all are on the same page	Contribute to meeting with supervisor and employee three to four times per year and as necessary to confirm agreement on priorities and goals and to ensure that all are on the same page
Bring problems/questions/concerns to PP and solicit communication from/with the PP, including reviewing problems, concerns, and successes	Bring problems/concerns/successes to supervisor and communicate as necessary
Facilitating professional development	On-the-job training about the work in the project area
Answer questions about what/when/who	Answer questions about how
Problem solving on entirety of job, including how to juggle both components and people problems	Problem solving on tasks and details

(continued on next page)

241

(continued from previous page)

Supervisor	*Project Partner (PP)*
Evaluation	Input on evaluation in area of oversight
Discipline when necessary	Letting supervisor know of performance concerns
Termination when necessary	Giving updates to supervisor on improvement or problems

This doesn't make all the problems go away, and it isn't always easy, but it eliminates a major element of confusion and accountability. It takes work, clear and open communication, and a focus by all on the mission and how the work supports it.

In the scenario above, when the organization decided to hire Mia for additional work, it should already have been clear who would be the supervisor and who would be the project partner. The default would probably have been that Mia's original supervisor would continue to be her supervisor, unless there were good reasons to shift that responsibility to someone else. The administrator would have become the project partner. When troubles arose in the administrative area, the PP would have immediately brought concerns to the supervisor, and they probably would have had a three-way meeting with Mia to address those concerns. The official supervisor would have conveyed clearly that she expected both the administrative work and the outreach work to be addressed. They would have worked together to address the problems, but there would have been only one supervisor. And that supervisor would have been responsible for making the entire job work.

The intention might be to make the work easier, but in this situation, dividing the work of supervision makes it much more difficult.

Make It Your Own

- What is the impact on the organization when some staff are unsure of their priorities?
- "Project partner" is the term I use to describe the not-official-supervisor role. Does that term work for you? If not, consider "job lead," "area mentor," "senior team partner," or "advanced work buddy." What works and doesn't work for you about any of these titles?
- What are the strengths and challenges that you see from the shared job situation? Under what conditions would it make sense to keep two separate part-time jobs, instead of combining them into one full-time position?

....

Your Staff Has Personal Troubles—Now What?

Troubles find all of us sooner or later. And the same is true for our staff. They may get injured or fall ill. They may experience a breakup or money troubles. They may face trauma or the death of a loved one. These inevitable scenarios present a dilemma for you as a supervisor. On the one hand, you want to be supportive and generous; you certainly don't want to add to anyone's difficulties. On the other hand, you must ensure that the work is getting done.

So, what's a caring supervisor to do? You know you don't want to revert to authoritarianism: "Do the work or get out." Yet you also know that you cannot look the other way forever. Not only does that fail to support the work, but it can eventually lead to resentment among other staff, who are not only doing their own work but probably picking up extra.

You and your organization will need to set policies, practices, and parameters about how to handle this kind of situation. The point here is to put those plans in place ahead of time so that you don't play things by ear and stumble into a place you never intended to go.

Here are a few dos and don'ts. Let's look at the don'ts first:

Don't

- **Don't give false assurances:** Don't tell the person who's having trouble, "I'm sure everything will be fine." You don't know that. And by saying that, you are minimizing their fears and their experience.
- **Don't make it about you:** This happens when people say, "I know exactly what you're going through" and then tell your story. This isn't about you; it's about them. And even if you have experienced the same sort of thing, it's a different experience for each person.
- **Don't impose your beliefs:** "Everything happens for a reason." Or "God doesn't give you anything that you can't handle." Your staff member may or may not believe the same things you do, and work is not the place to initiate this conversation.
- **Don't promise what you can't deliver:** You may want to take some of the person's pain away by promising them time or health insurance, or at least a guarantee that their job is safe. You can't do any of these things. You just don't know what's coming. Their troubles could get worse or go on for years. You cannot put an individual's needs over the work, even if you wish you could. And not treating staff in a way that's consistent with the organization's values and practices does not ultimately serve the staff either.
- **Don't tell them not to worry about their work:** This is another promise that you can't keep, at least not indefinitely. You may be able to adjust the person's work for a while, but you cannot do so indefinitely. At some point, they will need to do their work or take time off.
- **Don't let them ignore their work:** Some people will get so caught up in their pain that they forget they have a job to do. The mission and the work is bigger than any individ-

ual and must get done somehow. The staff is there for the work, not the other way around.

- **Don't let them take over the team:** The team may want to support and help their coworker, but some team members may not. That has to be okay too. Some people want (or need) to talk about their troubles all the time to anyone who will listen—and that is not sustainable in a work situation.

Do

- **Speak kindly, using a calm and even tone:** Acknowledge the difficult situation and be kind. "I can't imagine what you're going through. That must be really tough."
- **Let them be real at work:** If they want to share their situation, let them talk about it in a contained manner. Set aside an hour when those who wish to talk or plan for support can do so, but then bring it back to work. Make it a separate and optional meeting.
- **Offer support:** "How can we help?" or "Can I make dinner for you next Thursday?" or "I can't make any promises, but feel free to let me know what you need in terms of time off, and I'll see what I can do."
- **Offer resources:** Let them know what supportive benefits may be available, whether that is paid leave, insurance, a way for coworkers to donate time, help through your state, or an EAP.
- **Expect them to work:** While they are at work, they need to be productive. (Of course, you may be able to give them some flexibility on deadlines or expectations for a brief time, but that probably can't go on forever.) If they cannot do their work, they might have to take time off. That is probably what they need anyway if they can't focus on their job.
- **Remember precedents:** It is important to look at what has been done in the past when others in the organization faced a similar difficulty, and it is also important to look

ahead. If you give this person two months' paid time off, are you prepared to offer that same benefit to the next person facing a similar situation? Is the organization ready to do that? Are your donors ready to do that if you are a nonprofit?

- **Support the team and yourself:** Keep the team focused on work while allowing them to experience their own reactions and responses. If the event is traumatic, it might be important to bring in a counselor or a facilitator to help the team address their own sorrows and move on. Other staff (and maybe you yourself) might also need support through an EAP or outside help. Remind everyone what you are all there for.

It is never easy when trouble finds us. Nor is it easy when trouble finds one of your staff. You might feel like you are being mean or coldhearted when you hold people accountable. You aren't. You are doing your job through a difficult situation.

Make It Your Own

- Have you seen organizations respond to trouble in a coldhearted manner? Have you seen organizations take support too far? Either extreme is problematic. What did you see or experience in each response?
- Taken on its own, the statement "The mission and the work are bigger than any individual" may sound cold to some people. How does it land for you? Are there any exceptions to this statement?
- This is an area that requires individual supervisors to respond to each situation, but what happens if the response offered varies dramatically from one supervisor to another, or when one supervisor treats staff members differently from one another? How would that impact the entire team, and therefore the organization?

Valuing People *and* the Work

One of the things I love about working with social justice organizations is that they possess a clear understanding that people matter. The organizations I work with overwhelmingly value their staff and recognize that people have personal, as well as professional, lives.

Sometimes, however, managers get confused and act as though their staff are all that matters. I am all about how to work well with staff. Staff are important to the work. But when staff's personal needs take priority over the actual work, the organization has entered an alternate reality.

This is a tricky area, because of course we want to value people and all they contribute. We want to support them both personally and professionally. But sometimes we must make hard decisions when these types of support conflict, and the mission and the work must take precedence.

A few examples of these confusing situations happen when:

- A job has evolved past the skills of a particular staff member
- Performance has slipped to the point of being unworkable, but the staff member is in a difficult financial situation and needs the money the job provides
- The organization has shifted its work, and the job the staff member has is no longer necessary or relevant

In all of these examples, the supervisor needs to step back and consider the position, rather than the person. This is a critical step in finding the way forward.

Ronald Heifetz is the founding director of the Center for Public Leadership at the Harvard Kennedy School. He recommends a leadership practice of "going to the balcony." The idea is that by looking at your organization from above (from a different perspective), you can see things you can't see when you are in the midst of it. This is often my role when I come into an organization as a consultant or a coach.

I use this balcony image in my work with leaders and suggest that when they are on the balcony, they look at positions, not the people in the positions. If you look at the people, it is hard to find the way past the pain in front of you. When you look at the positions, it becomes possible to see the problem areas. When I have asked leaders what they see from the balcony, they often say, with sadness and certainty, "That position is no longer serving the work."

Then we can come down from the balcony and ask the next question: "Okay, so, now how do we move forward when we consider the people part of the equation?" From here, we might decide that we have to terminate someone but that we will line up resources for them before we take that step. Or maybe another position in the organization (or a sister organization) would better fit the individual's skills. We can be kind and creative while we still move forward in support of the work and the mission.

This step of considering positions first puts the mission front and center. It does not necessarily make the decisions easy, but it usually does make them more clear. Nor does it mean that people don't matter. We can support the staff *and* still recognize that the work must come first. That recognition also values the staff, even if it is difficult for them at times.

Make It Your Own

- What is the impact on the entire organization if leaders look only at the individuals and not the positions?
- How does it affect the other staff when one staff member does not pull their full weight, for whatever reason? And what if that situation goes on and on?
- How might overfocusing on individuals, rather than on the mission, replicate the habits of white supremacist culture? In your own words, how would you describe the way an organization can equitably hold the well-being of the staff and mission achievement simultaneously?

- Under what circumstances, if any, would it make sense to work around a staff member who is unable to do their job?
- Take a few minutes now to pause and "go to the balcony" to look at positions. Do you notice any problem areas? What else do you see?

The Impact of Ignoring Rules

I was flying back to California from Cleveland. We were about to land. They had made the customary announcement about tray tables up, seat belts on, and laptops stowed. The man across the aisle from me kept working away on his laptop. I waited for the flight attendant to tell him to put it away. I waited and I waited. She walked by our row, looked right and left, and said nothing. That did not sit well with me.

1. **I felt angry.** I felt angry that he got away with breaking the rule while everyone else on the plane had to comply with it. I felt angry that the flight attendant, whose role it was to repeat the rule, said nothing.

2. **I felt rebellious.** *Well, if he doesn't have to follow the rule, then I don't either.* (That's not really true; I am not a random rule breaker, so I knew I had to follow the rule.) It made me *want* to act out, though.

3. **I felt devalued.** The point of that rule is to keep others safe from flying items if a landing goes badly. So the fact that the flight attendant didn't bother to enforce it told me she didn't care about my safety—or anyone else's, for that matter. And I couldn't help but wonder if she didn't call him on it because he was a white man.

Now, think about how this scenario plays out in the workplace. I once worked with a group in which the managers felt frustrated by a rule that said staff could not use their cell phones during work hours. It felt unenforceable to them, so they were stuck making judgment calls about when and how to enforce it.

When staff feel angry about rules being selectively enforced, their work with other staff and clients will be impacted. Staff who feel rebellious will contribute to the further impossibility of enforcing the rule, or any rule. Other staff, those still following the stated rules, will start feeling resentful if they don't rebel themselves. Minor lapses end up impacting major rules. And when staff feel devalued, that impacts morale in a comprehensive and deep manner, which in turn impacts absenteeism, trust of supervisors, teamwork, and productivity.

Therefore, it is important to be thoughtful about the rules you make. Don't make rules if you're not going to follow through. If there is a rule, then do your best to hold people to it consistently, and explain why and how the rule matters (including being transparent about nuances if they are part of it). If the rule doesn't work or has outlived its intention, change it. If you can't change it, talk about how you will enforce it: "Okay, I'm not going to call you on it every time you use your phone, but I will definitely call you on it when you do it for a prolonged period or at an inappropriate time."

This is one of those actions that seem relatively minor but can lead to a major shift in a team's effectiveness.

Make It Your Own

- How do you react when you are following a rule and someone else is ignoring it? Think of a specific incident and notice your reaction—then and now, when you remember it.
- Is there a rule that you feel stuck enforcing? Talk about it. Make sure you and your staff understand why the rule is in place, and then talk about what's difficult. Is there a better

way to address the problem that prompted the rule?
- How does your organization show that it values staff? How might it inadvertently show that it doesn't value staff?

....

Breakdown!

It was so muggy. Hot and muggy—and then it rained. I was sitting in an open-air tent, and I felt alone, even though I was part of a small group, which was part of a larger team experiencing a dramatic breakdown of the planned schedule. I was a participant in this group, not the facilitator, and as such I experienced the breakdown of this team in a very different way.

It wasn't named as a team breakdown, but it felt like that to me. I didn't know what was going on or where we were going, because we weren't following the design or schedule outlined ahead of time and no one had announced any intention to do anything differently. I knew there was some unspoken conflict and that a schism had occurred within the team. But as a participant, I could feel only that something was off, that we weren't following the plan. I was told only the next step in front of me. As an introvert, I moved into receptive mode. I was taking things in, but I could not process the information fast enough to make sense of it. So I sat quietly, listening, noticing, thinking, but I did not talk. I did not advance the process. I did not do my best work. I have since thought a lot about what happened at that event, about my response, and about what my best work looks like in this kind of situation. What does *anyone's* best work look like in this kind of situation?

The details of this particular situation don't matter. In fact, since then, other, similar situations have occurred and raised the same questions: a spat with a dear friend, a process with a group that I did facilitate, coaching a leader about her fractured team, coaching another supervisor about her difficult relationship with her own boss. Even the national news has made me think about how we address disconnection and disagreements.

251

It is hard to generalize about any coherent response to breakdowns, because the variables are so important. The variables and the players matter. Whether the players are departments within an organization, unhealthy staff alliances formed to focus on the alliances' own needs above the needs of the organization, a friend who has hurt another friend, or people in any other situation that threatens the health of a unified group, those details matter and must be considered.

Nonetheless, there is a process that can support teams that find themselves in a disruptive situation within an organization. Add in consideration of the specific variables and people involved. Here are my suggestions for responding to a team breakdown:

Step 1: Identify and underline the shared commitment/goal/ mission. Ensure that all components are still unified and committed to a single focus. This might be an organizational mission, a shared goal, or the preservation of an important relationship.

To be effective, this step must be an activity, not just an assumption. We cannot assume that we are still united when we are in the midst of schisms. This requires a full-throated affirmation of our common ground—whether that happens through reading the mission, literally signing a written goal, making a statement that everyone values the relationship and expects it to survive this spat, or doing an activity underlining shared values. This step helps participants zoom out to the bigger picture and touch on their common ground, and lays out a shared intention of reaching that space again together.

Ideally, this step happens before the breakdown becomes entrenched, but it can happen at any time to refocus the unification of the group.

Step 2: Agree to a process. All parties must agree to a specific process to proceed together. This does not mean that every step needs to be taken together, but for every person to feel a part of the process, buy-in must happen. The process might be a mediation process, a problem-solving process, a research process, a needs-identification process, or a decision-making process. The process may be designed to take a couple hours, a couple months, or a couple years. Time for reaffirming agreement about the process can be built into it if some people don't feel ready to sign off on an extended process immediately or if the group (or segments of the group) can commit to only one step at a time.

Step 3: Practice deep listening. Any process needs to include a period of deep listening. If there has been any kind of a separation, breakdown, or activity that contributes to a sense of us versus them, this step is essential. In fact, it is probably *the* most important step of any process in a breakdown.

When people feel aggrieved, they feel unseen and unheard. This quickly leads to their feeling disrespected. And from there, actions tend to be defensive, reactive, or protective. We all need to feel seen, heard, and respected. Notice that I didn't say that we all need to *be* seen, heard, and respected from others' perspective; we must *feel* seen, heard, and respected.

This period of deep listening is therefore crucial. Each contingent must have an opportunity to speak their mind, make their case, list their evidence, and speak their truth. During this period, the other contingent(s) must simply (and deeply) listen. Listen to understand. Listen to empathize. Listen to hear the other people's pain and see their perspective. Do not argue. Do not interrupt. Do not explain or defend or counter their words. Listen. Periodically, let them know that you are in fact hearing them.

Pause after each presentation. Acknowledge what was heard. Then another contingent can take the floor to be seen and heard.

This process might take hours or days or weeks or months, but it will take far less time than it would if this listening did not happen at all.

Step 4: Develop a joint plan to move forward. Only after each group feels seen and heard can the group move on to this step. It is often helpful to start this step with some symbolic gesture to signify that all parties are letting go of the past and committing to the future. (Letting go of the past does not mean forgetting the past; it means letting go of the feelings that arose during the time when people did not feel seen, so that those feelings do not poison the future.)

During this step, you put your common focus in front of you and move into generating win-win solutions, based on what each contingent has shared and heard.

This step might involve everyone, or it might involve representatives of each sect. Everyone must have deep faith in the possibility of win-win solutions. It may take time, but there is a way for everyone's needs to be met and for their common focus to be the guiding star.

Organizationally, this might lead to new policies, practices, or procedures. In a friendship, this might lead each person to say, "Here's what I will do better next time"; in a government process, it might lead to new laws.

Step 5: Debrief. After a plan is in place, it is important to pause and acknowledge your good work and then come together to debrief on the process—not the particulars of the situation, which were worked out in the planning process. What worked about the process? What didn't work? Is there anything you could do to improve the process next time?

Step 6: Follow up. After some time, come together again and determine whether the plan is working. Has the original problem been resolved, or has the group at least made progress toward its resolution? Have any new problems come up? Are there any more insights to add to the plan and/or the debriefing? If a subset worked on the debriefing and the follow-up, make sure they report back to the entire group involved in the initial breakdown.

I cannot guarantee that this process will work in every situation or that all problems can be solved in this manner. I know this process will not be easy. But I also know that these steps remove some of the harmful actions that often follow breakdowns, which do not lead to healing or connection. This process prioritizes a common focus and emphasizes respect and connection for the people involved.

In my work with groups, this process has helped teams move forward together even when they are on the brink of dissolution. It accommodates the innate human need to feel seen, heard, and respected. Even if the process does not lead to a clear win-win, it can lead to a way to move forward with respect.

When I was sitting in that muggy tent, I did not know what I needed. I still do not know what the group needed. I was sitting with the unease and not-knowing that were part of the process. That part is okay. It's okay for people to feel uncomfortable during difficult processes. Now I have a better sense of what might have helped me, and perhaps the process: time to reflect, consider, and feel. Time to be seen and heard. And, just as important, time to see and hear everyone else.

When the rain came that muggy afternoon, it brought a shift in the climate and a sense of calm. That is what we often need in the midst of a difficult process.

Make It Your Own

- What is the difference between being told you're being listened to and *feeling* seen, heard, and respected? What happens when people do not feel understood?
- Have you been a part of a breakdown in an organization? What were the signs and the sides? How was it handled, and how did that help or hurt?
- Under what circumstances would it make sense to you, as a leader, to invest time and money in a process like this?

Avoiding Conflict

I am writing this book during the pandemic. The coronavirus is definitely something my family and I want to avoid. We are wearing masks and social-distancing and pretty much staying home. Likewise, when the weather is bad, it's good practice to avoid going out in lightning storms and floods. Some things are just good to avoid.

Then there are things that we want to avoid but shouldn't: going to the dentist, baby showers, colonoscopies. These are things that are not pleasant for many people, but we know that once we do them, we will feel better for having done them.

Conflict often falls into this second category. Most people would prefer to avoid conflict, even in situations when we need to solve a problem. And many organizations follow that tendency. In fact, some think of conflict as falling into the first category—something to be avoided at any cost. Our reactions to conflict are usually multifaceted and wrapped up with our personal history, our race, our class, our gender, and our dominant culture—all of which can make conflict avoidance seem like a viable option.

But conflict often has an important role, and we do harm as leaders when we avoid it. When we do so, conversations that need to happen don't. Issues that need to be resolved aren't. Solutions that could heal situations and relationships are not discovered. Concerns are not raised, because no one wants to go against their leader, so a better decision is left on the table.

In addition, conflict avoidance can do great damage. Avoiding conflict doesn't make it go away; it just pushes it underground, where it sits, ignored or undetected, and starts to stink and spoil. It will erupt eventually, and then it will be much messier and more difficult to address.

We often avoid conflict because we are afraid. We don't know how to handle it. We don't want to hurt people's feelings. We don't want to make things worse. We are afraid that the conflict will erupt, leading to actual danger. People often think of conflict as this dramatic and harmful erupting, which is usually more a result of its avoidance and suppression. But that doesn't mean that approaching conflicts, even without pent-up energy, is easy or comfortable.

However, the sooner conflict is addressed, the better. Of course, it must be addressed in a healthy manner that is infused with respect and a good process. Approach the conflict with respect for everyone involved. Learn how to resolve conflict. Train your staff to address conflict. Get help from a mediator, if necessary. Hold on to the conviction that win-win solutions are possible to resolve conflict.

It's bad enough when individuals avoid conflict, but when entire organizations do, the system becomes bogged down, bullies tend to rise to the top because no one dares to tell them no, and little innovation occurs, because people are afraid to take risks.

Don't barge into conflict unprepared, but once you have the training and the tools, approach it bravely in service of your mission and your team. In fact, it is often a good leader's job to unearth conflict. To actively watch for it and surface it so that it does not fester underground and become cancerous. To ask your team, "What am I not seeing?" "What is the flaw in this proposal?" "There is tension in the room; what is not being said?" "What is going on between Fiscal and Organizing?"

Be wise in avoiding clear dangers, and be courageous in facing what needs to be addressed.

Make It Your Own

- What are individuals and organizations hoping will happen when they avoid difficult conversations? How likely is that to happen?
- Under what conditions would it make sense for a leader to surface conflict, and under which conditions might it not make sense?
- Does your organization tend to avoid or embrace conflict?

How Did No One Notice?

The news was shocking and heart-wrenching. Another mass shooting with horrifying consequences: more than fifty dead and more than five hundred injured. As the week wore on, we heard more about the shooter and the victims. One news item stuck in my mind: The killer had brought ten suitcases full of weapons into the building.

How did no one notice that? I'm not blaming anyone; I'm simply wondering. And I'm thinking about how easy it is to miss signs that later seem obvious. This happens in organizations all the time, such as when a woman files a harassment suit and suddenly a bunch of other women in the company say, "Oh, yeah, he was awful to me too," but they didn't mention the behavior before or didn't even notice it as abnormal within the organization; it was just a part of the normal, accepted workplace culture.

Or someone quits, and when you look back, you realize that you knew they were unhappy but you didn't pay attention to it. There was always too much work pressing on your mind. Or, most relevant, when workplace violence or bullying occurs and people recognize the signs in retrospect.

We work in busy environments. Every person I work with is overwhelmed with work. There is always too much to do. So how can you look around and notice problems or unusual events?

You can't notice everything, and no one expects you to. You can, however, do your best to check in with people regularly. To ask them, often, "Is there anything else we need to talk about?" or, "Is there anything I should know?" (This means having regularly scheduled supervisor meetings; see chapter 3.)

Other ways to pay attention include:

Monitor Turnover

Notice if/when turnover starts creeping over 15–20 percent per year. I would also be curious about an organization that has zero turnover. Turnover rates should be monitored periodically so that you can notice any sudden changes. Turnover is tricky—there are often (maybe even usually) very good reasons for people to leave. But notice if turnover is happening in one particular department over others. Is it happening at certain times of the year? Or to a certain group of people? Is there a sudden spike in turnover? What's that about?

Notice Complaining

Is there a sudden, or gradual, increase in the amount of unhappiness among your staff? Compare notes with your peers. Are you hearing terms like "hostile work environment," "grievance," "discrimination," "harassment," "bullying," "stress," "overwhelm," "burnout," and "distrust"? What is going on?

Track Canceled Meetings

Is one staff member canceling or missing more meetings than usual, especially your one-on-one meetings? Again, they may have good reasons for doing so, or the situation might be circumstantial—sick kids, a doctor appointment, crossed wires on the time or place—but notice and be curious.

Note Changes in Affect

Is a usually perky person suddenly dim and quiet? Is a quiet person suddenly manic and hyper? Is a usually social person now more isolated? You don't have to be a therapist or figure out what is going on, but notice—and check in. Make questions open-ended so you're not forcing someone to reveal personal information if they don't want to, but you can still let them know you've noticed and open the door for communication.

Catch Gossip

Is an uptick in gossip and rumors going on in your workplace, either about individual people or about the organization? This is another sign that something is going on and needs to be addressed.

Having regularly scheduled meetings with your staff will help you notice when things start to go awry. Otherwise, changes might just become the new norm and problems could go underground and grow. You are not expected to diagnose anyone or be a babysitter, but you are expected to notice changes that could lead to trouble.

This is not about blame. This is about remembering to pay attention. When I teach harassment workshops, I remind managers that the liability burden is "Did management know about the harassment, or *should they have known?*" Pay attention, so you can respond to what you should have known. Catch problems early and address them. We can't prevent every problem, but we do want to prevent ourselves from ever having to wonder, *How did no one notice?*

Make It Your Own

- In this section, I state, "You are not expected to diagnose anyone or be a babysitter." Where is the line between noticing and being intrusive? Have there been times in your own life when you felt as if no one noticed, or as if someone was intruding into your personal life?

- How do you react to the idea of asking, "Anything else we need to talk about?" If you are afraid this might open an unending discussion, know that you can be the gatekeeper of what is discussed and what is tabled. Don't ask if you don't want to listen to the answer. If you ask and then table a response or discussion for another time, make sure you come back to it, or you will hear only silence the next time you bother to ask.

- Some of the changes I describe are individual and some are organizational. What needs to be in place to notice the organizational changes?

Don't Look the Other Way for Too Long

Sometimes you just need to choose your battles. There are times when people don't do exactly what they should be doing but you decide to look the other way, for whatever reason. You might not comment on every minute someone is late, or if they make a goofy comment, or if they forget a procedure.

You might have good reasons for looking past any of these particular behaviors. Maybe you know the person is stressed and working on a deadline; maybe you know that you just had a difficult feedback session with them yesterday and you don't want to hit them too hard; maybe they are in learning mode.

If this happens occasionally, it works. However, be careful. Any of these actions repeated over time can become a problem, and then you'll find yourself in the awkward situation of having to address behavior that you have previously tolerated. When you look the other way more than once or twice, you are saying that this behavior is okay. So when a few minutes late becomes twenty minutes late or happens every day, when do you decide to address it? When the goofy comment becomes snarky and disrespectful? When the procedural mistake becomes a pattern or a disregard for due process?

I am not saying you have to be an ogre and address every problem immediately, but I am saying that it is important to notice what you are tolerating, especially over time. Notice when you are letting things slide and when you have let them slide so much that you don't even notice anymore. It's also important to notice with whom you let things slide and if you are or are not consistent in your response to problems. This can be a double check for prejudicial behavior and/or the appearance of such.

This is why judgment-free feedback is such a critical item in your toolbox. When you can give (and receive) feedback in a neutral tone intended to convey important information that will help the other person be successful, you are doing your job as a supervisor. This way, feedback doesn't become rare and intense; it's just part of how you communicate with and support each other. Examples include:

"Hey, I noticed you've been coming in a little late the past few days. What's going on?"

"I heard you teasing Julie in the staff meeting, and I wanted to make sure you noticed her reaction. I don't think she appreciated your comments."

"I don't think you have to redo it this time, but I want to make sure you know that you skipped a couple steps in the closing procedure. The procedures are there for a reason, so make sure you follow them next time."

Simply supply the information that will help the person do a better job. Choose your battles, but pay attention and give your staff the information they need to be successful. And don't look the other way for too long.

Make It Your Own

- What is the impact on the organization when concerns are routinely overlooked?
- How do you approach giving feedback? Is it a big deal, or do you feel like you are "getting someone in trouble" when you give feedback? If so, how can you shift this to a practice of communicating information that they need to be successful?
- If feedback is one of the critical tools in your toolbox, what else is in there next to it?

Avoid the Triangle

Wikipedia describes the Bermuda Triangle as "a loosely defined region in the western part of the North Atlantic Ocean where a number of aircraft and ships are said to have disappeared under mysterious circumstances." Although the article goes on to debunk the concept, the stories and fear remain real for many people.

Also in organizations lurks a triangle that can cause enormous damage and sometimes make staff disappear, as they resign in frustration or are terminated for being identified as problem employees. In reality, this triangle is a problem with the system.

Here's how it most often works. Olivia is mad at, or has been hurt by, Lila. Instead of talking to Lila to clear up the issue between them, Olivia talks to Pat about the situation. Pat empathizes with Olivia. And then Pat goes to Lila and tells her what Olivia said. Sometimes Pat is trying to help the situation; sometimes they are simply gossiping. In any case, this scenario creates a triangle of Olivia, Lila, and Pat—one in which Olivia and Lila never talk directly to work out the initial problem.

The problem is that Pat is involved in a situation that really has nothing to do with her. This also happens when groups form alliances against each other. Team A doesn't like to work with Team B. Team C must figure out how to get the work done when the clearest path is disrupted. Sometimes the two teams will even try to get Team C to side with them against the other.

Triangulating is a pattern in which two people or groups who are at odds will appeal to a third party to take their side—not to help them work it out but to exacerbate the division and prove themselves right. The scarcer the resources in an organization are, or the more muddy the roles and responsibilities are, the greater the amount of triangulating. In politically charged situations, the landscape in which individuals or groups are siding with or against each other changes frequently.

And so it goes, on and on. Typically, such triangulation causes other people also to get involved, expanding the morass and sucking more and more victims into the swamp of messy communication. Triangulation is the classic "he said, she said, they said" situation. The amount of time and energy that this dynamic can devour in an organization can be astronomical.

Too often, the person in Pat's situation is the supervisor. There are certainly times when it is appropriate for a supervisor to be involved in a situation between two employees. Bullying, harassment, lack of follow-through, or accountability are a few such situations. But it is not always appropriate for a supervisor to jump in, especially in situations where the conflict is related to the personal relationship between team members or when a minor misunderstanding has occurred.

What's a supervisor to do? Stop! Stop being a part of the underground complaint system. This is a tricky proposition, because an important part of your job as a supervisor is to listen to people, support them, and help them. But listening and support cannot come at the expense of clear communication, or of teamwork, or of other staff members. As an HR director, I developed a practice of telling people, "I'm happy to hear your concerns and to help you develop a plan of action." The plan of action might have involved my helping them talk to the person, or it might have involved my dealing with the situation when that was appropriate.

Often the appropriate thing for the supervisor to do when faced with a triangulation situation is to simply say, "Let's bring Lila in right now so we can talk this through." Some questions that can help you figure out how to proceed while avoiding getting sucked into a triangle are:

- Is this a compliance, harassment, or bullying issue? (If so, you need to get involved as a supervisor or take the issue to HR.)
- How does this current situation impact the staff's ability to do their work? (The answer to this question will inform whether you need to get involved. It can help you to determine whether this is a work problem or an interpersonal conflict.)
- Were you there when that was said? (This question can detect gossiping.)
- When can the three of us talk about this together?
- How have you addressed the situation so far?

- What processes or procedures could we put in place to keep that from happening again in the future?

By not taking part in triangulating, you are helping to build a culture of direct communication and problem solving. You also won't make enemies by inadvertently taking sides in an issue about which you really have only partial information.

Organizations must build a triangle-proof system. Train people in communication and conflict-resolution skills. Make a process for the entire organization to follow when conflicts arise. Make a one-vent rule. This rule recognizes that sometimes we just have to let out our frustrations, so any employee can "vent" to a buddy about a frustration *one* time. Then the venter must either let the issue go or deal with it. If the same issue comes up again, the buddy must direct you back to the other person so that you can speak with them directly. (See chapter 4 for more about venting.)

Build a triangle-free environment so that no one gets sucked into the triangle and disappears.

Make It Your Own

- What is the impact on the rest of the team when people are involved in a triangle?
- What does the third leg of the triangle lose when they send someone directly to the person they have a conflict with (i.e., what motivates people to participate in situations that don't actually involve them)?
- Is there any policy or plan or discussion you need to have with your team to implement changes pertaining to this kind of interaction?

Getting Stuck in Guilt

When we see the isms that saturate mainstream culture and recognize their impact on our workplace, we can feel overwhelmed. We notice how justice has been denied and perhaps how we have been a part of the damage. For instance, white leaders must recognize the history and harm that our people have done historically, and look critically at how those harms continue and impact our organizations.

However, awareness of privilege and oppression can also sometimes wreak havoc within an organization. This happens when white leaders get stuck in the paralysis of white guilt and are unwilling, or unable, to deliver on their organizational responsibilities. Or it can happen in response to recognizing other historic harms and ongoing privileges, as when cis men start to recognize their complicity in toxic male culture or an able-bodied person experiences a temporary disability and sees the world differently. When we first realize our history and our complicity in inadvertently replicating dominant culture, it is normal—even healthy—to feel guilty. But when the guilt does not move to corrective action, it is unhealthy.

Instead of having hard conversations with themselves and others, some leaders are so afraid of being labeled unfair, sexist, or racist that they seemingly throw up their hands and give up. This can happen on an individual level or an organizational level. No doubt this stuckness can show up in any number of ways. I will mention five:

1. Silence/Shutting Down

The fear of doing or saying the wrong thing can lead us to simply be quiet. If the quiet is temporary and full of active listening, that's good. But when it leads to our tuning out or shutting down, it is a hostile act. It is prioritizing comfort and self-preservation over liberation. It is a refusal to be part of the solution. It is getting frozen in looking back, instead of looking ahead.

2. A "Poor Me" Attitude

The leader who gets stuck in guilt can carry the inactivity of shutting down to an internal focus that is unnecessary and indulgent. We must take time to feel the pain of our history and how we consider our own culpability. We must also recognize how we, both as individuals and as a group, have, for instance, also been injured by systemic racism, classism, and heterosexism that taught us that we are better than others. But getting stuck here helps no one. In fact, it makes us victims of history and prioritizes our experience over the experience of the historically oppressed.

3. A Prophet Mentality

Prophets want to tell everyone about their privilege and their complicity—for example, when they recognize the impacts of white supremacy, talking about it to BIPOC, who have seen and lived it all again and again. They want to educate everyone, but in doing so, they stop learning. They stop listening, they stop self-reflecting, and they stop addressing the actual impacts of systemic supremacy.

4. Inconsistencies

Avoiding uncomfortable conversations and situations can lead to inconsistent treatment based on identities. For example, in wanting to address historic inequities, supervisors seek to dole out perks and curry favor with people of color by treating staff members differently. Or they might look the other way when LGBTQ+ staff take shortcuts, or suggest extra time off for certain staff. Doing these things makes them feel good. This is a great way to create liability and resentment among staff, and the supervisor is still giving their own feelings precedence over the actual problems that exist in the organization.

5. Refusal to Hold Certain People Accountable

Supervisors must consider if and how racial (or other) dynamics are at play when considering accountability measures. Maybe a trans woman makes her boss uncomfortable, so the boss avoids addressing problems with her. Conversations about outcomes and practices must take place and ensure that the way the work is being done is not unfairly being held to white-supremacist or sexist or ableist standards. When stuck in identity guilt, managers can refuse to have accountability conversations with BIPOC or other staff, or to write them up, or even to terminate them following time and due process for change. These actions should not happen because of a staff person's identity, but they should not *not* happen because of that person's identity either.

All of these examples of being stuck end up focusing on a (white) leader's comfort, instead of addressing concerns about equity and the mission. They can happen across ethnicities and genders and orientation too. They can also exacerbate systemic inequities through avoidance and overcompensating. As white folks, as cis men, as straight people, as able-bodied people, as native English speakers or not recent immigrants, we need to do our own work and we need to have tough conversations. But most of all, we need to continue to move toward justice and liberation with our staff.

Make It Your Own

- What are the unintended consequences of one leader's getting stuck in white guilt (or straight guilt, or male guilt, or middle-class guilt, etc.)?
- What are the organizational consequences when leaders refuse to address problems that have been recognized?
- While perhaps they are well intentioned, what happens when leaders overcompensate, instead of addressing systemic issues of inequity?

CHAPTER 12:

IT'S A MARATHON, NOT A SPRINT

One time, I walked a complete marathon. It took me eight hours to walk the 26.2 miles. I trained for six months ahead of time. The first ten miles were pretty easy. The next ten miles were harder and slower. And the next five miles were endless—I just wanted it to end. But I was committed to finishing it. Then, when the end was in sight, the last 1.2 miles were exhausting but enthusiastic. I knew I could really do it.

I couldn't have done it alone. I couldn't have done it without hard work and commitment and a plan. The cheerleaders and the water stations along the way helped. Even better were the jugglers and the musicians en route. My walking partner helped; he knew I could do it and kept telling me so.

Leading for justice requires commitment, diligence, and sustainability. This is not quick or easy work. We need camaraderie, we need collaboration, and we need clarity. When you show up as a leader, you have a tremendous impact on your team and your entire organization. Recognition and celebration help people stay motivated. When you keep the conversation going and keep the work focused on the mission, people will be more engaged. When you make time for a little play, you give people a chance to connect. When it gets too hard, supporting the grief that must also be heard will allow people to take a deep breath and keep going. And when, together, you create a safer place for all staff members to be fully themselves while you all work together, there will be dancing in the streets. And justice will be a mile or so closer.

Respect the Drops; Recognize the Bucket

Some people say that a drop in the bucket is meaningless. But we say, No! If you have a bucket, those raindrops fill it up very fast. Being a drop in the bucket is magnificent. The problem is that we cannot see the bucket. Our work is to help people see that there is a bucket.
— STUDS TERKEL

Drops can add up to powerful action, and when we work together, in organizations and in the larger movement, we can create transformation. Helping people to see the bucket is an important step in creating momentum to continue the work.

Here are a few suggestions to help you, and your staff, recognize the bucket:

- Pause periodically to celebrate progress—both individual and organization-wide. We often get stuck looking only at our financial wins—this is about celebrating all kinds of benchmarks and goals, expanding our outreach, making an impact.
- Tell a story or two at staff meetings about wins by other social justice organizations or in the courts.
- Develop a partnership with another organization, and send staff to each other's staff meetings once a year to feel the energy of shared work.
- Once per quarter, start a staff or department meeting by having people share a success story (personal or professional—their choice). Applaud enthusiastically. Make it celebratory.

- Periodically publish statistics about how many social justice organizations there are in the country or world, and read the Studs Terkel quote together.
- Remember that drops of water can be life-giving and soothing for the thirsty soul.

Make It Your Own

- What happens when we don't recognize the bucket and focus only on our individual contributions?
- Think of a time when you felt the power of unified work toward a common cause. How did that feeling impact your engagement with the work?
- What is the impact on staff when they perceive leaders as partners with staff and with the larger movement?

Recognition Sticks

Eucalyptus. The smell wafted toward me as I hiked in the dry California forest: mint, camphor, oil, and sun. Memories of summer camp came rushing back. One particular recollection made me consider the strong impact that a woman named Marilyn had on my life.

I was a quiet fifteen-year-old when I worked as a counselor at a summer day camp. The camp was held just outside the city where I attended high school. The park was grassy, with several stands of eucalyptus. Counselors were assigned to either help a group of kids throughout the week or help a teacher for the week. Marilyn taught singing. I spent a week with her, as well as a week with the drama teacher, the nature teacher, and the crafts-and-dance teacher. At the end of the summer, awards were given for the best counselors in each area. The awards were hats that you could prestigiously wear all the next summer.

I was surprised and thrilled when Marilyn named me the winner of the singing hat. I am in no way an outstanding singer, but I was enthusiastic and did whatever she asked me to do. The award meant the world to me. It meant that Marilyn saw me as a leader, even though I was quiet. She saw me as a strong participant, even though I drew no attention to myself.

The impact of that recognition has lasted a lifetime. It gave me permission to be my quiet, strong self. It gave me confidence to trust who I was and how I worked. I didn't have to make excuses about how I chose to participate. I knew I could be a leader and still be me. I've been building on that confidence my whole life. Thank you, Marilyn!

Who among your staff could use some positive reinforcement? Who among your staff has been quietly doing a good job? Who among your staff has been exuberantly doing a good job? They all could use a little recognition.

Too often, supervisors wait until the annual evaluation process to tell people they are doing a good job, or they lead by focusing on problems and ignoring what *is* working. Either of these approaches leave staff wondering why they work so hard and contributes to disengagement.

People want to know how they're doing, especially when they're working hard and giving a little bit (or a lot) of extra time and energy. They want to be seen and recognized for making a difference in the organization. Even when they're not doing so well, make sure you give them clear and specific feedback about what needs to be done differently.

Your recognition doesn't have to be trumpets and parades, awards and hats. It can simply be a thoughtful notification, either verbal or in writing. When you give recognition, make it specific. Let them know what is working. Telling someone, "Good work" is certainly better than nothing, but your feedback can be better—not just "Good job on that report," but "I noticed that you turned the report in when it was due. It was well researched and well written. It will make a difference in our work. Thank you for your good work." Be specific about what you noticed they were doing well. This approach will help people to keep doing what's working, and most of them will feel seen and appreciated.

Your recognition could make a world of difference for someone, like Marilyn's did for me. Or it might just make them keep up their good work. Either way, it's a win!

Make It Your Own

- When have you felt recognized, and how did that impact your work?
- Some managers operate based on a sense of "I'll tell you if anything is wrong; otherwise, just keep doing what you're doing." What is the impact of that approach on their staff? Hint: Psychologists recommend a ratio of at least five positive comments for every negative comment.
- The need for recognition can vary widely from one staff member to another. What have you seen work for people who need a lot of praise?

Sustaining Passion

I still feel a little blip of joy when my beloved walks into a room, but after decades together, I don't experience the initial heart pounding, blood-rushing, weak-kneed hallmarks of first being in love. That stage of being in love shifts to a more calm and solid joy after the newness fades into normalcy. It might be fun to stay in the overwhelming head-over-heels feelings, but it would also be exhausting—and we would miss the depth of long-term joy and love that comes over time. Being in a relationship is not the same after a few years, whether it is with friends, lovers, or organizations.

I once had a conversation with a former client, an executive director, who lamented that her current staff viewed their work as a job, not as a mission. They weren't committed to the mission above all, and they expected to have a life and

273

leave for a better job whenever they wanted to. She missed the startup days when staff came together in fervent commitment to the work—working with passion and prioritizing work above everything else.

I told her, "I don't think that can last. That kind of passion is not sustainable." The ED didn't agree with me. She herself was maintaining that passion. She was tired but undeterred. The mission and the passion kept her going.

When I reflected on our conversation, I realized this didn't have to be an either-or situation. It is wonderful when founders and long-term staff live and breathe the mission and instill in new staff the joy and passion of the work. It can also be wonderful when new staff arrive, believe in the mission, give their best work for a time, and then move on. In both cases, the mission is centered and guiding the work.

The danger, as with so many organizational dynamics, is in the alignment and the expectations, such as when the passionate demand the same kind of passion from the newly committed. Or the long-term staff are tired and drained and the new staff arrive with energy and enthusiasm, and soon feel disappointed that all staff don't share their excitement. Or the elders expect explicit honor for carrying the flag so dramatically for so long. Or the original, grassroots staff mandate twenty-four-seven responses and all-hands-on-deck work on every project after the organization has grown.

Sometimes the newer staff (often younger, but not always) care deeply about the mission but their passion is in their work *and* their life; the mission is part of that, but not all of it. They expect respect for stepping up and doing the work. They most likely do respect and honor the elders who created the organization, but without mutual respect, that honoring is going to be cloudy and conflicted. They most likely expect some kind of work-life balance, desiring time off the clock. While they will gladly step up in urgent situations, they won't tolerate every day as an all-hands-on-deck scenario.

This lack of alignment can cause disruption and distance. It can sow seeds of discontent that, ironically, lead to more detachment. It can create within the organization fissures that feel like us-versus-them dynamics, instead of a united team fighting the good fight together.

To shift this disconnection, prioritize the mission and define passion. "Passion" is such a loaded word. Even in the early days, passion probably looked different from one person to another. Some people are outgoing and exuberant; others are quiet and steady. It doesn't mean that the quiet person cannot be fully engaged and committed to the work. It doesn't mean that people who want work-life balance cannot be strong and trusted staff members (in fact, that usually helps in the long term!). So define what you mean by "passion," hire for it, and hold people accountable to it *if* that is what you need. Here are a few considerations:

Demonstrated Commitment to the Mission
Hire people who understand, value, and support the mission. Make sure this is front and center in everything you do. Make sure the hiring candidates understand that lack of alignment with the mission is a deal breaker.

Full Engagement
While they are employed, staff need to bring their A-game to the work, work well with other staff, and be willing to prioritize work above personal matters when *necessary*—which doesn't mean always, or even often.

Collaboration
Staff are expected to keep the big picture in mind and collaborate with other programs and projects to move the mission forward. This is not a job for people who are lone rangers looking to make their next career move on the backs of other staff.

Transparency

When you understand and acknowledge that this job is not a lifetime vocation for every staff member, you can give and request transparency. When the mission is front and center, the organization can have annual conversations about where people see themselves going, how content they are with the work, and what they need to do their best work here and now. People can more safely admit that they are feeling restless and starting to look around while remaining fully engaged in their current role.

It can be a both-and situation. Some staff can bring the grassroots passion, and other staff can do good work in a rigorous way that helps the mission and then move on. Staff with a different level of passion (or style or speed or approach, for that matter) can work together for the common cause. If both modes can respect and honor the other, the organization can function with healthy, thriving relationships at its core, whether those relationships are long term or brand new.

Make It Your Own

- What are the joys and challenges of passionate relationships, with people or organizations?
- When you think of defining and mandating passion, what comes up for you?
- How do us-versus-them divisions in staff impact the work and the staff?

Making Play at Work Work

When I introduce an icebreaker at a training, I know that some people groan and some people laugh. Luckily, they usually keep both reactions quiet. Here's what I know about playing at work, when it's done well:

- It can get people in the room and away from their phones and their to-do lists.
- It can give people a break from the near-constant stress and overwhelm of so many workplaces.
- It can make room for joy and laughter in environments that are very serious and important.
- It can open the synapses to be creative and innovative long after the play itself is over.
- It can connect people—across generations, across departments, across positions, across hierarchies (and those connections can also last long after the play itself is over).
- It can bring literally every voice into the room and consequently help each person to participate more fully in the subsequent meeting. When people speak out loud in a group, they are more likely to speak again.

When people groan at the idea of playing together, they do so most often because workplace play has not been done well. This is not surprising, since play is not seen as an adult activity, and certainly not a professional activity, in our dominant culture. In those cases, these can be the results:

- People get competitive in the play, and it creates more disconnection and divisions.
- People are put on the spot, and trust is jeopardized; they are not given the option of adapting their participation.
- Leadership doesn't participate playfully, so it doesn't feel like real playtime to the rest of the staff; it feels like a test.
- Teasing is done in a way that is not playful and mutual but instead is judgmental and critical; our relationship to teasing is connected to our own complicated history and identity, as well as the norms we grew up with. Teasing is therefore often tricky and sometimes dangerous for people.
- The play is intrusive and pries into personal spaces, without giving anyone a chance to opt out without embarrassment.

- It lasts too long, and people feel like it's a waste of time.
- The play feels unsafe, and people are wary of participating.

I encourage teams to take a few minutes to play together here and there at work, but doing it well is important. Make it short, safe, connective, constructive, and fun.

1. Short: Two to five minutes is usually enough for a quick icebreaker. The start of a meeting is a good time—people are there to connect and share with each other.

2. Safe: Don't put anyone on the spot to answer a question or take a turn. Make everything optional, and make it easy to opt out or adapt participation. Don't let people comment on anyone else's answers or reactions. Shut down any negative teasing in a friendly and calm manner: "Let's keep this moving! Who's next?" "Hey—I spy with my little eye someone who is distracting the team." Be mindful of cultural and other differences.

3. Connective: Make sure the focus is on connection, not competition. Don't make it about right or wrong answers that reward and shame. Facilitate the play so that people talk to coworkers whom they do not usually work near.

4. Constructive: Ideally, the playtime will be related to the theme of the meeting—e.g., teamwork, creativity, assumptions. It doesn't always have to be a straightforward, logical connection, but it does always have to be something you can build on. Don't let it be divisive or exclusive.

5. Fun: If people are not having fun or if the environment feels tense, ask what's going on (and be ready to hear the answer) or wrap it up. Maybe the timing is wrong;

maybe cultural or generational awkwardness is affecting the dynamic. Have different people lead the activities for different meetings, introducing different styles of and approaches to play, but give staff these guidelines before you turn this task over to someone.

Lots of websites offer examples of icebreakers and play at work. These are usually well practiced and offer tips about timing and safety factors. It is well worth the time and effort to bring a few minutes of fun to the workplace. Doing so can offer rich benefits that go well beyond the actual investment of time. But it must be done well, or it will cause harm. Make sure you are authentic in modeling the safety and the fun. If it isn't fun for you, it won't work for your team. The bottom-line purpose is to connect people in a joyful manner. And that connection will support the work and the team long beyond playtime.

Make It Your Own

- When have you seen play at work work, and when have you seen it not work? What was different?
- Some people worry about wasting time on these kinds of activities. How else is time wasted during (or before) meetings? What makes the time wasted? When is non-work-focused time valuable?
- How could connection between people contribute to and improve the work?

Another Name for Morale Is Belonging

Cheers is an old TV show, but I can still hear the theme song in my head: "Where everybody knows your name / and they're always glad you came . . ." The show was about a bar, but these lyrics could ideally be about work too.

279

Belonging is not about permanence or being "a family" or always being positive; it is about being connected, feeling safe to be yourself, and having a sense of contributing to a greater good. When staff have a sense of belonging, they know that they matter—both as individuals and as components of the organization.

Many factors can contribute to this sense of belonging, and to high morale, but a common thread running through them is intentionality. Policies, practices, and the culture all align to support the mission *and* the employees. When there is a lack of alignment or the policies and practices seem haphazard or borrowed, any sense of belonging feels tenuous.

Some practices that contribute to high morale are listed below. This is not an all-inclusive list, and the particulars may vary based on the staff and the work, but in general these describe workplaces where staff feel good and safe.

Authentic People Work There

People feel safe being who they are. The workplace demonstrates much more than tolerance for differences; there is active joy about and celebration of how staff show up. Each person feels seen, heard, and appreciated for who they are and the work they do. This is demonstrated not only in how people treat each other but also in policies, responsiveness, and equity practices.

Communication Goes Up, Down, and Sideways

The organization is fiercely committed to sharing information, especially when it impacts employees. It has a practice of transparency regarding how and when decisions are made. Finances are not a mystery. Staff input is invited, heard, and valued when it is relevant—and when it is not, staff know why. Conversations, whether up or down or sideways, are two-way, not lectures.

The Work Matters

Staff are explicitly clear on how their work supports the mission and why it matters. They feel proud of their contributions, and they feel as if they are part of a whole that is making a significant difference in the world.

Competency Is Expected

Staff believe they have agency in their work; that is, they are not micromanaged. They understand the level of action they can take and when they need approval to proceed. They can learn and grow in their work and within the organization. The organization values training to improve individual skills and to support development, but also to ensure shared knowledge and approaches to the work. A level of mastery is expected throughout the organization—mastery of each individual in their work and mastery among the entire organization in supporting the mission and living the values.

Leaders Demonstrate Respect

Leadership is recognized as a particular role and not a badge of superiority. Leaders work in collaboration with staff. A tangible sense of mutual respect and appreciation floods the organization. Leaders own their power, authority, and privilege in a way that is of service to the organization. They accept the responsibility of their role and lead with vision, trust, transparency, and integrity.

Staff Have Tools to Do the Job

Staff have the tools they need to do their work. These include equipment, software, materials, and supplies but also space, responses, clarity, training, and respect. If they don't have what they need, they can ask for it. They have opportunities to learn from mistakes and from each other.

Clarity Abounds

Staff feel confident that all the pieces of the organization are working in harmony, that people are "rowing in the same direction" and reading from the same page. Very little, if anything, falls through the cracks. Very little, if any, duplication of efforts occurs. People know their own roles and responsibilities and understand the roles of others around them and how they impact each other. People understand their own and others' authority, when and how initiative and innovation are welcomed, and when they should follow protocols. They have clarity and consistency on process, conduct, and the handling of problems.

Feedback Is Commonplace

People know how they are doing. They can trust that good work will be recognized and problems will be addressed. If something they are doing is not working, they will know it. And they know that other people will also be held accountable and given information to improve, when necessary.

People Feel Safe

Staff feel safe, physically and psychologically. They may not always feel comfortable, but they know that they will not be in danger for who they are or how they show up, as long as they don't impinge on others or the work. Harassment, bullying, aggression, and threats are addressed and corrected immediately. People know that they will be heard and believed if they need to report danger. Leaders and supervisors at all levels are responsive and supportive.

Recognition and Celebration Happen

Staff know that good work will be recognized. They may not always see financial rewards, but they exchange frequent thank-yous. Individual, team, and organizational achievements are celebrated. Though there is always more work to be done, everyone understands that stopping to look back and appreciate what the organization has accomplished is important and nourishes the work ahead.

Equity Is Valued and Practiced

Equity has clear value. People can name what has been done and what is currently being done to address concerns. Every voice is heard, welcome, and considered. Hiring, discipline, and termination all follow a clear process that has been analyzed for bias.

Too often when we talk about morale, we think of employee happiness or occasional events. Morale that focuses on belonging is about so much more than an occasional potluck. It is about alignment and intentionality. It is about knowing everyone's name and making sure they feel good and productive being at work.

Make It Your Own

- What have you seen impact morale, and why does it matter?
- What happens to a sense of belonging within the organization when staff must be let go?
- How is happiness a flawed barometer of morale?

Grief

One day I was at lunch with a friend who happens to be a therapist. My assistant called me, and what she said made me stop in my tracks. She told me one of our beloved employees had been killed in a car accident. This was Barbara Love, one of the people to whom this book is dedicated. I was personally devastated, but I also had to figure out how to tell my staff before they heard it in some random manner. It happened that the ED was out of town and unreachable for a few hours.

There was no playbook for how to handle this situation. Barbara was known and loved by pretty much every staff member. I took the therapist back to work with me, and, with the other directors, we devised a plan to tell staff and support them through this horrendous news. This was no easy feat, as we had eighteen different sites—and we wanted to deliver the news in person. We immediately made space for staff members to sit together and process their immediate reactions. I found another therapist to sit with the largest group of employees.

We did not do it all perfectly. We were all stunned and feeling our own grief, but we did our best to make room for the grief that was varied and inevitable for staff. Over the next weeks, we developed a way for staff to donate vacation time that would translate into money to support Barbara's family, we held a staff memorial, we offered time off, and we created a permanent marker to commemorate this important person.

The point is that we made room for staff's emotional responses. We did not expect people to just bounce back as if nothing had happened. The need to grieve shows up differently in everyone, of course. Some people were tearful, some were quiet and distant, some seemed unaffected, but we didn't try to manage or analyze reactions. We simply made room for all of them.

The work had to go on, however. The organization ran child-care centers, as well as a health clinic that could not pause. We could not shut down the organization for everyone to take time off, but we did our best to support staff through that difficult time.

In a world where so much harm is done and where work comes with so much stress and sometimes heart-wrenching situations, it is important to make space for the sadness that will erupt at specific times and will perhaps sometimes be a river through the work. I know of organizations that bring in counselors to offer monthly meetings to staff. Others hold a specific (optional) staff ritual every month to honor losses. Many organizations offer an EAP as a benefit to support one-on-one needs.

Still others offer generous time-off practices so people can take mental health days as needed. They may practice moments of silence after local or national assaults, or host meetings to discuss and process frustration about specific incidents happening over and over again, such as acts of police brutality.

Social justice work is collaborative, and it is heart centered. We are analytical in our work and relentless in our goals, but we are also touched by our work. People don't work for social justice if they don't care about other people. Intentionally recognizing the need for grief, individually and jointly, is an important item to add to leaders' overall scope. Or perhaps it falls to a heart committee or wellness team to create ways to support the grief.

Making room for grief is another way in which organizations can support staff as vital people, not just cogs in a machine. When I received that upsetting phone call years ago, I did not have a plan, but I knew that staff needed support. That was my first concern. I hope you never get a call like that during your career, but grief will show up, one way or another. And when it does, make room for it.

Make It Your Own

- What do you imagine happens in an organization, or to an individual, when ongoing grief is ignored?
- What other ideas can you add to the options I suggested to make room for grief?
- People respond to grief, and other emotions, differently. How can you normalize that as an organization so judgment doesn't emerge from those differences?

Keeping the Conversation Going

Once, I was playing emergency helicopter rescues with my granddaughter but was simultaneously checking my work email. My granddaughter got frustrated with me and finally said, "Grandma, please put your phone down and sit on the floor and play with me." That got my attention, and I did just what she asked me to do. That was my intention, after all: to play with her. I was simply distracted by my phone. Nothing was urgent, and she is important.

How often have employees wanted to say that to their leaders? Leaders need to routinely put down both their literal and their metaphorical phones, be present, and listen to their staff and each other.

One of the most essential components of leading in general and leading for justice in particular is the practice of two-way conversations. Leaders must communicate information throughout the organization, and they must hear information from the staff. This happens in all kinds of ways, and the more you practice it, the more you will hear. As with most things in this book, this approach must be intentional and consistent. It does some good if leaders listen to their staff, but until it is a standard practice, you won't know what you don't know. When it is a standard practice throughout your organization, then it will become part of the culture and you can say, "That's just the way we do things here. Of course the ED has meetings with the staff."

In order for these practices to be effective, pay attention to safety concerns. It might not be comfortable all the time—either to speak up or to hear what is being said—and that's okay. Too often we forget that safe does not mean the same thing as comfortable. Safe means that no one will suffer harm from speaking up—they won't lose their job, they won't be retaliated against, they won't be bullied or teased. They might be held accountable if they say something discriminatory or against the values of the organization, but they won't be ostracized for speaking up. Uncomfortable means it is hard to say; it pushes you beyond what you would usually say. It pushes you to hear what you wouldn't usually hear. Uncomfortable is okay; unsafe is not.

And in order for it to be safe to speak up, the listeners must be safe to hear what they need to hear. Now I am not suggesting you have public feedback sessions, although some organizations do that. I am speaking more about pushback on decisions, or offering an alternative approach than the ED's favorite. Once we held a meeting to listen to the staff's reaction to how a move had been planned. We were hearing rumblings of discontent with the process, so we hired an outside consultant to facilitate the meeting. We wanted the staff to feel safe. And they stepped up and told us what they thought. The ED and the other directors had been instructed by the facilitator to simply listen. And we did. But it was hard. It was especially hard not to respond to rumors and assumptions and flat-out wrong information. But we did it and it was invaluable. Eventually we did have a chance to respond, but it was important for us first to just listen; for staff to know that they could say anything and we would listen.

Here are a few structured ways to make sure two-way speaking and listening are happening throughout the organization:

ED Talks

Depending on the size of the staff, these may happen at a weekly staff meeting or they may happen at quarterly retreats or an annual meeting. But make sure they happen. Staff need to know and hear from the top on a regular basis about what is new, what is important, and how things are going.

Surveys

Annual staff surveys are a great way to receive anonymous and objective information. These surveys might focus on engagement, satisfaction, commitment, or a specific goal/metric you are trying to obtain, like measuring your progress on becoming a welcoming and inclusive workplace. Each survey provides important information. It is imperative that if you conduct a survey, you share the results with staff and you respond to the information. When staff speak their truth, they want to know it was heard. If you ask for ideas or if you hear an area of discontent, tell staff what you are going to do about it. Even more informative than a single survey is looking at the same survey repeated year by year. Where are we improving, where are we losing ground, what new concerns are emerging. Staff know the organization isn't perfect, but if you listen, respond, and improve, they will be more likely to go with you.

Exit Interviews

Exit interviews conducted when staff are walking out the door can be a valuable source of information. They need to be conducted by an objective person who can listen deeply. Perhaps these are done by your HR staff member, if you have one, or by an external consultant; they should *not* be done by the person's supervisor or the ED. One of the things you want to hear is how their supervision worked; you are not likely to hear of any problems if the person asking is the person who they are being asked to critique. Nor are you likely to hear of concerns with the leadership if *the* leader is the one doing the interview. Determine ahead of time how this information will be shared. The person leaving has a right to know if their information will be shared directly or cumulatively or at all. If the information is to be shared directly, then do the interview on their last day (or close to it) and don't share it until they have moved on. And if you are not going to share it in any way, then why bother?

Stay Interviews

Why wait until people are leaving to ask them how things are going? Periodically, meet with staff and ask the same kinds of questions that you ask when people are leaving but instead of "Why are you leaving?" ask them "What would make you want to leave?" and/or "What would make you want to stay?" The same guidance about confidentiality and safety of the person answering the questions applies here.

Focus Groups/Input Meetings

When decisions impact staff, ask them what they think and listen to their input. These input sessions might be part of staff meetings, or they might be separate and specific to a certain initiative.

Facilitated Staff Meetings

Make sure that staff meetings are facilitated so that everyone has a chance to speak, and that they're not just dominated by the loudest, most insistent voices. The facilitation can rotate, or the meetings can be self-facilitated if people are trained and intentional about that approach, but if you notice that some people talk all the time and others rarely do, the facilitation might not be working. Start with a check-in question or icebreaker. Once someone says anything in a meeting, they are more likely to speak again in the meeting. And make sure these meetings are also two-way conversations, not just leaders delivering information.

Cascading Communication

The organization must have a clear plan for how information will move up, down, and across it. At the end of every meeting, check on any pertinent new information, decisions, or plans. Who has to know what from this meeting? Who will tell them? How will they be told? When will they be told? Make sure a plan exists, and then enact it. Plans can go sideways quickly if one manager shares information immediately and another saves it for a week or, even worse, forgets to share it at all.

Lunch and Listen

If your organization is large and your executive director is not a part of the everyday work, consider instituting a "fun" way for the ED to meet with line staff. One organization has monthly lunches that staff can sign up for (or be assigned to), where the ED meets with four to six staff members. Or the ED might attend a regular staff meeting and have a few minutes to speak and a few more minutes to listen. Or the ED has an open door—one that is *truly* open and inviting. (This won't work if no one knows the ED except as a figurehead.) Or maybe each department nominates someone to go to an annual one-on-one meeting with the ED.

Suggestion Boxes

Suggestion boxes are old-timey but still effective. Just make sure that if you institute one (either a literal box or an email box), someone monitors it. And respond to the suggestions, even if the response is "We'd love to be able to offer everyone full pay for a two-day workweek. That's not feasible at this time, but thank you for offering a fun suggestion!"

Innovation Forum

Once a year, offer an optional "lab" where people can brainstorm improvements to the way things are done. You can be clear that your organization may not have the resources to implement dramatic new ideas at all, or even good, realistic ones right away, but continuing to think and improve is still important. Make it fun, make it creative, and see what happens. This innovation forum might be just an hour or two long but could generate some good energy and connections. Maybe start with a seed question and then see where it goes—e.g., "How could we be more welcoming to LGBTQ+ folks?"

Data

Collect, monitor, and pay attention to data—data about your work, data about injuries and complaints, data about turnover and absenteeism, data about applicants. What do they tell you? Data might provide your seed question for the innovation forum: "Why has our turnover jumped since a year ago?"

Informal Complaints

Make sure staff know that they can tell leaders early and often about any concerns they have. And don't make them wait until they have a "formal" or "official" complaint—their supervisors should be asking them about any problems they're having. "Anything else we should talk about?" is always a good question. If your organization has an HR person, they should be someone safe to whom people can go talk without having to make any official statement. Once again, if you do hear anything, respond. Let them know what you will do to follow up on their concern, even if your response is simply "I am going to make a note of this, so if I hear of anything else like it, I will jump on it. Thank you for letting me know."

Formal Grievances

Sometimes a situation calls for a more formal complaint. Make sure staff know the "who," "what," "when," "where," and "how" of this process.

Partnerships take work, and they take a lot of honest conversations. Put down your phone and be present so your organization can demonstrate true synergy and thrive.

Make It Your Own

- Implementing any of these practices will take time. When time is scarce and people are overwhelmed, what can be gained by taking the time to listen?
- Getting input from staff on pending decisions or changes will surely slow down the response time. Under what circumstances is doing so worth the time, and when does it not make sense?
- What is the danger if you ask for input and do not respond?

How Can You Dance When the World Is Burning?

*If I can't dance, I don't want to be
part of your revolution.
A revolution without dancing is
not a revolution worth having.
If there won't be dancing at the revolution,
I'm not coming.*
—EMMA GOLDMAN

Those of us working for social justice are all too aware of what we must do. Of what is at stake in our work. We focus constantly on the huge mountain of work in front of us. When will we ever eliminate racism in this country? How will women ever be treated fairly? Will LGBTQ+ rights ever be secure? How will everyone recognize that the world must be made safe for people with disabilities? What will it take for trans folks to be treated with dignity? How can we redistribute wealth and disrupt the classism that underlies so much of the world? When will we invest in communities, instead of corporations? How can we ever reform our prison and police systems? When will we truly welcome newer immigrants? The list goes on: human trafficking, child abuse, reproductive rights, respect for religions and cultures, transportation justice, environmental justice, and much more. Can we build a world where every voice is heard and every person can be accepted and respected? The work is unending.

As the world cries out for justice, we must model the world we strive for while we work to create it. Our work is not a sprint; it is a marathon. Sometimes it is a marathon in a hurricane. We must be resilient, and our work must be sustainable. We must be sustainable.

One way we build our resilience, as individuals and as organizations, is by stopping periodically and looking at what we've done. We are making a difference. Bit by bit, step by step, we are changing minds, changing hearts, changing understanding, changing practices, and changing laws.

Trite though it is, we must be the change. We must actively and consistently appreciate people for who they are and what they do. We must continue to make our organizations places where justice and belonging are lived. We must do our individual work related to race, gender, class, ability, power, and privilege with joy and rigor. We must practice self-reflection and lead with intention.

Supervisors need to recognize their individual staff members' and teams' accomplishments. Organizations need to acknowledge the work we've done and take time to recharge. We must prioritize the recognition and celebration of successes, small and large.

And we must play. We must have space for joy at work. Supervisors and leaders set the tone of the organization. When work culture is infused with joy and pride, much can be accomplished. Laughter and a commitment to and recognition of success can help keep staff engaged and present.

So let's come together and dance our hearts out, and then get back to our justice-filled and joy-filled work!

Make It Your Own

- What do you personally need to be sustainable?
- When and how must an organization be resilient?
- Many people have a taskmaster inside them that frowns on dancing—both literal and figurative dancing. What is a hashtag you can create to quickly answer the taskmaster? #amdancing? #bethechange? #sustainability?

PS: Thank You!

Thank you for being a leader for justice. Thank you for all you do, day in and day out, to make the world a more equitable and safe place. Thank you for creating workplaces that model the world we need. Thank you for being thoughtful, intentional, and reflective. Thank you for reading this book.

ACKNOWLEDGMENTS

This book would not be possible without the seeds planted and watered by Barbara Love and Roberta Hunter and all the members of the Diversity Team at Community Action Partnership. We did good work together. I was profoundly impacted by that work and those people—personally and professionally.

My consulting colleagues have been teachers and partners. In working alongside you, I have learned more about myself, dove deeper into my work, and understood much more about the pervasiveness of racism and white supremacy in organizations. Special thanks to Emily Goldfarb, my fellow supervision fanatic, my mentor, and my friend.

I am so proud to be a part of RoadMap, a national network of capacity builders who work to strengthen social justice organizations. These brilliant consultants have challenged me to see and think systemically, to claim the power of human resources to influence change, and to trust my thinking and my voice. I want to name my partners on the RoadMap Racial Justice Action Team in particular: Nijmie Dzurinko, Bill Fletcher, Brigette Rouson, Terrill Thompson, Otts Bolisay, Susan Mooney, and Mala Nagarajan. Mala and I have worked together on HR policies, practices, and approaches. She has been a thought-partner and a friend. Thank you also, Mala, for writing the foreword to this book. It is a gift beyond measure.

I must acknowledge my clients who have trusted me to train, consult, and coach with them. When you brought me a concern, I was able to see a way forward, but the path would not have appeared if not for the question. The work you do, individually and collectively, makes our world a better, safer, and more equitable place to live. Throughout the tumultuous times, friends would tell me they were frustrated and feeling hopeless. I could share their frustration but I never lost hope, because I knew what you were all doing diligently, quietly, and powerfully. To be able to support your work has been my deep honor and pride.

Thank you to Rachel Sever and Mari Ryono who read an early draft of this book and gave me deep thoughtful input to make the book stronger and more relevant.

Thank you to the entire She Writes Press team who led me through this magical process of turning thoughts into pages: Brooke Warner, Samantha Strom, and many people whose names I don't even know but your work made this book what it is. Thank you to Rebecca Lown and Julie Metz for my beautiful cover design. My nieces, Heidi and Becky, provided thoughtful input about the cover. Thank you to Annie Tucker for her sharp editing and for teaching me more about how I think. Thank you to Esther, Donna, and Masha for help with proofreading. By the time it got to you, I needed your fresh eyes.

I cannot express enough gratitude for my readers—the ones who read my first book and the ones who continue to subscribe to my newsletter. You keep me thinking and writing and I am grateful for your time and attention.

Thank you to my coffee group, Susan, Donna, and Mary. The pandemic would have been way more bleak without our weekly visits.

Since I wrote the last book, I have lost two siblings, which makes me more appreciative of my remaining siblings: Bob, Jeannie, and Donna. You have been with me since Londonderry. When our dad's voice in my head told me I was being "too big for my britches," you knew the same voice, and cheered me on. I feel the rest of my family and friends behind me and next to me, offering sustaining love and support.

I give unending gratitude to my children, Isaac and Rachel, and their partners, Katri and Noon. Being in adult relationships with all of you is rich and deep and joyous. Dancing in parenting, friendship, camaraderie, and game playing with you has taught me much about how I show up. I have learned from each of you. And to my beloved grandchildren, Brayden and Skylar. You expanded my heart and taught me a new kind of love and joy.

And to Mark, who knows me best in all the world and loves me through it all. Thank you for building me a studio *and* an office so I can always have a room of my own no matter what I am doing. You have encouraged me to follow my dreams and urged me to trust my skills and use my voice. Our life together is the best dream I followed.

All of these people matter, not just because of their specific impact on this book, but because when it comes down to it, I teach and write about interpersonal relationships. I focus on work in general and supervision in particular, but it is all about how we show up and interact with each other. And I am grateful for what these people have taught me, about myself and about relationships, along the way.

ABOUT THE AUTHOR

Growing up the youngest of six kids in a low-income family, Rita often had the experience of feeling unseen and unheard. She became very focused on hearing and seeing others as individuals and within the groups that we live and work in. This led her to recognize the uneven playing field that the world calls "equal." This awareness has been part of her unified approach to human resources and organizational development for over twenty years. She worked as a staff member for nine years at an AIDS organization and another nine years at a community action agency. In her consulting practice, she works with social justice organizations throughout the US.

Rita has an MA in Organizational Psychology and is a certified professional coach. Rita approaches supervision as a primary leadership function. In addition, she sees the function of human

resources and the culture of an organization as essential components of organizational effectiveness. She works with individuals,
teams, and entire organizations to help the organization to be in
alignment internally as they work to achieve justice externally.
Rita works as an affiliate consultant with RoadMap Consulting,
a national group of consultants committed to strengthening organizations and advancing social justice.

Rita lives in Sonoma County, California, with her husband,
Mark, and their dog Lacy. They visit Portland, Oregon, and
Southern France as often as they can to visit their family. Her
first book was *Supervision Matters: 100 Bite-Sized Ideas to
Transform You and Your Team.*

Visit the author at www.supervisionmatters.com
or ritasever.org.

Author photo © Katharine Kimball Photography

SELECTED TITLES FROM SHE WRITES PRESS

She Writes Press is an independent publishing company founded to serve women writers everywhere. Visit us at www.shewritespress.com.

The Business of Being: Soul Purpose In and Out of the Workplace by Laurie Buchanan, PhD. $16.95, 978-1-63152-395-3. From a business plan and metrics to mission and goals with everything between—investors, clients and customers, marketing strategies, and goodwill development—this book clearly maps how to create personal transformation at the intersection of business and spirituality.

People Leadership: 30 Proven Strategies to Ensure Your Team's Success by Gina Folk. $24.95, 978-1-63152-915-3. Longtime manager Gina Folk provides thirty effective ways for any individual managing or supervising others to reignite their team and become a successful—and beloved—people leader.

Drop In: Lead with Deeper Presence and Courage by Sara Harvey Yao. $14.95, 978-1-63152-161-4. A compelling explanation about why being present is so challenging and how leaders can access clarity, connection, and courage in the midst of their chaotic lives, inside and outside of work.

The Thriver's Edge: Seven Keys to Transform the Way You Live, Love, and Lead by Donna Stoneham. $16.95, 978-1-63152-980-1. A "coach in a book" from master executive coach and leadership expert Dr. Donna Stoneham, The Thriver's Edge outlines a practical road map to breaking free of the barriers keeping you from being everything you're capable of being.

She Is Me: How Women Will Save the World by Lori Sokol, PhD. $16.95, 978-1-63152-715-9. Through interviews with women including Gloria Steinem, Billie Jean King, and Nobel Peace Prize recipient Leymah Gbowee, Sokol demonstrates how many of the traits thought to be typical of women—traits long considered to be soft and weak in our patriarchal culture—are actually proving more effective in transforming lives, securing our planet, and saving the world.